We Have to Talk

OTHER WORKS BY THE AUTHORS

BY SAMUEL SHEM:
  NOVELS
    The House of God
    Fine
    Mount Misery
  PLAYS
    Bill W. and Dr. Bob (with Janet Surrey)
    Napoleon's Dinner
    Room for One Woman

BY JANET SURREY:
  NONFICTION
    *Mothering Against the Odds: Diverse Voices of Contemporary
      Mothers* (co-editor)
    Women's Growth in Connection: Writings from the Stone Center
      (co-author)
  PLAYS
    Bill W. and Dr. Bob (with Samuel Shem)

WE HAVE TO TALK

Healing Dialogues Between Women and Men

SAMUEL SHEM, M.D.

AND JANET SURREY, Ph.D.

BASIC
BOOKS

A Member of the Perseus Books Group

All persons, places, names, or institutions have been changed to protect all identities. Any perceived similarity to real persons, places, names, or institutions is not intended by the authors and is either a coincidence or the product of faulty memory or imagination.

BASIC BOOKS
A Member of the Perseus Book Group
Copyright © 1998 by Stephen Bergman and Janet Surrey.
Published by Basic Books,
A Member of the Perseus Books Group

Designed by Jenny Dossin

LIBRARY OF CONGRESS CATALOGING-IN-PUBLICATION DATA

Shem, Samuel.
We have to talk : healing dialogues between women and men / Samuel Shem and Janet Surrey.
New York : Basic Books, 1998.
p.   cm.
HQ801.S5244   1998
306.7   21
ISBN 0-465-08063-4 (cloth)   0-465-09114-8 (pbk.)
1. Man-woman relationships. 2. Interpersonal communication. 3. Communication—Sex differences.

10 9 8 7 6 5 4 3 2 1
RRD 02 01 00 99

FOR KATIE CHUN AND HER WORLD

With special appreciation for the group of women of the Stone Center, Wellesley College, with whom Janet Surrey has worked for twenty years—Jean Baker Miller, Judith Jordan, and Irene Stiver—who together developed the Relational or Connection Model that is the foundation for this work.

As there is a Law of Gravity,
So there is a Law of Love,
Working at the heart of the Universe.

—VIMALA THAKAR

The meaning is to be found neither in one of the
two partners, nor in both together, but only in
their dialogue itself, in this "between" which they
live together.

—MARTIN BUBER, *The Knowledge of Man*

A truly respectful interchange based on the experi-
ence of both sexes can lead us along the path of an
enlarging dialogue. I believe that such dialogue is
the only path to the survival of us all.

—JEAN BAKER MILLER

Contents

Acknowledgments

We wish to thank Susan Bailey, director of the Wellesley Centers for Women, and Maude Chapin, Carolyn Swift, and Cynthia García Coll, former directors of the Stone Center at Wellesley College, who helped us create and sustain the Project on Gender Relations. We are grateful to colleagues in our work in schools: Nancy Beardall of Newton, Massachusetts, public schools; Nancy Goodman of Cincinnati Country Day; Carol Phillips of Montpelier, Vermont, public schools; and Joanne Hoffman, head of Moses Brown in Providence, Rhode Island. To Wendy Levine and Lynne Jones of Getaway Seminars on Cape Cod, thanks for organizing our first gender dialogue. Our editors, Gail Winston and Jo Ann Miller, have each done their part. Our agent, Joy Harris, has been greatly empowering. Of friends and colleagues, we thank Judith Abbott, Diane Aronson, Erica Bronstein, Mitch Cohen, Sarah Conn, Stephanie Covington, Mary Ellen Dolan, Cate Dooley, Kathleen Dyer, Miriam Greenspan, Leston Havens, Carter Heyward, Alexandra Kaplan, Jackson Katz, Kathy Kaufmann, Terry Kupers, Joanna Macy, Georgie McLean, Marsha Mirkin, Daeja Napier, Maureen O'Hara, Linda Pritzker, Chris Robb, Kate Seidman, Pamela Seigle, Jackie Simonis, Betsy Smith, Marion Solomon, Barbara and Burt Stern, Mary Watkins, Kathy Weingarten, and Tom Yeomans. Many thanks to Medical Portfolio Management.

We thank our parents, Rosalie and Alexander Surrey and Rose and Sig Bergman, with much love and gratitude for the lifelong lessons of relationship and mutuality.

For leading us toward and through the "we," we thank all the men and women and boys and girls whose words and spirit infuse this book.

Introduction: Three Decades of Dialogue

"You women just want the 'feminization' of us men."

—A MAN, IN DIALOGUE

"We're not saying be like us; we're saying be with us."

—A WOMAN, IN RESPONSE

"We have to talk."

To women, usually the ones saying this to men, these four words are often an expression of a desire to connect, to address something with a man on a deeper, more satisfying level. It often means, "Let's get together and see if we can move things to a better place." Saying this to a man can feel dangerous. As one woman put it, "Get ready for World War Three."

To men, these may be among the most feared words in the language. They often stimulate what we call *male relational dread*. One man's response was, "Let me out of here!" Another man said, "To me those words mean: 'Next stop, divorce.'"

These words often mean something quite different when they are said to someone of the same gender.

When women say to other women, "We have to talk," it can mean a multitude of things. If the other woman is someone new with whom the woman feels simpatico, it can mean, "Let's get to know each other." If it's an old friend whom she hasn't seen for a while, it can mean, "Let's catch up—do I have things to tell you!" And if it is a friend with whom she is in frequent, even daily contact, it can mean, "Ya-hoo—let's go for it! Wait'll you hear this. I've got to tell you about last night." It can also mean, "We've got something serious to talk about."

Men rarely say this to other men. When they do, sometimes it has a sense of invitation, as in, "Hey, let's catch up!" But often it has the connotation of "You're in big trouble with me. Get ready for a hassle."

Gender differences in the meaning of these words start early. In our gender dialogues between seventh-grade boys and girls, their comments and questions often focus on "talk":

> BOYS: Girls talk for most of the conversation so we don't have to talk.
>
> GIRLS: How come boys don't talk first?

How these gender differences can be used in dialogue to heal the relationships between women and men is the domain of our work.

Talk itself is not everything. The same words can bring men and women together or drive them further apart, depending on how they are used in relationship—and also on the state of the relationship, which often feels beyond words. Talk can be used for communication, but communication does not necessarily lead to connection. A "good communicator" may not be a person who can participate fully in good relationships, which are, at heart, mutual and growth fostering. And many of us have had the experience of silence being profoundly connecting. Silence too can open up a relationship or shut it down, depending on how it is used.

For the last ten years we have been privileged to share in the psychological transformation of many men and women. Since 1986, we have been conducting unusual workshops with men and women, some particularly for couples. We call them gender dialogues, because through them men and women learn how to talk with one another for a special purpose. Our goal is not to make men more like women—as the man quoted above feared—but rather to help both genders use their differences to create good connections with each other and thus to grow as individuals and as couples. But not only that. Our workshops are a microcosm of change in our culture. Disconnections in male–female relationships impact everyone: in families, schools, corporations, medical settings, courtrooms, and government. From the start our goal has also been to bring what we learn in our dialogues to the larger world.

For the vast majority of men and women who attend our dialogues it is the first time they have come together with others to explore gender differences and relationships. Many, especially men, are anxious; most, especially women, are frustrated but hopeful. Regardless of their previous conceptions of what it means to be a man or a woman or even to be in relationship, nearly all of them leave the dialogues with a radically new understanding of what the woman we quote above is asking for. Through dialogue they have learned to "be with" each other in a new way. They have learned the power of what we call "good connection." Connection is not a static thing but rather the movement of two or more people—two or more voices in dialogue—which heals.

These gender dialogues have taught us a great deal. As a psychiatrist and clinical psychologist, in our own dialogue for over three decades, married and parenting a six-year-old girl, we struggle with many of the same differences as the men and women we work with. We always lead the dialogues together—we have come to see that a man or a woman working alone cannot do this work as effectively. It quickly becomes apparent to us and to the men and women we work with that we too have gender foibles. For example, when the two of us are in front of an audience, introducing the Connection Model, our presentations are sometimes interrupted by laughter. Janet will be finishing up a comment, and as Sam starts to talk, the audience will laugh.

It turns out that this is a gender difference around transitions, which is all too familiar to almost everyone. Sam will think that Janet has finished explaining the point and jump in to shift to another topic, to keep things moving forward. Janet will not have finished wrapping up what she was saying—even though it had seemed to Sam that she had—and through body language or words she will show this. The men and women laugh because this is a familiar example of how the genders often handle transitions in different ways. Many of the men identify with how Sam, feeling the time pressure of the schedule, wants to get on with it, get to the "product" or "the bottom line" of the topic and then shift cleanly to the next, and how he feels "held back" by Janet's persistence in finishing up. Many women identify with Janet's way of "processing," making sure that in the transition no one feels left behind or left with unanswered questions and that there's no abrupt cutoff or disruption in the flow. We have come to see that our own disconnection around transition echoes that of many of the men and women watching us. These same gender differences show up in many ways in all of our lives—for instance, in what we call "Leaving the Party"—where women take much more time saying good-bye and getting out the door—or in "Moving out of Sex" after making love. The men and women watch us and realize that they are not alone in struggling with their differences and that we will offer them ways not only to respect and understand these differences but to *use* their differences, in dialogue, to heal.

It's not only that Janet and Sam as individuals are on display; our *relationship* is also on display—how we work with these differences, the back-and-forth between us when a disconnect around "transition" arises, our trying to find our way through the rocky places without either of us dominating or withdrawing. Being real in public is challenging and humbling. We try to remain open and authentic about our own struggles and to stay in dialogue with each other as we work together. Every moment presents an opportunity to stay in connection and grow, or disconnect and retreat to old patterns of unresolved or avoided conflict. Staying in this creative tension is not easy, not always graceful, and not always possible in any given moment. But staying with it eventually gives birth to something new.

Our purpose in writing this book is to share what we've learned from the men and women we've worked with. It is our hope that bringing to the printed page what we have discovered will help you, the reader, to understand more about relationships and about the power of dialogue to heal. Disconnections between men and women are inevitable—no one ever gets it right the first time, or all the time. It's not only what you do that matters, it's what you do *next*. The couples who grow learn to move through the disconnects to create better connections. Those couples who stagnate move from disconnect to more serious disconnect, and then impasse. We will share our understanding about what distinguishes one path from another, and we will show how it is possible to stay in the healthy movement of your relationship.

What do we mean by "using differences" for a positive purpose? Why does this concept carry such weight in bringing about transformation? Differences of gender can divide, but facing differences in the spirit of dialogue can connect. Judith Jordan writes, "The movement toward the other's differentness is actually central to growth in relationship. . . . Growth occurs because as I stretch to match or understand your experience, something new is acknowledged or grows in me."[1] Connecting through diversity is at the core of healthy relationships.

The crucial step is men and women together holding the sense of a "we" between them, greater than each or both of them. This allows them the space to open to each other's experience, understand each other's point of view, and value and validate each other in a respectful way. When both people hold the "we," something happens—something new. Differences start to *add*. Both people and the relationship grow. Both feel more connected *and* more themselves. If they are in the "we," their differences, which previously divided them, now connect them—in fact their differences may be appreciated even more. Men and women move together from stereotype, judgment, and blame to curiosity and compassion, from shame and guilt to healthy self-awareness and acceptance of responsibility. We call this process "the shift to the 'we.'"

The "we" becomes a vessel for the interplay of their differences, and at the same time the differences enrich their "we." Using differences in this way moves men and women from impasse to deeper connection, to an enlarged sense of being human together. It's a paradox: working through our differences gets us to what we have in common—our desire for good connection, the way our isolation brings suffering, and our legacy of past hurts and wounds in relationships that make it difficult to risk starting, staying in, and sometimes leaving relationship.

Our dialogues are based on the groundbreaking work of the Stone Center at Wellesley College (where we are both on the faculty) and on the pioneering ideas of its founding director, Jean Baker Miller, and her colleagues Judith Jordan, Irene Stiver, and Janet Surrey. In the last two decades Stone Center researchers and clinicians have articulated a radical paradigm shift in psychology that has had a powerful impact on thousands of women and men. The shift is embodied in what has come to be known as "the Relational Model" or "the Connection Model." The main ideas of this model are:[2]

1: Human connection, not individual autonomy, is at the center of a healthy psychological growth. Our psychological health and happiness are related directly to the quality of our connections, shaped by our capacity and opportunities for engaging in mutual, growth-fostering relationships.

2: In addition to the "I" and "you," there is a third element in human experience called the "we." This "we"—the connection, or the relationship—has qualities of its own that can be described and developed.

3: Psychological development is shaped by our experiences of connection and disconnection in relationships and the meanings we construct around these. These experiences in relationships are shaped in turn by personal, familial, and cultural forces.

4: Male and female relational development is shaped differently, along different pathways. In Western culture women have "carried" responsibility for relationships and for fostering the development of others. This orientation has been a hidden strength and a "different" voice described by Carol Gilligan. She and her colleagues at the Harvard Project on the Psychology of Women and the Development of Girls have beautifully documented the distortion of girls' relational voice at adolescence in dominant, mainstream culture.[3] Boys' relational voice, too, has been denied and distorted in the dominant culture.[4]

The idea of using difference for a positive purpose represents a radical departure from much of today's thinking about gender. In the past few years a torrent of popular psychology books have swept millions of readers up in the message that men and women's best hope for creating satisfying lives together is to acknowledge their differences as biologically determined, "instinctive," basically unchangeable. Their underlying message: we all might as well accept the barrier between men and women and figure out how to live respectfully side by side, like boys and girls in parallel play.

In the beginning of the nineties, writers like Robert Bly[5] and Sam Keen[6] even suggested the differences weren't distinct enough. Their solution to the difficulties men experience in relationship—especially with women—was for men to become more male, not more relational. The problem, they said, was men's identity, not men's relationships. In terms of their identity and role, men had gotten "soft," which often was translated into men having gotten "feminine." Men must embrace the warrior within themselves and let the chips fall where they may in the effect on their relationships. As the decade draws to a close, best-selling authors like Ellen Fein and Sherrie Schneider ask us to return to prefeminist mind games.[7] In *The Rules,* they recommend exploiting the male hunting urge by playing hard to get.

But what about men's and women's common needs and urges? Deborah Tannen's landmark 1990 book, *You Just Don't Understand,*[8] showed us that men and women are so inherently different in thought, action, and communication styles that even the same words and sentences have different meanings for them. Tannen described brilliantly the typical gender differences in conversational style; bridges across the communication gap were not her focus. A few years later, in 1992, John

Gray went a step further. In his phenomenally popular *Men Are from Mars, Women Are from Venus*,[9] he painted a familiar and often comic picture of worlds so vastly different that men and women might have hailed from different planets. For many, this notion provides comfort. One woman we talked with explained: "A lot of nights my husband sits on the couch and channel-surfs, and I read. I always wondered why he didn't listen to me or talk to me. I always thought it had to do with me. Now I know it's not because of me; it's just because he's a man."

Gray is a masked return to the stereotypic 1950s couple: father being "Father" calling the shots, mother being "Mother" by going along to get along. Men have an instinctive need to "go off into their caves," women to "go down into their wells." Father needs to isolate, Mother needs to get depressed. When Dad comes back from his isolation, Gray says he needs to be admired; Mom, back up out of her depression, needs flowers and respect. There is little hope for getting to the deeper human connections, no way to work with differences creatively, to build something better.

We reject this pessimistic view. In the pages that follow, you will find a picture very different from the silent man-in-front-of-the-TV and despairing woman, quiet and alone across the room, wondering whether she should call up a woman friend. In our picture, isolation is replaced by authentic relationship that fosters growth for both partners. Our woman and her partner will be doing the work of "getting to 'we'" in their lives so that she can turn to him as he channel-surfs and say, "This is our danger time. I'm feeling lonely. Where are 'we' right now?" For his part, the man will break his silence. Invited to remember that there is a "we" in the room, he can respond, "I hear you. Just let me finish watching this show, and then how about we take our walk?" This is a small step, but with a large effect: it stops the slippage toward relational death. Having worked with more than twenty thousand men and women, boys and girls, we have learned that it is possible to find simple ways to create, from different voices in dialogue, healthy mutual connections.

It is noteworthy that with few exceptions none of these popular authors takes into account the power differential inherent in gender and its impact on relationships. *Mars and Venus* presents a kind of peachy-keen light comedy between men and women. This is in the face of the great violence and abuse in our culture, much of which is directed by men against women and children. Judith Herman in her 1992 *Trauma and Recovery*[10] describes the tragic underside of power-over relationships, based on a system of dominance and entitlement.

The historical roots of the male–female relationship are thousands of years old and are imbedded in power-over systems that profoundly affect us all. As old systems of relationship break down, new visions are called for. In her 1987 book *The Chalice and the Blade,* Riane Eisler[11] envisions the creation of a new form of relationship—moving beyond a power-over, "dominator" model to what she calls a new "partnership" model. It is essential for both men and women to move out of a sense of personal deficiency, pathology, or blame—we are *all* called on to participate in this cultural transformation of relationship. As the century turns, American culture is trying hard to embrace equality, where we can be different but still equal. We acknowledge the importance of this effort and build on it with the suggestion that we also embrace mutuality as a new kind of partnership. In mutual relationships power struggles can be transformed to shared power, or the power of the "we."

The idea of the mutual "we" is new and emerging. Contrast the 1950s "we" with the "we" 2000. The old "we" was male-dominated, "Father Knows Best," with very distinct gender roles and responsibilities. The '50s "we" was a family circle with distinct boundaries, the man at the center and everyone else within his perimeter. The mutual "we" of the year 2000 emerges from two (or more) voices in dialogue, building on disconnections to create new connections. It is always in motion, either growing toward greater shared authenticity, empathy, and empowerment, or losing altitude, spiraling downward toward isolation. Roles and responsibilities are based on how they impact and are impacted by the "we." While there are signs of this new movement, the blossoming of spirituality around creative relationships—in the work of John and Myla Kabat-Zinn, Derek and Darlene Hopson, Gay and Kathlyn Hendricks, Harville Hendrix, John Welwood, and Thomas Moore, among others[12]—the creative powers and energy of this new, "millennial we" have yet to be fully realized.

Nor are we as pessimistic as Bly, Keen, and Gray about men's potential to participate fully in mutual, growth-fostering relationships. The research of Daniel Stern[13] and others suggests that all babies—both boys and girls—have as their primary motivation a desire for connection. In many families, both boys and girls grow in relationship with nurturing men and women for several years, at which time there is a fork in the path of development, girls continuing on, boys walking quite a different road. Our work, too, suggests that men and women share the same great potential to be empathic, relational beings.

What about stereotypes? When we write about "men" and "women," we are describing group differences, those that are apparent in groups of men and groups of women. No individual man or woman will fit these descriptions. Sometimes a quality we say is more typically "male" might turn out to be more characteristic of a particular woman. Why do we talk about these group gender differences? Because whatever his or her individual characteristics, the man or woman will be impacted by cultural attitudes toward men and toward women. And because we have found it remarkably helpful, in bringing men and women together, to introduce the suggestion that the conditionings of male or female development may be affecting the interaction. Simply put, gender has an effect on connection. We have come to realize that, paradoxically, it is only by looking carefully at these group differences that we can erode stereotype and encourage the full expression of individual qualities. We try to hold gender differences lightly, knowing that only such lightness can heal.

While biological differences are important, biology is malleable, and our attention is on this potential for change. Our focus is not on every aspect of gender but on gender-in-relationship: how gender affects men and women as they try to relate. In the maelstrom of men and women co-creating connections, their differences become all too apparent and powerful.

We also acknowledge that to focus on gender without taking into account race, class, sexual preference, and ethnicity, among other factors, has a particular purpose but is not meant to suggest that these factors do not have powerful impact. While we have sought diversity along these lines and have worked with people of many different ethnicities, most men and women we have worked with are white, middle or working class, and heterosexual. Frequently we have had other race, class, and sexual orientations represented in our dialogues, but not in the majority, certainly not to the extent that we can draw conclusions here about the intersection of gender with these qualities. The men and women who come to our dialogues are a self-selected sample, drawn by their interest in working out their questions around gender and relationship. The men are a particularly select group, invited by women or having a rare curiosity about these questions. Though the sample is limited, the lessons learned may be of help to those with whom we do not have direct experience. If we can understand how power moves in the relationships between these men and women and how to alter the movement of power to a more mutual endeavor, this might be a model for helping to change the destructive power relationships across these other differences in our world.

Pervasive and profound relational disconnections—or *impasses,* as we call them—have their roots in the different early developmental pathways of boys and girls. They grow in the fertile soil of a patriarchal culture that shapes our institutions, our thinking, and our relationships. In our gender dialogues and couples work we use the Connection Model to challenge the inevitability of this pattern and to heal the sometimes fierce split, sometimes lonely divide, between men and women. We give our men and women—whether in couples or not—the opportunity to explore, embrace, and grow through the interplay of their differences.

We have not, in this book, written about the gender issues particular to gay and lesbian couples. We hope and believe that many of the ideas and steps to connection in this book will be applicable to these couples as well.

As you will see, this is not an academic exercise. We provide a structure, tools, processes, and examples that allow men and women to engage around differences in the service of healing. One of the most compelling ways we have discovered to help men and women do this is to have them ask each other, "Where's the 'we' right now and what does it need?" That is, we show couples how to hold their "we" through the disconnect they are experiencing—the confusion, the harsh feelings of loneliness, anger, shame, and frustration, the vicious words or icy silences, the self-centered and self-righteous judgments and bitter accusations. This will often move them from disconnection to a better connection.

As you read the chapters of this book, you will hear the voices of real men and women in dialogue. You will witness their stuck moments, their grieving the loss of that bright promise of their first meetings and courtships, and their moments of suffering that, if not healed, will spread throughout their families and communities and echo down through future generations. You will also see their moments of understanding and love, of laughter, of quiet realization and dazzling release. It is a chronicle of our helping men and women to meet these moments head-on, *really in it with* each other, finding ways to allow things to move in a healthy direction once again. We hope that your reading this, and trying our suggestions, will bring you into this circle. From our work with these thousands of brave and persistent men and women, we have the experience and the faith based on that experience to offer men and women a way to dialogue, heal, and grow together. Our faith is in the power of that core yearning for good connection that cuts across the fault line of gender, core to all human beings. And you may learn to partake not just in your own "we" but perhaps partake in the larger "we" of your family, your community, and our planet.

We are envisioning a new dimension of relationship: each of us seeing, being in, and holding the perspective of the "we." The Navajo have a saying:

> When we do not agree, perhaps it is because none of us sees far enough. People living on opposite sides of a mountain rarely see the land the same way until they meet at the top.[14]

Over the years we have come to realize that we are not talking only about couples, or even just about men and women. We are talking about a new view of the world: a shift from "either/or" to "and," a shift from "self/other" to "we," a new paradigm of how we can learn to live together. Healing dialogue seems to be a vital step for creating this new "we." Once we make a shift to the "we," our world changes in radical ways. Once changed, it tends not to change back.

1

Differences Between
Men and Women

USING DIALOGUE TO UNMASK INVISIBILITIES

What's going on in there?

—A WOMAN, ASKING THE MEN

What's so important about connection?

—A MAN, ASKING THE WOMEN

Our journey into the jungle of woman–man relationships began in the summer of 1986 on Cape Cod. The women clinicians at the Stone Center—including Janet, Judith Jordan, Alexandra Kaplan, Irene Stiver, and Jean Baker Miller—had been leading workshops on the Relational Model of women's psychology for many years. At the end of one session the organizers asked Janet if she would like to do an additional workshop the next summer.

Often at these summer workshops the women participants would ask, "But what about men?" Up until that time, Sam had never taught at the Stone Center, and we had never worked together professionally.

This seemed a wonderful opportunity to explore how the Connection Model might apply to men and how it might be useful in strengthening the woman–man relationship. With a sense of curiosity and daring mixed with foreboding, we agreed to do a workshop focused on bringing men and women together using this model. Our workshop was publicized as one of many in a mailing to mental health professionals of many different disciplines throughout America.

Fifteen people showed up for the weekend workshop—nine women and six men, including four couples. It was held in the small attic of a motel during a broiling hot weekend in August. We soon found out that unless we turned on the air conditioner the room would be stifling, but that if we did turn it on we couldn't hear each other speak. Some of the men seemed reluctant to be there, sitting in defensive postures—arms across chests, knees crossed, heads back. Their body language seemed to be saying "Let me out of here!"

The women, on the other hand, were leaning forward and seemed eager to begin. They had probably tried hard to get their men to pay attention to the issues in their relationships and were glad to be finally taking action. Their body language seemed to say "Let's go!"

We went around the room with each person introducing him- or herself. It turned out that indeed each of the six men had been brought by a wife or partner. One man's wife had told him that he was coming to a tennis weekend on Cape Cod. Only as they crossed the Bourne Bridge onto the Cape did she tell him the truth. He was not happy.

The men and women were from all over the country. They ranged in age from nineteen to seventy-two, from working class to upper class, and were of several different ethnicities. All were heterosexual and white. Many of the women and some of the men were in the field of psychology, mostly social workers, psychologists, and school counselors, with interests ranging from psychoanalysis to college education, from substance-abuse treatment to hypnosis. One man introduced himself as a geophysicist, then introduced his wife: "This is my wife, Charlotte. Uh, what exactly do you call yourself, Charlotte?"

"I'm a Jungian psychoanalyst, dear."

We were startled that he had to ask.

Friday night we talked about the Connection Model and how we would try to apply it to the male–female relationship for the next two days. We had worked in the peace movement in the 1980s, trying to get groups of Russians and Americans into constructive dialogue, and had decided to try the same dialogue process across gender. If it could work with countries, why not with genders? If through dialogue we could engage around gender differences, would this lead to better connection?

On Saturday morning we broke into same-gender groups, the men in a cubbyhole near the fire escape with Sam, the women staying with Janet. We then asked each gender group to form smaller groups of three, appoint a reporter for their small group, and come up with consensus answers to a few simple questions about men and women. We emphasized that we were not asking them to stereotype men and women, for no individual man or woman would fit what they might come up with. But we suggested that looking at group differences might be helpful. While no one person would fit exactly, it might be useful to make the cultural forces that act on all men and women more explicit. They went to work.

Once the men and women split up, the whole atmosphere changed. What a relief, for each gender, to be away from the other! They loved it! The men immediately shook hands and each started writing down his own individual answers; the women started talking noisily in small groups, with a lot of laughter and waving of hands. The men, too, were soon laughing at the answers they were coming up with, though they soon got into serious issues, like their puzzlement at women and their sorrow at not having meaningful connections with their fathers, friends, wives, and children. The talk was so loud and enthusiastic that it drowned out the noise of the air conditioner.

After the small groups had finished, all the men met with Sam and the women with Janet to discuss their small-group answers. The men especially were surprised at how similar their answers all were, and how thoughtful.

After an hour, we brought the groups back together. It was as if the men had been transformed: no longer withdrawn, sullen, skeptical, they were now animated, curious—almost cheerful. One of the women said, "My God, you men all seem so much more *dimensional*."

Next, to the surprise of the participants, we asked the men to sit on one side of the room in a semicircle, facing the woman sitting in a semicircle on the other side. They did this reluctantly. Why, if we were trying to get men and women together, were we separating them?

As soon as the men and women faced each other, there was once again a sense of tension. Nervously, a woman said, "It feels like a junior high school dance."

"Yeah," said a man, "ladies' choice."

One of the men looked particularly tense. We asked him what was going on.

"I'm afraid," he said, looking at his wife and the eight other women focusing their attention on him.

"What are you afraid of?" we asked.

"I'm afraid that . . . well, that *something might happen!*"

We all laughed, as did he.

His wife said, "Eddie, I'm *hoping* that something might happen!"

Again we all laughed. And then we started the dialogue.

(*Note:* In what follows in this chapter we will not only be using the voices of the men and women in that first dialogue but additional voices from other similarly structured dialogues we have done since. The observations we make and conclusions we draw about gender invisibilities come from hundreds of other gender dialogues. The content and process of this first gender dialogue has turned out to be typical of what we have seen since, although today we understand it much more thoroughly.)

Without saying who should go first, we asked that one of the small groups begin by having its reporter read their consensus (and thus individually anonymous) answers to question one: "Name three strengths the other gender group brings to relationships."

The women hesitated, looking around at each other and at the men. They were trying to decide whether or not they should go first. As they were doing this, one of the men said, in a begrudging tone of voice, "Ohhh-kay, I'll be a good soldier, I'll start things off."

This was a good example of how power gets taken or deferred based on gender: the women had held back, leaving the initiation of action to the men and then resenting it. The man who spoke up did so without getting any sense of how the other men felt and without a real awareness of the women's process or the implications of what he was doing for the power balance. He felt he was doing everyone a favor and taking a big risk. The women, holding back, got to see the men "put their cards on the table" and thus retained some power of their own. From this first instant it became clear how relations across gender imply power; you can't talk about gender without talking about power. In mixed-gender groups—in couples, work, school, church—this playing out of power is complex and sometimes invisible.

Question One: Name Three Strengths the Other Gender Group Brings to Relationships

Men's Answers

The men said that this was the easiest of the three questions to answer. The reporters for each group read the group's answers. Women bring:

> Nurturance; empathy; capacity for feeling; sensitivity; speaking emotional truth—they have *inspired* emotional energy; realness; self-revealing; interest in working on relationships; courage to raise issues; ability to deal with more than one thing at a time; incredible memory for past incidents; capacity to ask for support; seeing both sides of a situation; warmth; tenderness; skill at noncompetitive interactions; women are the "waker-uppers" in relationships; women have more patience with children; relational resiliency; able to listen well in a nonjudgmental way; they organize the social stuff, they create community—they're better able to network.

When the men finished, the women sat there, a little surprised. They had rarely heard from men the things that men admire about them. They felt seen. Then they got animated. They started asking the men about the answers they'd just heard, wanting to go deeper into it with them. "What do you mean by 'inspired emotional energy'?" "How do we 'wake you up' in a relationship?" "How come you resist this?"

The men, feeling they'd done enough, grew defensive and silent. They seemed to be experiencing the women's questions as threatening. When we prompted them to say what was going on, they said they felt the women's questions were like "bullets," "arrows," or "darts." They felt judged as inadequate, under attack, and criticized. The women then asked to hear more about their feeling criticized, which just made things worse. The men withdrew. The group stopped dead in its tracks, in an awkward, angry silence.

Male Relational Dread

Something invisible was going on in the relationship between them, something based on a gender difference. We call it a relational invisibility.

As Sam listened, he realized that the men had alluded to this same phenomenon in their small-group discussion with him: in a close relationship with a woman, when asked to go into what he feels or thinks, a man may be overwhelmed with a sense of male relational dread.

But now, stuck in silence as they faced each other across the room, neither the men nor the women knew what was going on. The men's sense of dread was largely invisible to the women and not really visible to the men themselves: although they felt it, they hadn't named it.

We asked the men what was going on. One man spoke up:

"I feel that nothing good can come of my going into this; it's just a matter of how bad it'll be before it's over."

"And," another man said, "it will *never* be over!"

The group laughed. Sam said that he had seen this before when men faced women's yearning for "more," a sense of "male relational dread."

Nervous laughter. Both the men and women recognized it and started to comment on it. The tension broke. People joked about what had happened, said how familiar it was from their own relationships. Someone called it "the Big D."

Janet pointed out that it had been the women's yearning for a deeper connection that had stimulated the men's dread: dread came about *between* people, not in one person. And the situation was not symmetrical: while the women's yearning had been articulated and made visible to both the men and the women, the men's dread had been mostly invisible, masked in silence, in withdrawal behind stone faces.

This was our first breakthrough. We suggested to the group that masked differences could lead to disconnections and that unmasking them could help men and women connect. We felt we were all discovering this together: when an invisible gender difference remains invisible to one or the other gender, it can lead to disconnection and suffering. People silently conclude that there must be something wrong with them personally. If the invisible gender differences can be made visible, there can be relief—laughter—and things start to move toward connection again.

This is what therapists—and any healers—try to do, session after session, day after day, dialogue after dialogue: to help move people from the idea that what seems to be their personal defect, shame, or sickness is not apart from, but part of, the human condition.

Women's Answers to Question One: Name Three Strengths the Other Gender Group Brings to Relationships

For the women, this was the hardest question of the three to answer. One woman said, "We found it really *difficult* to find three strengths of men."

Since it was the easiest for the men, they felt even more criticized. One man said, "You couldn't even come up with *three?*"

"It depends on how they're used."

"You couldn't even name three," a man said, "without *qualifying* them?"

The men were not happy. They had just spelled out their appreciation of women, without any qualification, and now they were being told that for women to talk about men's strengths was difficult. Again the tension rose. The group seemed stuck once again. We too were puzzled.

"Go ahead," one of the men said, "read your answers."

The reporters for the women's small groups read:

> Caretakers; deep loyalties; humor—true humor, when it's funny and not used as a put-down or an escape; relationship through action and projects; de-emphasis on connection—which is also sometimes really destructive; lifting heavy objects; removing dead animals from the attic; killing spiders; objectivity—but that can be terrible when you're trying to connect; focusing on one thing at a time; they can see the big picture; honesty; directness; can let things go and move on; breadwinners; protectors; know how to deal with fear; power-brokers who can run interference for us with authority, like a plumber; not so overwhelmed by feelings; they can cut through all our emotions—cut to the chase; strategic; product makers; purposeful; stabilizers of the relationship, more or less; their sex drive—they make us feel frisky about sex; they have internal heaters at night; being free of the "bog" of emotions so they can skim across the top—their being distanced is both a strength and a weakness of course; boyish in the best sense of the word.

The men, after hearing these answers, were not too pleased. One man said, "That makes me feel really good, being able to lift furniture and get rid of dead animals."

"Yeah," another man said, "it makes us sound so boring—no emotion, no understanding, no depth."

For a while the dialogue went on in this irritated, resentful way. But then a man said, "But maybe we haven't been able to use our strengths with them, maybe that's why they have trouble naming them. We've never had real permission to do so."

A woman: "You mean in relationship with us?"

Man: "With you, with other men, and with our children and parents too."

This helped. It shifted the focus to one of the main dilemmas of men as a gender: men's strengths *have yet to be brought fully into relationship*. That is, in the service of strengthening or nurturing relationships. This was why the women had had such a hard time with naming men's strengths.

The Relational Context

For almost every strength the women came up with, whether or not it was a strength depended on *how it was used in relationship*. Many of the strengths on the list were qualified: "true humor, when it's funny," or "objectivity—but that can be terrible when you're trying to connect." Objectivity is a weakness when feelings are asked for; humor can be a deflection of deepening contact.

A strength can be a weakness, depending on the relational context.

Again we felt we were discovering a major gender difference that was visible to women and invisible to men. The women were thinking in terms of the relational context, the effect of something not only on each person but on the relationship.

The men, answering question one, never qualified their answers because of the relational context. For example, they quickly listed "sensitivity" as a strength of women, despite the fact that one of the things they disliked most about women—and joked about accusatorily in their own small groups—was that women are "oversensitive." The men had *not* thought, "Well, sensitivity can be a strength or a weakness, depending on how it's used in relationship." And the men had not been aware that they had not thought that. On the other hand, the relational context, clearly, was part of women's awareness much of the time.

If we look back at the men's answers to question one, we can take just about any of the qualities listed as strengths and turn them to weaknesses, depending on the relational context. But men almost never think of that. In their view, it's not relevant to the question.

As we pointed this out, one of the men lit up and told this story:

My wife and I were having a couple over for dinner last month. By East Coast standards they were a little strange: the woman, Faith, a friend of ours, was a homeopathic healer, and her partner, a man, was into acupuncture. We had a wonderful evening, and then, afterwards, we were joined for dessert by a distinguished psychiatrist and his wife, an internist. The psychiatrist sat next to me on the couch, facing the two other guests. He challenged them about what they were doing, subtly devaluing their work. When everyone left, I said to my wife, "I never realized that Faith was so awkward and, I don't know, thick. She sounded so fuzzy—stupid, even." And my wife said, "Don't you understand? That was how he was relating to her made her seem to you?" It was like a lightbulb went off for me. Is this what you're talking about?

We said that it was. The other men and women immediately recognized this and began to discuss it. The difference had been unmasked in dialogue. When it had been hidden from the men, it had caused anger and frustration and had stopped the process. Unmasked, it not only was a relief but it served to connect the men and women even further. Rather than it being a defect of the men or an example of the hostility of the women toward the men, it was, clearly, merely a fact of our shared gender learning: what girls are trained and valued for, and boys are not.

Once unmasked, it had been understood. Once understood, it brought the men and women closer. Most of us tend to forget mere knowledge; we never forget what we truly see and understand. With this new understanding, there was a growing sense of the women really *valuing* the men for their clear strengths—seeing the big picture and the bottom line, staying calm during emotional storms, and so on.

The group then talked about the cultural imperative—reinforced by Bly and Gray and others and taken up with predictable enthusiasm by the dominant male culture—for men to become more male: strong, powerful, "heroes" (in contrast to being "soft" and vulnerable). But it's not a question of changing the male role or identity or making men *more* male. It's enlarging men's strengths into relational strengths, available not only for the good of the man or the woman but for the good of the relationship. The way out—and the way these men and women, given a chance to talk together, *wanted* to find—was not to stop being strong or powerful. It was to be strong and powerful with an awareness of the effect of their strength and power not only on the woman but also on the relationship, to be *with* others, rather than to be in their caves, alone. Further, there was a glimpse of the idea that real strength and power, if brought into relationship, empowers all, men and women both.

As they went on, the group relaxed. They discussed moving on to the second of our three questions, this time with the women going first.

Question Two: What Do You Most Want to Understand About the Other Gender Group?

Women's Answers

The women said that this was the easiest of the three questions for them to answer. One woman said, "Everything! I want to understand everything about men! I've been waiting my whole life for this!"

"Our main question," one woman said, "is this: What's going *on* in there?"

"And," said another woman, "what isn't?"

"And why isn't it?" added a third.

Again, laughter.

In this spirit, a man answered:

"You really want to know what goes on inside us men? I was sitting at breakfast the other day, and Myrna asks, 'What are you thinking about?' 'You really want to know?' I ask. 'Yes,' she says, 'you have such a thoughtful look on your face.' 'Okay,' I say, 'I was thinking, Today, when I mow the lawn, do I mow it this way—back and forth from the street to the front of the house, or this way—back and forth from one fence to the other.'"

MAN: I read the other day somebody saying that if all the men in the world suddenly told all the women in the world what they were actually thinking, the planet would collapse.

MAN: But my really interesting—and insightful—thoughts come when I'm talking to my wife. When I'm alone I'm thinking of things like What's for dinner? and Will the Lions win? Talking with her I get stimulated.

WOMAN: Then why do you avoid it?

MAN: Good question. I'd like to know that myself.

Men's internal experience was the major mystery for these women. Other ways in which the women put it:

> Are you aware of what's going on inside, and does it matter? What happens between receiving a message and sending back your response? What moves you deeply? Do men feel?—if so, how, and what? What do jokes really mean? What do sports really mean? What's it like to live in a man's body? Are men lonely? Why are men so private? What is the process going on in your heads when you're not able to answer my questions? Why do you clam up just when we get to the real meat? What would it take to get men to open up? Why are men so silent—what does your silence really mean?

It turned out that the women had the misconception that men's internal experience was invisible to men, too. Men often joke about this. But as the men answered this question, it became clear that this was not really so:

MAN: My silence can mean a lot of things; you need to ask me.

MAN: I've expected my wife to magically know.

MAN: But when she asks me, it's like when I'm thinking about the answer to that question, another question comes—"Why are you so silent"—and I get all screwed up.

MAN: Silence for me is fear I won't know the answer; silence is safe for me. My fear is that if I speak up, something will happen which will be worse. No action is better than what will come.

MAN: I wouldn't dare initiate conversation around feeling, because it would be a step I couldn't defend. Now, the consequences are worse if I keep my mouth shut. To my amazement, the times I have initiated conversation—she *likes* that! It was astonishing to me! Jesus, it's this easy? But that initiation is real scary.

MAN: If there's something wrong and she's talking about it, it's like if I can't fix it, I won't say anything. It's almost like the problem goes away if I don't say anything. That's why I'm silent.

MAN: It's like a tough question in an algebra class we never took.

WOMAN: You mean there's a right answer?

MAN: My right answer, to a woman, always seems to be the wrong answer. If I really say how I am, there'll be another question, and another, and I know, but I can't articulate it under that kind of pressure, and a little dread gets mixed in, and I stop talking.

MAN: It's hard to interact in a sphere where we don't know the result. If we go in there, we have a big fear of the end of the relationship, we think it's gonna be a disaster. We stay out of connection to preserve the relationship, to keep something from happening.

MAN: I get afraid that if I go into it with her, I'll lose myself, and if I don't have that, I don't have anything!

MAN: Yeah, me too. I'm afraid that if I put myself in the other person's shoes, I lose myself, it's going way too far. As a result, I don't express the real me.

MAN: But where *else* is there to go? *(A long, thoughtful pause ensued.)*

WOMAN: The next relationship is not going to be any better, is it?

WOMAN: I say to my husband: Bob, I'd hate to be inside your head—it must be so lonely!

As they went through this, it became clear that the men often knew what was going on inside, both their thoughts and feelings. The problem was not that men didn't listen to women or to their own internal experience. Rather, the problem came in *responding*.

Once this was pointed out, it became fertile ground for the group dialogue. Both men and women tried to figure out why responding was so difficult for men. The women, fascinated, listened as the men—probably for the first time in their lives—talked about how they wanted to respond but could not. Dread played a part in this, as did the whole devaluation of boys and men learning to "hang in," that is, participate fully in relationship.

Not that it all went smoothly. As the differences arose in dialogue, disconnections occurred, and there were outbursts of anger and frustrated hostile silences. It was just at the point when the men and women were deadened and flattened by the anger and dread and pain of being stuck that one of us or one of the group would say something to suggest that "we're not getting anywhere" and "we can find a way out of this." The group moved back and forth through power struggles, polarized attitudes, defensiveness, avoidance tactics, despair, cynicism, grief, and hopelessness.

As the differences were made visible, we pointed out how they were examples of what women and men had been valued for in the "normal" culture rather than anything pathological. The differences we were seeing "came with the territory" of being a man or woman in the culture.

When they got stuck, we suggested the specific ways that gender might be playing a part and asked if these stuck places were familiar to them. Often someone would say that he or she often got into the same kind of stuck place with a partner. We helped them hold the idea that there was a "we" here—the "we" of the group—and that "we" could find a way through the disconnection. "Hanging out together in the disconnection" could lead to a better connection.

And it did. Whenever the group got back to a sense of "we," it would start to move again.

The women had a long list of other questions for the men, such as:

> What are men's real fears? How can you separate your feelings from your actions—like in sex? Why the urgency for sex? What is the burden of needing to be successful? Why won't men go to doctors? Why won't men stop and ask directions? What is the most effective way to teach the harms of patriarchy? How can we engage men in dialogue? What goes on between men that you don't want women to know about? What would it take to get men to become relational without major bloodletting? Why can't you reach out when you're hurting? Why do you hang on to your power at the expense of your health and your relationships? Why are men so violent? How do you develop the ability to be so impressed with rational authority, the weight of the rational approach? What's it like to be feared? Why can't you pick up the phone and call a friend?

The dialogue then focused on one of the women's questions: "What goes on in men's friendships with men?"

> MAN: *(joking)* Hey, we're really sensitive together. I say to him, "Hey Ralphie, how 'bout we go out for a cup of tea and talk about our relationship?"
>
> WOMAN: Why are you joking about it?
>
> WOMAN: We really want to hear the answers—your friendships with other men are a mystery to us.
>
> WOMAN: Friendship with my women friends is a good model for me for what I want in relationship. I don't hear men say that about male friendship. For me it's joining, cultivating listening, empathy, soothing to the soul, it's like being in a desert and going to a well. Isn't that why men like to go to women?—we do that? And now I want it back from men.

WOMAN: For women this is life-blood, the essence of life, essential. Someone I love the most in the world, if I don't have it with him, I don't want to live. There's a longing, an essential feeling about that connection.

WOMAN: We live in this war culture, where the ideal is a warrior. The ideal for men is not faith or love, it's John Wayne.

MAN: I have good friendships with my men friends, but it's a lot different than with women. I can work on a car for a whole afternoon with a friend in his garage, and we won't say two words to each other, but we'll be connected. Or when we go fishing. It's not worse than with women, it's just different.

MAN: *(angrily)* I disagree, I mean I really disagree. I spent Saturday after Saturday when I was a boy with my father in our garage working on the family car, and I don't know my father at all! Not really at all, and it pisses me off! It's not any kind of friendship that I would value. It's a bunch of bullshit, sitting in a boat fishing all day and not saying a word. We men have to talk!

MAN: It's true. I like spending time with my guy friends okay, but if I really want to connect, and feel understood, I always go to a woman.

MAN: I've been playing golf in the same foursome for almost ten years, and it's great, but if you had a videotape of the interactions, the conversations, the tape of the first time we ever played would be just like the last time, last week—nothing, you know, like *progresses.*

MAN: I went to some Bly workshops, drumming and chanting out in the woods, and it was cool, and I felt close to the other men, especially talking about what our fathers never gave us, but when I came back from the woods, it didn't help with my relationship with my wife, or with other men or women. I started a men's group, and we drummed and chanted and talked a little, but nothing, you know, *grew.* One of the things I suggested once was for each of us to call up the other guys on the phone in the month between meetings. Well, it was as if I had suggested we wear dresses or something. Right away one guy says, "I don't do phone too well," and another says, "I'm pretty busy." Never happened. We mock how much time women spend on the phone, but they get connected a lot deeper than men. It's not enough to white-water raft together or get naked in a sweat lodge—I've been doing that in every locker room since I was a kid. He's right—we have to learn how to talk, how to go back and forth, ask and listen—like we're doing right now. I hate to say it, but we men need to learn to just sit on our butts and *talk*. So we can do it when our lives depend on it.

MAN: I agree. It's really sad. For fifteen years I've been going to work out at this health club, and there are some friends I see there. If anyone asks me how I'm feeling—which they don't do, much—I always say "Fine." And if I ask, they always say "Fine." I mean he could've just been diagnosed with cancer, or his kid could have just been picked up for dealing drugs, and he'd still say "Fine." Male–male friendships are one thing, but if I really want warmth, and meaning, to find out what I'm really feeling and thinking, I go to a woman. Don't get me wrong—it's crucial for me to be with other men, but I need women too. It's best if we have both.

As the group felt more connected, the major question that the women came back to was about men's loneliness:

How do you get through the day without intimacy? What takes the place of it, if anything? If men don't express feelings, what *are* you doing with feelings? What does it feel like to be nonrelational? How can you get by in life without close friendships with other men, like we have with women? Are you lonely? Do you really want us to leave you alone? How can you put yourself first so much of the time? Do men feel there's something missing? Is life worthwhile for men?

The men, now feeling more safe with the women, started to describe how sometimes in groups with other men they could begin to be open about the losses in their lives—the loss of relationships with wives, children, and especially fathers. The men talked about how they found it difficult to be open about grief and loss with women—and then started to *do* just that!

As men were going back and forth in dialogue, the women began leaning forward with exquisite attentiveness. One man said, "All you women are listening really hard, and it's really quiet, like you can't believe we men have grief, or are lonely."

WOMAN: Are men lonely?

MAN: God, don't you *know*?

WOMAN: I thought so, but we're been waiting a long time to hear it—about a millennium, in fact.

WOMAN: I'm drawn toward you, but I'm pulling back too, because I just don't want to take care of you anymore.

MAN: I can understand that. But we're not asking you to take care of us anymore. Just hear it, that's all.

At this the group was quiet. No one said anything for a long while. There was a palpable shift in the room.

And then, as people began to talk again, it became clear that something had happened. There was now an intense sense of people really *being there,* really *present.* After a while we asked them how they would describe it:

A sense of release; comfort; caring; safety; sharing; peaceful; easy, enjoyment of different styles; hopefulness; spaciousness; nurturance; energizing; movement; insight; softening; appropriate confrontation; clear recognition of others' experience.

Over the years we have found that such a shift invariably happens in the gender dialogues (to a greater or lesser extent depending upon the length of time in dialogue). We call this movement the *shift toward mutuality.* The group had moved to a different dimension of being in relationship.

With this shift, the group said they wanted to move on to the men's answers to question two. But then someone noticed that we had been in dialogue for four hours! It was time to break for lunch. We reconvened with much energy.

Men's Answers to Question Two: What Do You Most Want to Understand About the Other Gender Group?

The men began by saying that this was the hardest of the three questions for them to answer. (It had been the easiest for the women.) As they talked, it became clear that the reasons for this were many: women are trained and valued to be more "other-oriented"; men have been valued much more for self-referential thoughts, questions, and actions than for questions about the other's internal experience or about the relationship; men are leery of asking questions of women because of their fear of the answers they might get or further questions from the women. And so it was difficult for the men to come up with questions. The first one was "What do you women want from *me?*"

The men elaborated:

> What do you want from us men, and how are you so sure you want it? Why is what I do never enough? How do you expect us to be powerful and sensitive both? How do I get close to you without losing myself? Why so many "whys" for us? Why do you demand I be vulnerable and then see it as a weakness? Why do you say you want the sensitive guys and then go for the macho jerks? What do you really want?—one thing is being discussed, but it turns out what's *really* being discussed is different. Why do you always bring up the past?

The women started to answer:

> WOMAN: What I want is to be understood, listened to. Men get a lot of that from us, so it must feel pretty good to you. Give it back.
>
> WOMAN: I want more emotional presence, not more money to be thrown at the problem.
>
> MAN: Do you have a model for someone who meets your high expectations?
>
> WOMAN: We have a model of other women, those are the things we want back.
>
> MAN: So you want us men to be more feminine?
>
> WOMAN: No! We want men—and women too—to be more *related*. If that's taken to mean "feminine," the world's in big trouble.

This was a surprise to men. They assumed that to be asked to be more *relational* was to be asked to be more "feminine." But the whole point of the gender dialogue between men and women was not to get men to be more feminine or women to be more masculine. The point was to get each, men and women both, to bring their different strengths into connection, to be more fully in connection with women and men both.

The second question the men had was the one that provoked the most intense dialogue:

> What's so important to women about connection?

The men put this in other ways:

> How do women remain so intensely involved with each other without getting overwhelmed or bored? How do you stay with

your feelings so well? How do you gain satisfaction with empathy rather than problem solving? How do you come to personalize relational failure to such a degree? How do you care so much without losing yourself? What's this yearning all about?

The women responded with energy:

WOMAN: There's a lot of hurt, underneath that yearning.

WOMAN: And sometimes it makes us crazy and too angry to listen to you.

WOMAN: You might as well ask why we have so much of a need to live.

WOMAN: If I'm not connected, I'm not alive.

WOMAN: The real answer is, "Why don't you?" How can you live without it?

MAN: Like we said before, we don't, very well. Under this Lone Ranger shit I feel like the Lonely Ranger.

WOMAN: For us, connection is not such a big deal as it seems to be for you men. You think it's a whole big thing, an involved thing, something that you have to *do*. For us it just *is*, it just happens.

WOMAN: You men seem to feel that if you did a little connecting, you'd be swallowed up—but you don't understand—I too get bored with talking about this stuff all the time—it's not about talking about feelings, it's about being connected. If you're connected, you feel better. I'd have more energy to focus on the rest of my life if I were connected to Ed better. He says, "All you want to do is talk about the relationship"—but I don't, I really don't.

MAN: But why do you need so *much* connection?

WOMAN: That image—"so much"!—why didn't you marry some vacuous woman who'd sail your boat and just haul in your sheets, so to speak. But I know that's not what you'd like.

WOMAN: It's no fun hounding a man to connect. The only way it works is it becomes a shared thing, both of us nurturing the relationship.

WOMAN: When there's no connection in a marriage, it's the worst of both worlds—both dealing with another person and being alone.

WOMAN: My husband doesn't want to share my sorrow because he feels it will double his sorrow. I feel that sharing it halves it.

WOMAN: To have someone holding it with me makes it feel bearable. It's the difference between being in pain and being devastated.

WOMAN: Do you men know what we're talking about?

MAN: Yeah. In twenty-seven years married, the best time has been the past year. When it's been good lately it's been *great,* the feeling that we're a really powerful unit. When that trust drops for a second it goes like a freight train to hell, but the more I do it the more I feel I *can* do it.

WOMAN: The first few years we were in a kind of *National Geographic* guide to marriage. I felt disconnected and isolated and blamed myself, that I wanted too much.

WOMAN: When he does show his feeling, let me know what's going on, his anger and tears are so important, each tear is gold to me. They make me feel him, and I feel connected.

MAN: So why the need for the constant question?

WOMAN: Because we never get an answer.

(Laughter.)

MAN: Seriously, why do women want to process all the time?

WOMAN: It feels good—I feel alive.

WOMAN: And it feels bad not to.

WOMAN: Processing things, it's having a conversation where everyone is engaged. If you don't answer, something gets dropped between us, like a load of mashed potatoes on the floor.

MAN: You want us to move quicker?

WOMAN: No, as long as you tell us why you aren't moving.

MAN: Let me ask the ladies a question: Are you enjoying yourselves now?

WOMEN: *(together, with great enthusiasm)* Yes! Yes!

MAN: Hey, this is easy!

(A lot of shared laughter.)

MAN: Yeah, we can do this, even though you're the experts.

WOMAN: I'll tell you a secret: we don't always know what to do. *(Passionately) We're not experts in relationship, either.*

With this growing sense of really working together, the group went on to some of the other questions the men had posed:

What are you so angry about? Why do you expand your processes *ad infinitum?* Why do women talk "extra"? When you're with your friends, how do you know when to *end* a con-

versation?—do you actually ever get anywhere? Why are you so
tied to verbal expression? What supports you? What is it like to
be tied to your cyclical bodily functions? Why is the sharing of
feelings so important? How can your emotions be so fluid? How
can you do three things at once? Why do you fake orgasm?
How can we understand your sensitivity to subtle cues, verbal
and nonverbal? Why do women tend to tolerate men's behavior? What's it like to have babies? What's the purpose of sex for
women? How do women keep up their strength when they
shop? Why do women go to the bathroom in groups?

This last question is also one that boys often ask, starting in grades
six or seven. In one dialogue the women answered:

WOMAN: It's a safe place to talk, without men being present.

WOMAN: It's peaceful, doing the bathroom thing, and talking.

WOMAN: If you're out to dinner and you go to the bathroom with
the other woman, you can find out what is *really* going on at the
table, the things no one is saying.

WOMAN: And you don't have to walk across the restaurant by
yourself, you feel safer walking with another woman, and you
don't feel as stared at, so much.

WOMAN: I can find out more about a woman in five minutes waiting to go to the bathroom than in five years with my husband.

WOMAN: Don't men talk when they go to the bathroom?

MAN: Never. We can be in the middle of an animated discussion at
a meeting and then we break for a pee, and we stand there at the
urinals side by side in total silence, no one says a word.

WOMAN: Really?! Why?

MAN: With your pecker out you don't feel like talking.

WOMAN: I get it—it's just like marriage. *(Laughter)*

WOMAN: Don't you make any eye contact?

MAN: Pecker eye contact? Oh, God!

The flow of this piece of dialogue is instructive, and typical. As the
men asked questions of the women, as the dialogue went on, both the
men and the women listening, attending, and responding with real
authenticity, something else had begun to happen that was invisible to
the men and women both.

Relational Curiosity

The men would ask the women one of their questions, and for a while the women would start to answer. But then, inevitably, like the ballast of a ship in a strong current, attention would shift back onto the men. The women would wind up asking the men about *their* response to what was being discussed, even though the questions were directed at the women. There was a continuous flow toward focusing on the *men's* experience. This was partly because the women kept asking more questions, partly because the men did not.

Both the men and the women were subtly colluding to shift the group's focus to men. This collusion was a real barrier for the group "getting to mutual" in their dialogue. The men were reluctant to respond in relationship and disinclined to explore the women's internal experience by asking follow-up questions that would open up the relationship. The women sacrificed their need to talk about their own experience in order to try to draw out the men.

The process of "trying on the feelings" of the other person as a way of knowing the other and connecting with the other was familiar to the women, foreign to the men. Without realizing it, the women were trying to help the men do that; they were denying themselves for the sake of relationship.

As we saw this happen, we pointed it out to the group, calling it *relational curiosity*.[1] We suggested that women are more valued by the culture than men for being curious about the internal experience of others. The result was that over and over the focus was turned back on the men. Sometimes this one-sided relational curiosity was visible to the women, sometimes not; it was not visible to the men. The men didn't realize how much time and energy the women had been spending in drawing them out.

We asked if this also happened outside the group, in "real life."

"Of course it does," one woman said, "we do it all the time—it's one of the secret tactics we learn as girls, to pump up the boys. And they hardly ever notice."

"You can never go wrong with a man," another woman added, "by asking him about himself."

"And when we don't get it in return, it makes us angry."

"But," said a man to his wife, surprised, "you always seem so *interested* in my experience. It's great."

"See?" his wife said. "It works. And besides, I usually *am* interested."

We pointed out that once again this had implications for power imbalances between women and men: if one gender receives more attention than the other, the power of that group is enhanced. The focus of the attention on the socially dominant group (men) by the socially subordinate group (women) was visible to the subordinate, invisible to the dominant. While making it visible to the men may make things more authentic, the power that accrues may not be something that men want to give up. (This nonmutual power structure, seen in whose experience gets attention and is most visible, is also familiar in differences of race, ethnicity, class, and sexual preference.)

Several times in the group we urged the men to "ask" the women more about their experiences. The men often had had great trouble asking.

Question Three: What Do You Most Want the Other Gender Group to Understand About You?

Women and Men's Answers

Suddenly it was quarter to five. We were running out of time. In the last fifteen minutes we decided to simply read to each other the answers to the third question. Just listening, without discussion.

The women spoke with deep feeling, clarity, and power. They said that they wanted men to understand that:

> We are not the enemy; even if I'm not clear, I have a point; to know what my experience of disconnection feels like; that conflict is an invitation to engagement which can bring closeness and resolution; conflict does not mean the dissolution of the relationship; how frightening men's power for violence is in limiting women's actions; don't trivialize my experience—go with my female creative processes; what it feels like to make sixty-seven cents on the dollar; that my way is not wrong, just different; that we are angry because we are hurt; that my sexuality is far beyond the physical; that I just want you to be there; that I am a human being too; we want to share, not take over; that we're not experts at relationships either.

As we all listened, we realized that most of these comments had already been covered in the day's dialogue. Listening now, there was a sense of all of us openly affirming what the women had said they wanted to be understood.

The men, also with much more feeling than initially, then said what they wanted the women to understand:

> I am not your enemy; how many of my actions are acts of love; my difficulties communicating feelings; my need for solitude; my difficulties in admitting powerlessness and asking for help; that I need space; that I need time; I'm scared too; not to have to censor my maleness; I love competition and play; how I feel about responsibility; the heavy burden placed on men to be successful and not look foolish; that being a man is often difficult; my sense of intrusion that often comes with relationships and my sense of shame for feeling that; I want to change; we care about relationships as much as women do; men are scared of other men too; men have different priorities; the complexity of masculinity; our relational yearnings; our grief over losses; that I will come back after I go away.

We all sat quietly. Some of the women, and a man or two, had tears in their eyes. No one wanted to say anything. Finally one of the women said, "Thank you. There's a glow now. You gave us the other half of the string, and now we can make a tie."

Lessons Learned: Ten Years of Gender Dialogue

We came away from that first rocky dialogue on Cape Cod with a sense of affirmation about using the Connection Model to bring men and women together. By actually naming the "third element"—"the relationship," "the we," or "the connection"—and then describing its qualities and the gender ramifications, the men and women had shifted from a focus on individual concerns and antagonism to mutual concerns and mutual authenticity, empathy, and empowerment. It was surprising to us how powerful this simple model was, how gender differences, unmasked in dialogue, could be used to create better connections. The applications to working with individual couples were obvious.

As we went back over our notes on the first dialogue, we realized that while we had easily identified qualities that were based on the different gender conditionings of men and women, we had just touched the surface of identifying what happens to these differences when men and women try to connect. The key to working with men and women was to shift the focus from the qualities of men and women to the *qualities of the connection between* men and women.

The major insights from that first weekend were that:

- From early in life men and women in our culture are valued for different things, which deeply impact men and women in relationships.

- Male relational dread and women's struggles with their relational yearning are vital parts of the experience of most of us.

- To talk about relationship it is helpful to introduce gender.

- It is useful to men and women to envision a "we" (especially during conflict).

- We had discovered several "invisibilities" based on gender that, once unmasked, helped move men and women from conflict to collaboration.

Finally, we learned a profound lesson: give men and women a chance, in a safe holding space, to participate in a respectful dialogue around differences, and there will be a shift or expansion into mutuality. Men and women will feel more connected *and* more themselves.

This expansion into mutuality can be experienced as a deeply spiritual opening. Isasi-Diaz described this: "If I sit down with someone to talk and I feel that I'm being taken seriously, I go away with a deep sense of experiencing the divine. I believe that in the taking of each other seriously we go beyond ourselves."[2]

.   .   .

It was surprising to us how quickly and widely word about our first gender dialogue spread. People—or, rather, women, for it was the women who turned out to be the organizers of the dialogues—were hungry for the chance to dialogue with men. Women did the "relational" work of calling us, setting up the dialogues, and getting men to attend. In fact, one of the real problems with this work has been "How do you get men to pay attention to this?" Various schemes have been tried: from discounts for men, through "bring a man with you for free," to (for example, in the gender dialogue we did in Istanbul) our actively searching for a few brave men who might want to come.

We held another dialogue on Cape Cod the next summer—a fiery, turbulent dialogue reflecting the rage women felt toward men, several of whom in the group were deep into the men's movement, asserting their "maleness." Then we had dialogues in Holland and in student groups at American universities, where we were awed and energized by the fresh energy that the young men and women brought to the endeavor as well as by the distance they moved in a short time from fragmented, resentful subgroups to a mutual working team. Finally, we moved to groups of professionals (psychologists, psychiatrists, social workers, counselors), to state and local psychology organizations from Maine to Arizona, and less formally (sometimes in people's homes) in Beverly Hills, Miami Beach, Washington, D.C., and rural Ohio, among others.

Over the years, using the same three questions and structure with all these people, groups, and institutions, our experience in that first dialogue on Cape Cod has been reaffirmed. While the details and effectiveness have differed, the core is always the same: bringing men and women together in dialogue inevitably leads to some shift toward mutuality between them, where disconnections can lead to better connections.

The same gender invisibilities reappear: men's dread, women's yearning, the relational context, men's internal experience, relational curiosity. In addition, we have consistently noticed three other invisibilities that we will describe later: around power, in the continuity of connection, and in relational timing.

Over the years, as we started to understand what we were seeing and tried to work with these eight major invisibilities, we realized that we needed to take the notion of the "we" a step further. The key to helping men and women create good connections lay in something else we discovered in that first dialogue as we looked at how men and women got disconnected, then stuck.

The Connection Model suggested that the problems in relationship came from difficulties not in one person or the other but in the way they were meeting. We came to realize that the focus of attention for us, and for the men and women, had to be on this relational meeting place.

We had noticed over and over again how men and women had gotten stuck, how the dialogue stopped dead in its tracks. The most obvious example of this was how women's yearning was met with men's dread, men's withdrawal provoking women's further attempts to connect, men's redoubled withdrawal, and so on. This "stuck place" turned out to be all too familiar to the men and women from their experience in couples: each of them could identify with that shared experience of being trapped, together, with no place to move, no way even to start to move.

While we didn't yet fully understand how to break through these stuck places, we did know that we had to focus our attention on understanding the "stuckness" itself. We called the place where men and women get disconnected and stuck—the place where this stymied meeting occurs—the relational space. And we called the process in which men and women try to connect—but get stuck and disconnected with residual feelings of anger, shame, humiliation, and rage—a relational impasse.

Before we go on to describe our work on relational impasses, we need to answer a question that came up at the end of one of the dialogues. A man, seeing the striking differences between the women and men and how they played out in the relationships in the dialogue, asked, "But why did this happen? How did we get here?"

To explore that question, we turn our attention to boys and girls.

2

How We Got Here

WHAT HAPPENS IN THE DEVELOPMENT OF BOYS AND GIRLS

Please see my heart.

—ELEVEN-YEAR-OLD BOY,
IN DIALOGUE, TO GIRLS

We're not some toy you can push around, and when we're moody it's not all PMS.

—ELEVEN-YEAR-OLD GIRL,
IN DIALOGUE, TO BOYS

By seventh grade, in the fresh undertow of hormones, girls and boys are trying to get back together. At this age, eleven or twelve, they have a good deal of trouble, for from about the age of five or six they have walked quite different and separate paths of development, boys with boys and girls with girls. From kindergarten on, except with their brothers and sisters, boys play mostly with boys and girls play mostly with girls.[1] There are, of course, exceptions—a girl and boy being "best friends," playing together, having sleepovers—but as time goes on, the shaming and teasing from other boys and girls pressure the friends to join the mainstream and not be with each other in those ways. Contact between boys and girls, for five years, has been glancing and shallow.

Their same-gender peer group, then, has been their learning ground—and proving ground—perhaps as much so as with their mothers and fathers and brothers and sisters and adult friends. In their friendships, they have learned not only about their identities and roles as boys and girls but also about relationships. In general in these years, what relationships are to boys is learned in relationship with other boys; what relationships are to girls is learned in relationship with other girls.

When the time comes to try to connect with the other gender in about sixth or seventh grade, the two different ways of being in the world—the two different senses of identity and relationship—collide. The collision will echo all the way into adulthood, and is, in many ways, similar to the difficulties adult men and women have trying to make authentic connection. These "years of missed chances" for cross-gender relationships take their toll.

When we bring seventh-graders together in a gender dialogue to ask and answer questions of each other, two main themes emerge.

The first is the mystery of each gender to the other. As we listen to their answers to one of our questions—"What do you most want to understand about the other gender group?"—we are struck by how mysterious the other gender's experience is.

Boys, for example, put these questions to girls:

"What do girls do all day?"
"What do girls think about?"
"What do girls talk about?"
"Why do girls have exaggerated mood swings?"
"What do girls think of boys?"
"What would girls want to do with you?"
"Why do they have more get-togethers than boys do?"
"Why do they talk more than we do?"
"Why do they gossip?"

Girls ask boys these questions:

"Why do boys go only for looks?"

"Why do boys beat each other up?"

"Why such big egos?"

"Why don't boys cry?"

"Why do they always follow someone?"

"Why don't boys talk to us first, before we talk to them?"

"Why don't they ever talk about anything interesting?"

"Why do boys try to be so masculine, so, like, macho?"

"Do they really just want to be friends with some girls?"

"Why do some boys not appreciate us, make fun of us, and think we're just, like, little people?"

"Why do boys act up in class and get destructive?"

When the boys and girls ask and answer these questions with each other, the attention level is high. Each gender is more or less a mystery to the other. They really want to hear the answers.

The second theme is how strong the cultural forces are on each gender, and how difficult it is to connect. This theme comes out in their answers to another question—"What do you want the other gender group to understand about you?"

The girls' answers reflect their struggle at that age with self-esteem. They feel devalued, objectified, and angry.

"We can do everything you can—for the most part."

"We aren't all wimps."

"It's okay to be in a bad mood."

"I don't whine all the time—just sometimes."

"We're not stereotypic feminine images that come up."

"Boys think everything we do is connected to them, but we're not on earth so you can go out with us."

"If there were no women on earth, boys would be nonexisting— we do everything! We do most of their work in their lives."

The boys' answers to this question are heart-wrenching. Over and over we hear from boys their core conflict: between the way they act and the way they are; between their "public" persona and their "hidden" one:

"I may act like a macho asshole but I really care."

"Don't believe my actions, I'm really a nice guy underneath."

"I tease you and make fun of you but I really want to be your friend."

"We are nice."

"We may fool around but we really are nice people."

Boys also put forth, strongly, the qualities of the more "public" self, their role and identity in the world:

"Girls are one of our priorities, not the only one and we have other things to take care of."

"Why we use excessive violence—to let out emotions."

"We are more physical."

The boys and girls are in quite different places. For the first decade of their lives, in families and play and schools, they have learned different ways of being in the world, different roles, and different ways of being in connection, with their own gender and with the other. Both sides have a sense of not feeling seen by the other gender, of separation from the other gender, and of inadequacy in relationships.

How did they get here? How do we make sense of what we see?

The Connection Model

The old and outworn theories of human psychological development have been written largely by the men of the dominant culture and have not accurately described the experiences of *most* men and women in relationships. They have defined healthy development as the growth of a self-sufficient, independent, emotionally controlled, and well-bounded self. At some later date—unspecified—this self should be "ready" for a mature relationship. This approach has many problems. For instance, that later date may never come; the worst thing for a mature, mutual relationship may be a self-sufficient, independent, emotionally controlled, and well-bounded self; and such theories leave out the experience of most women and of many "relational" men.

Freud's basic assumption—that we all come into the world driven primarily by the instincts of sex and aggression—has been shown to be insufficient. The careful neonatal studies of Daniel Stern[2] and others have shown that both boy and girl babies are primarily motivated by a desire for connection. Another problem with these outmoded theories is that they center on the self and the need for self-actualization. Self at the center creates an inevitable split: self/other. This split invites comparison, and comparison inevitably invites a power differential.

Theories centering on self-development perpetuate the status quo, implicitly valuing and privileging the dominant groups (men, the rich, the white) and inherently devaluing subordinate groups (women, the poor, people of color). And this status quo—hierarchical, violent, fragmented, disconnected, and isolated—is unhealthy not only for women and other marginalized groups but also for its main beneficiaries, men. Men also suffer psychologically in patriarchies: "It's lonely at the top." But the dominant voice is not the majority voice. The kindergarten bully may dominate the class, but does not truly represent the majority of the boys.

What about biology? What about differences between men and women being "hard-wired," genetic, or innate? Obviously there are clear biological differences between the genders at birth, which spool out over the life span. But in this book we focus on learning: what is learned, and what can be.

We are attempting to make sense of what we actually see in the men and women and girls and boys with whom we work. For this reason we try here as much as possible to stay with their voices. We are touched by how far they can move toward mutual connection when given the opportunity. We believe that we need a new theoretical model to account for this.

"The Connection Model"[3] grew out of the work of Jean Baker Miller,[4] who suggested that the very qualities for which women have been pathologized (emotionality, sensitivity, focusing on the well-being of others at the cost of focusing on themselves, caretaking of relationships, and so on) could actually lay the foundation for a more healthy way of living. Jordan, Miller, Stiver, and Surrey suggest that a desire for connection is at the heart of healthy human development.[5] Jordan has described growth at all stages of life as "through and toward" better connection.[6] Miller and Stiver describe this as "a new model of psychological development within relationships in which everyone participates in ways that foster the development of all the people involved, something we might call mutual psychological development."[7]

Mutuality is central to healthy, growth-fostering relationships. This describes a movement or dynamic of relationship, a shared activity in which all involved are participating as fully as possible. Surrey describes mutuality as "a creative process in which openness to change allows something new to happen, building on the different contributions of each person."[8] Jordan describes mutual empathy as occurring "when two people relate to each other in a context of interest in the other, emotional availability and responsiveness, and cognitive appreciation of the wholeness of the other; the intent is to understand. While some mutual empathy involves an acknowledgment of sameness in the other, an appreciation of the differentness of the other's experience is also vital."[9] Carter Heyward has written of mutuality: "the experience of being in right relation . . . sharing power in such a way that each person in the relationship is called forth more fully into becoming who s/he is . . . a whole person with integrity. Mutuality is a process, a relational movement, not a static place, because it grows with/in the relationship."[10]

We (Bergman and Surrey) have worked extensively with what we have named "the third element of relationship," or "the 'We.'" In addition to "I" and "you," there is always a "we." That "we" can be recognized, described, nurtured, and made a central priority in building mutuality. The "we" is shaped by the qualities of connection between individuals, and, in turn, the individuals are shaped by the "we."[11]

Miller describes "five good things" that come from a healthy connection. In such a meeting, each person feels:[12]

An increased sense of zest or energy.

Increased empowerment to act.

Increased self-knowledge and knowledge of the other person.

Increased self-worth.

A desire for more connection.

In this model, energy, power, knowledge, and worth are not qualities that only reside within a person, they arise in the movement of connecting, for all persons involved.

Healthy connections occur in relationships that are moving toward mutual empathy and mutual empowerment, and where disconnections are a stimulus for new growth and reconnection. Destructive relationships are characterized by rigidity, lack of movement, and chronic impasses around disconnections.[13] Rigid role differentiation and power-over contexts set the stage for such unhealthy relationships. These chronic disconnections are the seeds of psychological suffering. All of us have been impacted by living in a culture where our societal structures and modal relationships have not been grounded in the search for mutuality. As a result, all of us, men and women alike, have developed protective actions and reactions of disconnection that profoundly complicate our attempts to make healthy relationships.[14]

At best boys and girls are nurtured in connection as babies and continue to grow in connection for a few years, even though there are already significant gender differences. By the age of about three or four a crucial fork appears in the path. From here on the normal development of boys and girls is markedly different. The most profound differences are in what boys and girls learn about growing in relationship with others. Most theories speak to the development of male and female identity and role. We speak to male and female *relational* development (which encompasses identity and role), that is, how men and women, boys and girls, are shaped to participate in relationships.[15]

Men's Relational Development

Why don't boys cry?

— SEVENTH-GRADE GIRL, ASKING BOYS

Bill, one of our clients, describes a pivotal event in his life when he was six:

> I had been beaten up at school, and I was walking home along the railroad tracks. I hadn't been hurt physically, much, but had been humiliated by the other boys in my class. Waves of feeling rose up, came out in sobs which I tried to choke off. I knew that my mother would be home, and I couldn't wait to tell her what happened. I came to the house, and went around to the back door. I entered the kitchen. My mother was standing at the sink, back toward me. She heard me come in and turned around. I saw her seeing on my face my dried tears, I sensed her sensing my pain. She asked, "What happened? What's wrong, dear?"
>
> In that instant something shifted in me. I had been yearning to tell my mother what had happened, but as I saw her concern in her face, as I sensed her moving toward me with concern, I stiffened up inside.
>
> "Nothing," I said, and turned away, and went back out the door.

This is a fairly typical incident of "normal" male development in our society. It is an early example of the "male relational dread" seen in the men in our dialogues. It is destructive for the boy, for his mother, and for their relationship. How did six-year-old Bill get to this place and where does it lead him?

Boys' Learning Not to Listen and Not to Respond

Despite biological differences, for the first two or three years of life boys and girls develop in similar ways: in connection with nurturing persons (if they are fortunate).[16] Recently in the dominant culture in nuclear families this person has primarily been the mother. While fathers are taking a greater part in nurturing their sons and daughters, it is frequently still the mother who fulfills that role in a primary way.

The first few years of life see both the little boy and girl growing in connection with their mother. To a greater or lesser extent, the child's yearning for connection is rewarded, and growth takes place in the current of that yearning. Both genders experience that yearning, often in closest relation to a woman. Thus, *both* men and women have, some place within themselves, the potential to grow in empathic, mutual relation with others and to foster the growth of others. Many girls stay on that path, continuing to grow in connection. Especially around the age of three, though, boys start to walk a different path.

Even at that very young age, all the forces of the culture—represented in toys, TV, books, movies, computers, etc., and the way they are expressed through interactions with adults and other children—demand that a boy begin to deny the importance of relationship in order to become "a man." Boys are shamed, humiliated, and bullied for being vulnerable, "babyish," or "sweet." We call this process disconnecting from relationship. It leads not just to disconnecting from mother; but *disconnecting from the relationship* with mother.[17]

What is the difference? By disconnecting from relationship, the boy begins to deny the importance of relationship and to affirm the primary importance of a particular notion of self. Self often means what a boy *does:* his actions, competencies, and products. He is disconnecting from the very process of growth in relationship. He learns to turn away from the whole relational mode. Healthy, "normal" development from that point on is toward strengthening the self, seen by the boy as in opposition to relationship, or even "held back" by relationship. Rather than growth in mutual connection, the little boy strongly senses that growth takes place out of connection. From then on he starts to become an *agent of disconnection* and is rewarded for this behavior.

This turning away from growth in connection means that the boy never really learns how to do it, how to be in the process with another and grow. Unlike girls, whose relational development is grounded in the practice of attending and responding to others' feelings, boys frequently do not get as much practice in this arena of empathy. Not knowing how to do it, they avoid it, devalue it, and even deny that it exists.

A quality of this violation of the relational process is a declaration of difference, of maleness. Difference, at least in this culture, implies comparison. It easily becomes "better than" or "worse than"; it implies one person having power over another, including power to determine standards. This can open the door to the disparagement of mother and other women, of the relationship with mother, and even of relationship itself.

While this is the overarching issue of boys' development, different boys take different paths through it. But the majority of boys sooner or later "go underground" with their yearning for growth in connection.[18] Their "above-ground" talk and behavior disguises the yearning. Of course some boys are supported by relationships that value good connection above all else, and such boys grow with less need to mask it. This doesn't mean that boys are not emotional. Boys have feelings and express them. But boys are not valued and encouraged for bringing their feelings, thoughts, and responses into the give-and-take of relationship.

The Male Relational Paradox

And so in the "normal" development of boys is a relational paradox:[19] on the one hand the boy experiences joy and love from growing in connection for several years; on the other hand the culture demands that this yearning for connection be stifled for him to grow. The boy has powerful relational experiences of shame, humiliation, abuse, and violation when he acts on these yearnings. One fourteen-year-old boy said, "If you don't act macho, you really get beat on. The only way to protect yourself is to pretend to be tough." The result is that the boy disconnects from the expression of his yearnings, begins to devalue relationships and is encouraged to sacrifice relationship for his idea of self. "Self" comes to mean "who I am in what I do" rather than "who I am in being with others." In the service of maintaining status and thus acceptance in relationships with other boys and men, boys begin to develop ways of maintaining disconnection.

Simply put, while deeply wanting connection, boys find themselves disconnecting.

This may bring isolation—but it sometimes seems that boys are almost innoculated to tolerate isolation. This comes at great cost.

The implications of this paradox for boys between the ages of three and six are staggering. Being caught in the paradox may push the boy to devalue connection, his mother, and women in general. Once a young boy starts to feel that he himself, his strivings and his achievements are more important than connecting with others, he may have a nagging sense deep down that as far as relationship goes, he is not enough.

The world of games is clear and sharp; the world of ongoing connection, of "hanging in" with another person through words, through attending and responding and asking about and joining with the other's experience—especially on a feeling, empathic level—is fuzzy and puzzling. As he grows more competent in the world of boys and men and the male-dominated structures of TV and computers and institutions, the boy may feel a parallel sense of incompetence at being in the process of relationships. This can promote a deep sense of "I'm not enough in relationship." He may disengage from the verbal and emotional give-and-take of relating in order to engage in self-affirming activities. This disengagement leads to further discomfort in relating and strengthens the choice of self-striving. The yearning for connection may in fact surface in the boy's quest to be competent, to compete, or to achieve—or to command respect, not to be "dissed." It is a vicious cycle: even if the boy is loved in relationship with his mother and father, he may flee those relationships and try to do things in order to be loved in the relationships whose love he is fleeing. Again, paradoxically, he flees love to do something to win the love he is fleeing. But no achievement can win love.

Freud would put this in terms of the Oedipal conflict: the little boy wants to have sex with his mother and kill his father; above all else he fears that his father will castrate him and so he disconnects from mother. Even now the dominant cultural idea is still that boys need to "separate" from mother to become healthy men. Olga Silverstein's *The Courage to Raise Good Men* (1994) documents the falsity and unhealthiness of this view.[20] But the issue is not Mother but relationship. Mothers are not "the problem." The "problems" in the mother–son relationship arise as the cultural forces skewed toward shaping a separate self filter down into the relationship and play out in it. "Mother-blaming" takes place when men (and some women) buy into the primacy of self-focused development. This, we have seen all too often, is destructive to boys' and girls' and their mothers' full psychological development.[21]

Bill and his mother's disconnection in the kitchen is one of thousands of similar interactions they will pass through as Bill grows toward manhood. It will be replayed in various ways and with various people, in the family and in the world, over a period of many years. We call this "normal male development." It shortchanges boys. It sells boys a bill of goods, setting up an artificial dichotomy between reliance on the self and relating to others, between competence, "coolness" (or achievement) and being with and helping others grow. And it has resulted in a very sad state of affairs.

If you ask mothers of sons of this age about their experience, over and over they say things like, "It is as if a wall is going up between me and my son"; or, "My son is spiraling out—what can I do?"

Often the boy learns not to listen to his mother's attempts to maintain connection—or to listen with a certain suspicion—and not to respond to her. As Bill described it:

> I remember my mother facing me, asking me something, and my not knowing what to say. And then she got angry, or maybe she started crying. But she kept asking me, and the feeling I had, it was like she was ripping at my heart, my guts. Not only could I not say anything, but I had to steel myself against showing her any reaction. I made my face freeze, showing her no reaction, and tried my hardest not to respond, saying to myself: "Stay like this and it will be over." I felt like something horrible might happen. I wanted desperately to respond to her, but could not, because if I said anything it would only get worse. I was in the searing spotlight of my mother's love. I froze.

If we look once again at Bill's walking into the kitchen after being beaten up, we see that Bill clearly wishes to share his pain with his mother. He yearns for the kind of connection with her of which he has a sense-memory from the first several years of his life. He yearns for comfort, caring, holding, and love from this woman who has comforted him and held him and loved him from the beginning. And yet he has gotten the message that he must deny this yearning; "big boys don't cry," that he has to "tough it out," "go it alone," or "fight back." But this is only part of the story.

Just as important as Bill's not showing his feelings is his *not being moved* by the feelings of someone else, in this case the person most dear to him in the world. He is afraid, on a deep level, of being affected, of being tipped off his newly found path of self-reliance. He needs to keep his "boundaries" intact. The result? He denies the feelings, cuts off the relationship, pretends, denies, bluffs, turns and walks away. This is not John Gray's instinctual need for men from Mars to "go to their caves"; there is nothing instinctual about this. If anything is instinctual, it is men's desire *not* to go to their caves but to connect.

As his mother approaches, yearning to be there with him, trying to make a connection that will comfort her son, the son starts to feel an overwhelming sense of dread. It's a vicious cycle: as mother comes toward son emotionally, he feels dread and withdraws emotionally; she tries harder, he withdraws harder; she tries really hard, and he runs out the back door or up to his room.

Note that this dread is *relational*. Bill did not feel dread when he walked in. In fact, his intent when he walked into the kitchen was to connect. It wasn't until she moved toward him, seeing his pain and showing her feeling, that his dread arose. Dread arises in the connec*ting*.

Dread is not carried inside him like a sickness. Dread arises not in the "I" or the "you" but in the "we." This is a radically different view from that of traditional theory, which views pathology, or neurosis, as residing within the person. In fact, male dread is not even pathological but something that often arises in the field of "normal" relationship, when men and women attempt to open up to each other, often in the most intimate situations.

The implication is that if dread is a by-product of the attempt to create a "we," then the solution to the impasses around dread are in the "we" as well. The old solution would be for little Billy to undergo child psychoanalysis to dig out the deep roots of his dread; Billy's mom should also undergo analysis to get over her neurotic hunger and inability to "let go" of her son. It won't help, because the odds are that nothing is "wrong" with either of them as individuals. Now, of course, the treatment of choice might be to start them both on Prozac.

That was Bill's first memory of a process—male relational dread arising in approaches to connection—which will happen thousands of times in most boys' lives. In most encounters, and more and more frequently as his faith in connecting dissipates, with a certain inevitability he will choose to focus on himself and come to see relationship as a hazard to that self. This often describes men struggling with women in marriages: they are "good men" with clear strengths—loyal and faithful and helpful and honest—but not easily able to engage in "good mutual relationship." Women in these situations want more.

The alternative is mutuality. What would that look like?

Billy would move toward his mother and open up about his pain; she would move responsively toward him, listening, attending; he would allow himself *to be moved* by her feeling and concern; she would be moved at a deeper level by his authentic feeling and his honest words. A mutual movement toward greater connection would be established. Instead, Billy and his mother move toward greater disconnection and finally isolation: he leaves. They will be less and less able to create connection between them. This sad dynamic is not unfamiliar to couples.

The Question Mothers Always Ask: "What Can I Do About My Son?"

In the 1950s, mothers were told not to try to hold on to their sons. The implicit fear was that sons could turn out to be weak or gay. "Cut the apron strings!" was a thinly veiled threat. Currently there is more permission for mothers to stay in connection with their sons.[22] In some groups of courageous, like-minded mothers, doing this is valued (again, Olga Silverstein's book is a landmark). Yet many mothers still suffer enormous doubt about what they can do to help their sons live and grow in relationship.

We have several suggestions. First, mothers can hold the connection with their sons no matter what. "Holding" means keeping it in the forefront of mind and heart and soul, no matter what message the culture gives. Holding is not a passive process but an active and artful one. It uses every opportunity, whether the son is closed to it or opened up, to validate his increasingly hidden yearning to connect.

Can you get "too close" to your son? As Jean Baker Miller has put it, "You can never have too much of a good connection."[23] It is the quality of connecting as well as the process of connecting that matters. Although the process may differ, holding the connection with a son has essentially the same qualities as with a daughter.

Second, it's helpful for mothers to make contact with like-minded others, both mothers and fathers. Fathers need to give priority to fostering good connection with both their sons and daughters. Unlike mothers, fathers have not been primarily valued by our culture for doing this; they have been more valued for fostering independence, competence, and action. As in any alternative or "resistance" activity, there is power in numbers—and in America today mothers and fathers who try to hold the priority of good connection with their sons are in resistance. Find like-minded others.

Finally, it is crucial that both mothers and fathers not only talk the talk, but walk the walk. The son (and daughter) learns about relationship not only from relationship with mother and with father but also from seeing the relationship between mother and father. That has to be an example of a good mutual relationship where connection is the top priority.

What About Sons and Fathers?

The new fatherhood movement, which gives men permission and recognition for actively and intensively fathering their children, is a great gift to boys—and girls, too.[24] Fathers are crucial to helping their sons find someone to be *like* in many ways. They can, along with mothers, teach sons and daughters how to be competent in the world, how to be loyal and team players, and how to make "objective" decisions and take action. The joys and impacts of fathering have been well described in many books and articles.

Yet most fathers as boys have gone through the male relational paradox and more likely than not were valued more for themselves—their accomplishments as "men"—than for their ability to engage in mutual relationships. And so a father may not naturally teach his son mutuality—mutual empathy, mutual authenticity, and mutual empowerment. If the father too is recovering from the normal boyhood trial of enforced focus on self and has spent decades keeping his yearning for connection a secret, underground, it may be particularly difficult for him to teach the boy how to value and stay in connection with others. A father might say to his son:

> That little girl on your soccer team has every bit as much a right to be on this team as you do. You have to give her her chance, respect her efforts, let her do as best she can. Be nice to her. She's an equal to you.

This endorses the notion of equality but does not move toward mutuality. Simply put, mutuality is when differences add. Both or all voices are heard and responded to. In dialogue or group process something else is created, larger than anyone or all, which helps all. In a mutual connection, the "five good things"—zest, worth, knowledge, power, and desire for more connection—arise. And so in this example, to help his son move toward a mutual connection with the girl, the father might put it this way:

> That little girl on your soccer team has every bit as much a right to be on the team as you do. Try to *help* her to do her best, and *let her help you*. She probably has different ways of playing the game, and if you and she put your different ways of doing things together, both of you will get better, and the team will be stronger. You watch—it'll be more fun.

According to male coaches of girls' sports, girls bring different sensibilities to the game. In fact, in a truly mutual connection on the soccer field, the game may be quite different in terms of how feelings, injuries, and competition are handled. The son might come away saying to the father, "But, Dad, it'll be a different game." Of course there are differences between team relationships and other kinds. A team tends not to talk about feelings (rarely during the game); it is brought together most intensely when against another team, and outside the event there is not always the felt necessity for continuity of connection. While fathers have a similar capacity for empathy and mutuality as mothers, they have not been valued for relating to their sons in this way. Fathers may feel less competent with their sons in these more purely relational arenas.

An aspect of fathering, pointed out by Deborah Tannen,[25] is that the way fathers talk to sons and daughters is quite different from the way mothers do. In general, fathers engage in product talk, action talk. There's less eye contact and less back-and-forth, less affirming body language and fewer "uh-huhs" and "rights." Empathic words and actions around feelings are fewer, speeches are longer, and there are fewer interruptions. When we speak of the father–son "we" or the father–daughter "we," the qualities of that "we"—the tone, texture, facts conveyed, movement, and feeling—are greatly affected by the particular style that fathers use. The mother–son "we" and mother–daughter "we" may have strikingly different qualities.

In sum, fathers—like mothers—can help a great deal by consistently validating and fostering the relational development of boys in many different arenas.

The Terrors of Boyhood

By the age of six or seven, the "normal" boy in our culture is being moved down the path of individual competence and action, which he often feels (in tune with the dominant culture but mistakenly) is opposed to connection. This "self" path is affirmed by the patriarchal culture at every turn. For example, as the boy starts to have friends—almost always of the same gender—the group of boys reinforces the culturally mandated notion of what a man is. Groups fall into little patriarchies and hierarchies, with up–down, power-over rules, and orders. Talk to most men about boyhood and you will hear tales of bullying, brutality, and perhaps abuse. Boys learn this certain *kind* of relationship in boy–boy culture.

The boy arrives at adolescence more or less at home with a focus on himself, not having been valued for the care and feeding of relationships with others, for attending to the "we." (An exception is the sports team "we.") But the self-focus of the boy can carry the man only so far. Most men seem to struggle with the male relational paradox in relationships that matter to them. It may flare up around commitment to marriage and in relationship with children. A man who primarily values himself and the comfort of his aloneness may be surprised to find himself, in his late thirties or forty or fifty, becoming desperate in his isolation. The male "midlife crisis" is a natural playing out of this self-focused way of living, the sanctioned male quest. It is often a sad announcement that a man has hit a wall, or the four walls of what Miller has called "condemned isolation."[26] Luckily, the desperation sometimes unearths the long stifled yearning for connection that most men dearly hold inside. Riding that yearning, a man might wake up and seek mutual connection, often with a woman. He will still have to learn to work with his powerfully learned ways of disconnecting.

Women's Relational Development

Why do we *have to talk first?*

—SEVENTH-GRADE GIRL, ASKING BOYS

Women's psychological development is different.[27] At age three to five girls do not face the same cultural imperative to disconnect from relation-

ship in order to grow. For girls, the overwhelming crisis of self and relationship, connection and disconnection, hits as adolescence approaches.

Judy, a fifty-year-old client of ours, looks back upon a crucial time in
her life, just as she entered adolescence at age eleven:

> Up until that time, I was a spunky, self-assured little girl. My
> favorite activities were writing and acting, my most favorite
> class was English. I was really articulate and focused on my
> writing. I won prizes for my stories—I *loved* reading them aloud
> to my class, my friends, even my family. I was a passionate
> writer and actress. At the start of seventh grade, everything
> changed. I didn't know why. I feel like I lost myself. I wouldn't
> even raise my hand in class even though I knew the answers. I
> couldn't talk with my parents, my teachers. I felt lost, unhappy,
> and desperately lonely. My language, once the thing that I was
> most proud of, that was most *mine, me,* all of a sudden was
> gone. I stopped writing totally. I had friends and boyfriends, but
> somewhere I lost me. For years. I think that I and all my women
> friends are still in recovery from our adolescence.

Carol Gilligan, Mary Pipher, and Catherine Steiner-Adair have been in
the forefront of describing and understanding this transition to adulthood
in girls in our culture.[28] Parents and educators try urgently to understand
how this transition from active, happy, self-confident girl, to gloomy, self-
doubting, quiet, and even depressed, suicidal, and substance-abusing,
young adolescent takes place for many girls.

The first years of life for girls are a process of growth in connection,
similar to that of boys. Girls rarely pass through the dramatic struggle
starting around age three that boys do. The culture allows and encour-
ages girls to continue to grow in connection with their mothers and
fathers and others and to focus attention and learn about relationships.
Other aspects of development are encouraged (creativity, initiative,
exploration, interests, and talents, etc.) in the context of relationship.
Girls do not perceive the need to disconnect or to sacrifice relationship
for self. The fact that girls continue to develop as strong, self-assured
people for the first decade of their lives is living proof that "self" does
not suffer from "connection" but is enhanced by it. For the first years of
their lives many girls are wonderful examples of a blossoming creativity,
perceptiveness, sensitivity, and achievement—physical, intellectual, and
aesthetic. These may be some of the best years of many women's lives.

In this culture, most girls and women develop in the context of relationships. Relationships are central to their growth and well-being. Healthy growth in connection (what we call a relational pathway of development) implies a deepening capacity for participating in mutually empathic and mutually empowering connections. Empathy—the motivation and capacity that Judith Jordan describes as being aware, attuned, resonant, and responsive to others' feelings—is a crucial feature of this model of women's development.[29] Rather than empathy being an instinctual "earth-mother," "essential" quality of women, it is something learned and practiced in relationship with the support of this cultural "norm" for women. This emphasis can have a downside for girls who then do not fit this dominant cultural model. The centrality of relationships can be used to discourage full expression of girls' development while emphasizing being "nice" and "good" in order to create conflict-free relationships. And most problematically it can lead girls and women to carry a one-sided responsibility for the care of their relationships with men.

Early relationships such as mother–daughter, sibling, and girl–girl friendships can be seen as models of growth in connection.[30] The mother–daughter relationship supports the process of learning mutual empathy through the girl's ongoing emotional desire to be attuned to and to impact her mother's feelings. Remaining open to the feeling states of mothers and others can and often does create challenges for girls and women. A client described her three-year-old daughter's frequent questioning of her: "What are you feeling, Mommy?"

The mother would respond thoughtfully and carefully to the question. She was pleased to be asked but also worried about "burdening" her daughter with her answer. She was also puzzled that she hardly ever recalled such an interaction with her five-year-old son.

Her daughter seemed to have a sense of reciprocity as well. When the mother asked, "How was your day, Lizzie?" the little girl would tell her, and then, likely as not, ask, "And how was *yours,* Mommy?"

Her son never took this step toward adult mutuality.

Girls' Learning to Listen and Respond

This early attentiveness by girls to their own and others' feeling states and to the state of the relationship—and the mother's or other woman's corresponding ease with and interest in emotional sharing—may form the basic sense of "learning to listen," to orient and attune to the other person through feelings. (How different this is from men, who often describe their childhood experience as "learning *not* to listen, to shut out my mother's voice so that I would not be distracted from pursuing my own interests.") For girls, "being present with" emotionally and psychologically can be experienced as self-enhancing and relationship-enhancing; boys may feel it as self-diminishing. At the same time, girls may feel overburdened by attention to and responsiveness to others. Relationships with mothers in particular can come to feel too powerful, stifling, and obstructive.

"Being present with" someone means "seeing the other person," "feeling seen by the other," and "sensing the other person feeling seen by you." It creates a sense of joining, of truly "being together" or "moving together" in an emotional and psychological dimension. This sense of joining and mutual impact and responsiveness we call mutual empathy. Usually this open connection is more allowed and in some families encouraged between mothers and daughters. When this process does not develop in a healthy way, the psychological well-being of girls and women can be profoundly disturbed.

Thus, girls develop more in the context of relationships rather than toward an autonomous sense of self. This relational way of being is two-directional; it becomes as important to understand the other as to be understood, to be impacted by the other as to impact. Clearly all women in this culture do not necessarily follow this pathway or follow it in the same way (individual families and cultures vary widely), but in general this relational pathway is more highly encouraged for girls than for boys. A consequence is that girls and women are hurt and diminished in relationships that cannot move toward mutual empathy. They also feel shamed and devalued when the prevailing or dominant culture views or judges this relational way of being as "dependent," "oversensitive," "overemotional," "needy," or "immature."

The Female Relational Paradox

At adolescence—under the demands of the culture and prompted by the onslaught of media and advertising—the girl begins to sacrifice her full connection to herself and others for less authentic and limiting relationships, with both boys and girls. She begins to try to shape herself and her relationships—literally in terms of her body as well as emotionally and intellectually—to "fit" the cultural image of male–female relationships. In interacting with her friends, her yearning for connection and her terror of isolation is intense. The new focus of the yearning, a boy, may stimulate that yearning even further by his unavailability for connection with her—a symptom of his disconnection from his own yearning for the same thing. In early adolescence she may begin to suppress or distort her own being in order to be in relationship with the other gender.

Simply put, girls sacrifice expression of their whole being for relationship; the fullness of personal expression for the sake of relationships that then precludes the possibility of authentic relationships, exactly what they yearn for.[31] Simultaneously they are faced with the cultural valuing of developmental goals of independence, separation, self-reliance, and self-direction. Girls' yearnings for connection are twisted on the spindle of the cultural image of "a real woman," who is supposed to walk an impossible line precisely balanced between male and female models of development: ambitious but subordinate, warm but not overemotional, strong but nurturing, responsible for herself but not too independent. These cultural imperatives for girls are highly contradictory.

In trying to follow conflicting cultural mandates, girls suffer on an epidemic scale. If they are lucky, they will begin to come back to themselves and their families to a certain extent by the end of high school. Yet the shadow of this paradox falls across them for the rest of their lives and influences to a greater or lesser degree all their relationships. Still, it is important to note that for girls, this relational paradox takes place years later than for boys.

Even girls who are not bound for heterosexuality in adulthood face this patterning of relational development in adolescence. Girl–girl friendships in preadolescence and adolescence are often one of the arenas through which this relational paradox is shaped. While girls deeply value and rely on their relationships, they are often also enormously vulnerable to rejection, triangulation, and loss. Girls play out a powerful dance of inclusion and exclusion, who is "in" or "out" of connection. Relationships feel precarious, and girls feel a terrible danger of isolation when they do not live out cultural norms for "ideal" female development that get enforced by girls. Girls learn this certain *kind* of relationship in girl–girl culture.

The precarious drop in self-worth and confidence associated with female adolescence impacts overall school performance, with particular loss in math and science achievement. Among other important variables, race, class, ethnicity, sexual preference, and geographical location impact girls' relational and academic development. In particular African American girls do not evidence the same overall drop in self-confidence as Caucasian girls.[32] These girls are not as subject to the tyranny of "good" and "nice" at the expense of their intensity, anger, and strength. While girls in nondominant cultural groups may have a certain freedom from these particular limiting relational images (African American, Latina, lesbian, and many others), they also contend with many other limiting stereotypes and "isms."

There is currently the beginnings of a girls' movement. Literature, magazines, after-school programs, videos, and school curricula abound that challenge gender stereotypes, envisioning gender equality and encouraging girls' strengths. Mothers, fathers, teachers, and adult friends of girls have an essential role to play in helping girls resist this terrible relational paradox. By attempting to create mutually authentic relationships with girls that challenge isolation and disconnection and "hold" the possibility of continuity and creativity of relationships, adults can help girls to stay connected. There is much to suggest that girls with strong relationships to families, especially with their mothers, are least in danger at adolescence.

Fathers have been talking a greater part in their daughters' development—in school, in sports, and in the arts. Since fathers are the dominant power in the society, when fathers become concerned about their daughters' problems in school, they can be powerful in changing school systems. If they join with mothers to bring about change, change can happen. To help their daughters, fathers can do similar things to what we have suggested for mothers: hold the connection and the vision of an alternative to the cultural norm, find other fathers of daughters who are struggling to stay in connection themselves, and of course walk the walk—demonstrating to the daughter a good male–female relationship with her mother.

We believe that programs for girls that support the possibility of authenticity, collaboration, and problem solving in girl–girl friendships are essential. Creating opportunities for exploring, building, and sustaining authentic, empathic, and empowering relationships with boys at every age is also essential in fostering girls' development. Healthy relationships between boys and girls are a powerful arena for both genders' development.

Given these different "norms," what happens when these two different pathways of development meet?

Gender Collisions: When Boys and Girls Get Together

Gender collisions occur earlier than most of us think. Here are two examples, one from childhood, one from adolescence.

One sunny spring morning several years ago, we were doing a gender dialogue with four-year-olds in a preschool, six boys and six girls. We used our usual format, asking boys and girls separately to answer three questions about gender, modified for their level of understanding. Then the boys and girls sat on the floor facing each other. We asked the boys, "What do you like about girls?" They said:

"They like to play what *I* like to play."
"They always play with me and help me with things."

Then we asked the girls, "What do you like about boys?" They said:

"We like kissing and hugging boys."
"We like when they chase us and tie us up and they thought we
    were dead and we faked it and then we liked sneaking away
    and getting away."

We found this somewhat appalling. But then something else started to happen. The boys were fidgeting, not paying much attention to the girls, and the girls began to tell a story, together, each adding lines. The story was about how one girl had tricked a wicked baby-sitter. Soon the boys were listening wide-eyed. The girls had found a way to connect.

Next we asked the girls, "When you play a game with boys, who goes first?" One girl said, "Boys go first." She looked to the other girls and then, giggling, started to chant, "Boys go first! Boys go first!"

Soon all the girls were getting into it, "Boys go first! Boys go first!"

It was remarkable to us how they were simultaneously enforcing gender patterns and debunking them. But the joking and teasing again served to keep the boys' attention and to keep the group connected.

After the dialogue there was a free-play period outside in a field. Soon the teacher, surprised, said to us, "This is amazing! I've never seen this before. The boys and girls are playing together. And there are no hierarchical patterns among the boys." He pointed out that the girls and boys were running around holding hands—sometimes a foursome would run by—and that the "top boy," the one usually heading the hierarchy of play, was now all by himself. No one was paying attention to him. It was clear that something had shifted during the group dialogue, and the shift was being incorporated immediately as more interconnected play.

It was striking to us how strongly this relational pattern is in place even at age four. Here is the playing out of the relational paradoxes: the girls moving out of their own most authentic ways of speaking to focus attention upon, entice, and connect with the boys. The boys, fairly unaware of what the girls were doing, were happy to be at the center of attention. For the boys, self-interest was more important than attending to the connection ("Girls like to play what *I* like to play"); for the girls it was more important to attend to making the connection rather than to say or to play what they might have if only girls were present.

In this example, something worked, although it was somewhat at the expense of the girls' wholeness and authenticity and the boys' relational awareness. The girls gave and made the connection without the boys realizing what was going on. In the children's free play in the field there was more connection, but perhaps at some price—loss of wholeness, manipulation, and lack of awareness. This is not unknown to couples.

Gender Collision in an Eighth-Grade Classroom: Alleged Coeducation

In the second example an eighth-grade English teacher is at his wits' end. His coed class has an equal number of girls and boys. When he asks a question, many of the boys' hands shoot up. The same few girls always raise their hands. He has tried everything. To his dismay, he finds that many boys will raise their hands even if they don't know the answer, hoping that by the time they are called on some answer will come to them. If he tells the boys not to raise their hands, they will sometimes raise their elbows! The girls are reluctant—even though he knows from tests that they are at least as capable, as a group, as the boys. Finally he gets fed up and says in an irritated voice, "Okay, girls. You have to answer. I'm not calling on the boys at all this time. Let's go." The girls become more silent and shamed.

Eighth grade is a sad and dramatic collision of the two pathways of development. Not only are male and female roles and identities more or less solidified by this time, but boys and girls now have some firsthand experience of relationship with the other gender. Girls are shaped away from speaking and acting in ways that might threaten relationships. Boys are shaped to defend and grow the "self," although they still yearn for connection. Again, one series of answers to the question "What do you want girls to understand about you?" reveals this most poignantly about the boys:

> "Don't believe the way I act—I'm really a nice guy underneath."
> "I may act like a pervert, but I really care."
> "I act like a jerk around you because I'm nervous."

And the most poignant, said softly and shyly, a real plea:

> "Please see my heart."

Eighth-grade girls, on the other hand, are in the throes of their own relational paradox; more and more they are twisting themselves out of authentic connection with what they know and diminishing themselves to "fit" the image that they are told will succeed in relationships with boys. Here are some of the girls' responses to the same question, "What do you most want boys to understand about you?"

> "We act happy, but it's just an act. Do you know how many of us go home and cry into our pillows at night?"
> "I may act like I don't care, but it really hurts girls when you tease them about body parts."
> "Just because I show my feelings doesn't mean I'm not smart too."

These eighth-grade girls and boys are coming from very different places. When the teacher asks a question, the boys are thinking of the answer. The girls are thinking about the answer too, but in addition they are thinking, in their words:

> "I don't want to seem to be too smart."
> "What will Chip think if I speak up and show him up?"
> "The teacher doesn't really like me anyway."
> "I'm not good at English."
> "I might hurt someone's feelings."
> "I might embarrass my friends."
> "My enemies are just waiting for me to say something, to tease me."

"I don't *believe* what my mother said to me this morning! I'm
still angry at her!"

The girls are intensely aware of the relationships that exist in the
room and in their lives. A girl's whole relational context—peopled by
the teacher, boys, friends, "enemies," her mother, her father, her sib-
lings—impacts her classroom participation.

In this case it is not only the girls who are being shortchanged but the
boys as well. When boys are encouraged to focus mainly on classroom
or athletic achievement as it is narrowly defined (good behavior and
performance) rather than being praised for being responsive to others
and working with others, both boys and girls suffer. Our classrooms
echo our culture. Boys and girls both are not valued in the classroom
for their relational strengths and yearnings. True coeducation would
center on using the differences between boys and girls to create connections in the classrooms, allowing both boys and girls to be more creative, alive, and empowered to learn. A truly mutual coeducation would
occur when gender differences *add,* making the whole greater than the
sum of its parts.

With this new view of the different developmental pathways of boys
and girls, we again turn our focus to the collisions between men and
women, what we call "relational impasses."

3

Women's Yearning
Meets Men's Dread

THREE RELATIONAL
IMPASSES

"It's not just a yearning for connection, it's a burn-ing yearning."

—WIFE, DESCRIBING WHAT SHE WANTS
FROM HER HUSBAND

"When she asks me what I'm feeling, it's like a five-hundred-pound gorilla has just walked into the room."

—HUSBAND, DESCRIBING HIS
WIFE'S ATTENTION

An impasse occurs when a relationship is stuck, static, unmoving, and there is a sense that it may never move again.[1] Things go dead, each participant retreats into his or her self. Everyone feels the relational space close down, the closing down closes down more space, and a neg-ative spiral is created: women's yearning leads to men's dread leads to more yearning leads to more dread. Each person has a sense of being trapped, deadened. Things become more polarized; things also fall into more gender-stereotyped behavior, often with accusations like:

WOMAN: You're just like all men!
MAN: You're just like your mother!
WOMAN: Your father!
MAN: Italians!

This results not only in the impossibility of contact but also in the impossibility of *working with the conflict.* As we have seen, impasse is relational in that it does not reside only in one person or the other but in the process between them. While there might be a "transference" component (your partner seeming to be like your mother or your father) and a "projective" aspect (seeing in your partner the qualities you dislike in yourself), these are not always helpful concepts when couples are in trouble. An impasse is not mainly projective or transferential but rather the result of one relational style meeting another quite different one. The stuckness is the result of what the man and the woman have been learning about relationships over the course of many years.

Miller has suggested that relationships are always in movement, either toward fuller connection or greater disconnection.[2] In all relationships, minor disconnections are inevitable. Nobody gets it right every time. The couples who grow find ways to turn disconnections into better connections; the couples who wither rarely do.

In growth-fostering relationships, disconnections become a stimulus for relational growth. The challenge is to let go of the past—past learnings, past resentments, past images—and to create new connections, which are by their nature in the present. We call this growth *through and toward connection.*[3] In growth-hindering relationships (nonmutual ones), disconnections lead to further disconnections, and to impasse.

Couples tend to have their own particular areas of impasse. They can be provoked by the cap left off the toothpaste, the dishes in the sink, the underwear on the floor, the different approaches to limit setting or protectiveness with the kids. With your own relational impasse, you each know that if you start down a particular path it will end in disaster—and still you start down that path, and it always ends in disaster. You each wind up feeling more alone and isolated and less able to act effectively in the relationship. Either or both of you might feel angry, bored, frustrated, confused, disappointed, lonely, hopeless, and a complete failure as a human being. Or you might feel that the *other* person is a complete failure as a human being, either through what could only be bad genes, a warped family history, a personality or moral defect, or what seems in the moment to be a particularly barbaric cultural heritage. Over time, unresolved impasses constrict relationships so that there is less space for any real movement or authentic meeting. They begin to define the *whole* relationship.

After several years of doing gender dialogues we noticed that the ways in which men and women got stuck could be described by three main impasses, which we called *dread/yearning, product/process,* and *power-over/power-with.*

Mostly, men identified with one part of an impasse (dread) while women identified with the other (yearning). But sometimes a man would be more on the yearning side, a woman more on the dread. Yet the *way* women described their experience of dread was often quite different from the way men described it, and the setting, too, was often different. For instance, female dread seemed to be stimulated more often in her male partner's sexual approach to her (as described in chapter 6), while male dread arose in the face of women's attempts at emotional connection. There is much overlap among the three impasses. Dread and yearning are deep-seated and play a part in most other relational impasses between men and women.

The examples of the three types of impasses that follow come from couples in our gender dialogues. First we will simply show what they say to each other; next, we will show in each impasse what is going on in him and in her.

The Dread/Yearning Impasse

Alice and Phil are at the beach. A young couple, married two years, they've just finished a wonderful picnic lunch and, sitting side by side, are staring out at the gulls, the waves, children splashing, and the vast ocean. They both feel relaxed and happy.

ALICE: What are you feeling, hon?
PHIL: *(startled, says nothing)*
ALICE: Can you tell me?
PHIL: *(pause)* I don't know.

ALICE: Sure you do. Please, talk to me?

PHIL: *(tensely)* Don't . . . spoil . . . it.

ALICE: *(angrily) I'm* spoiling it?!

Now we look at what is going on in each of them:

ALICE: *(motivated by this good feeling between them, wants to affirm it, continue it, and asks)* What are you feeling, hon?

PHIL: *(is startled, and blinks his eyes, suddenly feeling tense. He doesn't know what to say to this. A pause. He tries to think but comes up with nothing)*

ALICE: *(goes on)* Can you tell me?

PHIL: *(his tension rising, remembering similar exchanges between them in the recent past, says tightly)* I don't know.

ALICE: *(says with growing urgency)* Sure you do. Please, talk to me?

PHIL: *(in a cold, measured voice, barely in control, says)* Don't . . . spoil . . . it.

ALICE: *(is taken aback and in an eruption of anger screams) I'm* spoiling it?

Things deteriorate to the point where Phil gets up abruptly and walks off down the beach, leaving Alice alone, now in tears.

This is an example of a man being overwhelmed with a deep sense of dread, a visceral sense in his gut and his heart. Invitation starts to seem like demand; curiosity like criticism. It's also an example of a woman lashing out in anger when her yearning is rebuffed, a result of repeated past experiences of this. The more Alice comes forward, needing to explore things relationally, the more Phil feels dread and wants to avoid things relationally. As one of the women in a dialogue put it, "Men don't give women enough information to keep us from going crazy."

"That's because," a man answered, "you're always asking us for more."

What is Phil's experience in this scene? From our dialogue work we know that men do listen, at least until dread takes over. Further, men do have feelings and are often able to sort out what these feelings are, but this usually takes some time. That's where the "pause" comes in. Unfortunately, women often seem to be on a different time sense and, in the midst of the man sorting out what he is feeling, may ask again, "Can you tell me?" This makes the man feel pressure, and his "I don't know"—or even, as one man put it, "I don't know, I'll tell you tomorrow"—may be an attempt at buying time to stay focused on what he feels and say it. In a very real sense, he is trying to stay in connection. But then when the woman says, "Sure you do. Please, talk to me?" the man's original feeling gets all mixed up with the feeling of being under pressure to respond. Here is where things begin to fall apart. The dread starts to take over, feelings become blurred and homogenized into a wish to escape, and further listening becomes almost impossible.

The woman, on the other hand, starts out with a general yearning to be more in connection, to be closer. In the face of the man's first withdrawal, she feels a heightened yearning, and then when he says "I don't know," she is hit with a difficult choice: to continue to pursue him and take care of him and the relationship, or to withdraw also, in anger and shame. When Phil says, "Don't spoil it," Alice gives up in hurt and anger. She says, "*I'm* spoiling it?" and withdraws. Disconnection leads to further disconnection. He leaves, and she is left alone.

Suddenly we're in the wasteland of disconnection. Things come to a dead stop. The relationship goes flat.

Dread arises not from the woman reminding the man of his mother but from his being in a relational process where things are happening quickly and complexly on both sides, a movement where one relational style (men's) is meeting another quite different one (women's). As we have seen, a man's dread is the result of his learning to avoid really being in the process of relationship with another person, repeated tens of thousands of times, day in and day out with few exceptions, year after year. Phil's every *intent* was to be in good connection with Alice, much as the little six-year-old boy who had been beaten up *intended*, as he walked into the kitchen, to open up to his mother about his pain. For each of them, the boy and the man, the woman moving toward him created the relational context that brought out a response of dread. His response was the opposite of his intent. And repeated dread now dulls even his intent.

Alice's intent was to connect. Phil's stiff silence brought out a response of more frantic yearning, desperation, and anger. In the words of Phil after working later on the impasse, "That day on the beach we were in dreadlock!"

Aspects of Men's Relational Dread

Over the years we've heard thousands of men talk about dread.[4] Men consistently use similar images, so that when other men hear a man talk about his own experience of dread, they feel a sense of relief. Listening to each other brings men who think they are out on the edge of the so-called "sick" into the current of the human. A man starts to move from feeling different from everybody else (and especially from other men) to feeling that he is *like* other men. Hearing these aspects of dread, men start to move from a self-centered shame toward connection. They tend to describe this process in certain terms:

Inevitability of disaster: "Nothing good can come of my going into this with her; it's just a matter of how bad it'll be before it's over."

Timelessness: "And it will never be over!"

Damage: "The damage will be immense and irreparable."

Closeness: "The closer I feel to the woman—even, the more I love her—the more intense my dread becomes. When my wife says to me, 'I love you,' my back starts to sweat."

Precariousness: "Even if it starts to dissipate and clear and feel better, it can turn at any moment back to dread, betraying me."

Process: "This is a shifting, time-warped terrain, and I'm not sure of the validity of my perceptions, let alone being with her while I'm in it. It's a quick, forward-moving process, and I can't seem to find a firm foothold for myself, and I'm scared that something out of control might happen."

Guilt: "I'm not enough. I have not been enough in these relationships before. I feel I've let women down all along, and I feel guilty."

Anger: "I feel like fighting back but I can't. She's going to bring up everything from the past and forget how hard I've worked to be there for her in my own way; nothing I do is ever enough."

Denial of and fear of aggression: "If I'm trapped, pushed too far, and unable to withdraw or leave, I might panic or get violent and hurt someone. I feel like I'm all dressed up in my power with nowhere to go."

Incompetence: "All my life I've been taught that I have to be competent in the world, and I don't feel competent at this. She's better at this than me, verbally and relationally—not only does she know the general territory better, but she seems to know *me* better than I know myself. Sometimes she seems to be able to see right into me, or through me. I could focus on one thing at a time, but this is many things all mixed together, and vague things at that. She insists we talk about patriarchy and our health plan and the Middle East and the kids' school and our relationship—all at once! It's baffling!"

Shame and humiliation: "I'm ashamed of my incompetence. I ought to be able to function in this, but I can't. I ought to be able to take action, to fix the flat tire of this interaction. Before I can say anything, I have to be sure of what I'm going to say—usually I can go off by myself and get sure first, but in this I can't. And I have to be accurate."

Paralysis: "As each of these things comes up, my dread is redoubled. Trying to fix things under the pressure of feeling I have to fix things fast. I fumble things even more. If I can't fix it, I can't admit that it's broken—the problem doesn't really exist. I'll keep quiet about it, not even acknowledge that it's there."

And so, through these various aspects of dread, even though a man may desperately want to connect, he becomes an agent of disconnection. Men tune out and withdraw. In some situations, under the influence of alcohol or other drugs, they may escalate to violence—the ultimate, tragic disconnection.

Aspects of Women's Yearning

When women, who are often much more at home in the process of dialogue leading to good connection, describe aspects of their relational yearning as it encounters male dread, they speak of frustration, blockage, rage, despair, and isolation. One woman called this place a "black hole."

Suddenness of disconnection: "It's like when you're peddling fast on your bicycle and suddenly the chain slips off and you're left peddling hard, going nowhere."

Disbelief: "I start to feel 'I don't believe this is happening!' When I keep wanting to go into it, to get at it with him, he gets this glazed look, he starts to look at me like I'm a vegetable in a market. As I keep at it, he starts to look at me as if I'm the enemy. I say, 'Yoo-hoo, it's me—remember me? Your wife? Your friend? How did I get to be the enemy? I mean things were fine a second ago; what happened?' It makes me feel like an alien, trying to make contact. But it makes me feel really sorry for him too."

Feeling frantic: "When I feel that silence, it's like a chill goes through me, and I feel I've *got* to do something, to take care of this and to keep the thing moving. It feels like life or death."

Desperation: "I get totally focused on him, and on what's going on between us and him, and I can feel myself getting really desperate, as if it's a life-and-death matter to get it going again, and that if I can't, and if I'm left alone with all these feelings and this sense of failure, to retreat into myself at a time like that, with you withdrawing from me—is like falling off the edge of the world."

Bargaining: "If you talk to me, we'll make passionate love all night long."

Shame: "I know I shouldn't be doing it, working so hard to take care of him and the relationship, I know from all the other times I've done it that it's unhealthy—and then I go ahead and do it. I know I sound like a bitch, a broken record, a nag—I hate myself! It's humiliating, but I can't stop."

Anger: "Why do I need this? I'm sick and tired of being sick and tired of being the caretaker of this relationship. I'm out of here."

Rationalization: "Maybe it's just impossible, between men and women. Maybe the only sensible position to take is that guys are aliens. I mean if you start there, you don't expect them to change—you can't expect to change a dog into a cat, right? You stop trying. There are a few mutants—I thought you might be one—some guys you can have bridge conversations with, bridging the differences, at least at first. But sooner or later you find yourself beating your head against a wall. I'm telling you—you have a lot of energy when you break up with a guy, because you stop trying to turn a dog into a cat."

Rage: "Respond! If you don't respond to me I'll kill myself or throw something or rip your eyes out!"

Women's Anger

In the gender dialogues, men always have questions about women's anger, such as, "What is women's anger about, and what to do about it?" In one dialogue, the men and women tried to get clearer on anger, together:

MAN: What level are you angry about? We always feel that what we see is the tip of the iceberg. How deep does it go?

WOMAN: When we're angry, you could *ask* us what we're angry about.

MAN: If her car keys are lost and she throws a fit, I try not to take responsibility for it. But then she's *so* angry that I start to think that her anger is not about the car keys, it's about something else. So which is it, the car keys or the something else that's going on in her?

WOMAN: She might not know yet which it is. It could be everything. Life doesn't come in clear little packages.

WOMAN: Can't the *process* she's in be where it's at?

MAN: Rather than the car keys?

WOMAN: *And* the car keys.

MAN: It's mind-boggling.

MAN: Why don't you just *tell* us when you're angry?

WOMAN: Because sometimes we don't know. How are we supposed
to know how we feel except by talking about it?

And so one of the problems in the dread/yearning impasse is that
when women's anger starts to come up, women want to get through it
in connection, while men want to get out and let things calm down and
come back to it when anger is not so hot.

Anger is often a difficult feeling to deal with in connection. We have
found that when anger arises in the man–woman relationship, it can be
helpful to reframe it in terms of hurt in the relationship:[5] rather than
anger being a primary feeling of aggression, of wanting to hurt, it can
be seen as a sign that someone is hurt or that something is wrong in the
relationship that needs to be changed.

From the gender dialogues we discovered that another aspect of this
impasse is mostly invisible to women but visible to men.

Relational Timing

Men and women are on quite different relational time scales, with
women's being faster than men's. As we've seen, the process of *responding*
about feeling or with feeling takes longer for men than women. Women
have more rapid access to their feelings, as well as a greater fluidity of feeling and multiplicity of feeling—lots of different feelings flowing, sometimes
together, sometimes apart. Women can not only identify and respond more
rapidly but they can listen to the next question while they're processing the
last. This is the "focus on more than one thing at a time" strength that men
readily identify in women. As, in general, women are more bilaterally inte-
grated in terms of cortical brain function, this may perhaps be a biological
difference between the genders, or perhaps learned.

Women's quickness in processing feelings and responding is visible to
men and women both. But men's process of relational timing is largely
invisible to women. Women, of course, realize that men often fall silent,
but they may not realize that this is because it takes men more time to
organize feelings for response, especially in the face of dread.

Women respond with the sense that their final formulation can take place in the process of responding, *with* others (usually women) free to brainstorm, to speak and think simultaneously;[6] men have been trained to come up with the answer *before* they say anything, to respond without "public" processing. Rather than forming a response *with* others, men often are valued for responding *despite* others. "Draw a line in the sand," or "Stand tall," no matter what anyone else is saying, feeling, or doing.

In our gender dialogues, when the men and women in small groups of three fill out the questions in their same-gender groups, the men often *each* fill out their own answers, and then the group shuffles or lists them for a "group or consensus" answer; the women, on the other hand, talk together, and then as time nears the end they together write down the group's answers. Once, in a dialogue at a noted medical school, a doctor came back into the mixed group and announced that he had refused to join the men's small group but had filled out his answers on his own.

"I don't agree that there are significant differences between men and women," the doctor said, "so I filled out my answers by myself so you would not be able to tell if it was filled out by a man or a woman."

"*That*," Janet said, "is how we can tell."

In another of the dialogues, a man observed how the women quickly processed what they were hearing from the men in terms of snatches of conversation, one woman building on what another was saying, non-verbal cues, and so forth. He then said:

> Our model is the stoic male, the steady private thinker. Women jump in so much more quickly, it's amazing to watch you—you all have a five-minute conversation in twenty seconds, and it does result in connection, though I'm not sure how it results in direction. When I give an answer I have to really think it out myself first, as if it's gotta be valid for one hundred years.
>
> WOMAN: You men just don't see our women's logic.
>
> MAN: "Women's logic" is an oxymoron.
>
> MAN: I disagree. They have "pot-logic"—throw everything into the pot and see what cooks up.
>
> WOMAN: We have the faith that if everyone gets involved, if we really go into relationship, we will all be enlarged, and the best answers will shine through!

When men's slower relational timing and different logic is made visible to women, it can be a great help to couples.

"I" versus "You"

Dread/yearning impasses can be the most harsh example of how a couple can slip into an "I" versus "you" stance.

Gail has awakened earlier than her husband, Bo. They are hard-working graduate students in their late twenties, with a small child. She comes into the bedroom. It is a Saturday, and she is full of hope and expectation that they will have a nice family day together.

GAIL: Good morning! We're going to have a great day!

BO: Let's hope so. Is the washing machine already on?

GAIL: Yes, why?

BO: I wanted my jeans washed today.

GAIL: If you wanted them washed, next time put them in the laundry bag.

BO: *(says nothing)*

GAIL: What is it? Do you want to say something?

BO: I feel scolded.

GAIL: Who cares! I give up! *(leaves the room)*

BO: *(lies there in silence)*

Now, we look at what is going on with him, and with her:

GAIL: Good morning! We're going to have a great day!

BO: *(has other things on his mind but, feeling her expectation, tries to react; he is feeling slightly depressed, but won't say that to her)* Let's hope so. Is the washing machine already on?

GAIL: *(feels a little defensive for her good mood not being acknowledged or appreciated, especially since she's been up for an hour and has done so much around the house already)* Yes, why?

BO: *(her tone alarms him; a bit of dread, but he doesn't want to show any external expression; he tries to divert the conversation to avoid feelings, and says matter-of-factly)* I wanted my jeans washed today.

GAIL: *(defensiveness grows, irritated)* If you want them washed, next time put them in the laundry bag. *(irritation turns to anger as she speaks; she feels herself setting a line between the two of them)*

BO: *(feels attacked, blocked, doesn't know what to say, and thinks, "I was afraid of this happening and it did"; wishing it would all go away by itself. He says nothing.)*

GAIL: (*feels anger at being shut out, feels hostility from him, suggesting he was hurt; reacts on impulse to abandon the conversation—but that's not what she really wants—she doesn't know whether to try to save it at this point or not; takes a chance*) What is it? Do you want to say something?

BO: (*feels she is looking for inflammatory words; this is a declaration of war; something very bad is about to happen, what to do? She is closing in, yet he attempts to say what he feels—attacked*) I feel scolded.

GAIL: (*eruption of anger, with abandon*) Who cares! I give up! (*exits, overwhelmed, her heart filled with this wretched feeling of the sum total of all past bad experiences with this man—and other men; the day might as well be over*)

BO: (*lies in bed, overwhelmed with regret and shame and anger, understanding there is nothing to say—which at that moment reaffirms his initial feeling that he'd better not say a word to her, ever again*)

In this and the previous example of the dread/yearning impasse, the movement is from "we" to "I," from an attempt at connection to an ending in total disconnection, polarization, accusation, where the language has devolved into "I" versus "you." This is true of any impasse.

The Product/Process Impasse

This second type of impasse is very common for men and women, familiar in couples, families, and work. As detailed by Deborah Tannen[7] and as seen in our gender dialogues, men are trained and valued for getting to the bottom line or fixing things, or being competent at getting results ("making a product"). Women are often trained and valued for working in process, with others, to reach a goal.

Men will often say that "women don't get anywhere" or that "your process will get in the way of getting to a product." Women respond that the focus on process can help to get to a more shared, understood, and effective product, *if* the process works well.

One of our couples sketched out the following product/process impasse.

Deb and Richie are a couple in their early fifties, moving out of the house in which they've raised their children. Together, they are carrying the last box of their belongings to the car. Again, first their words, without interpretation:

> DEB: It's sad to say good-bye to this old house.
>
> RICHIE: Yeah, but think about where we're going!
>
> DEB: *(slows down, stops, starts to cry)*
>
> RICHIE: Uh-oh.
>
> DEB: Please, Richie, can we talk?
>
> RICHIE: Not now, we've got to finish this.
>
> DEB: I really need to talk. I need to know where you are.
>
> RICHIE: I'm right here. Moving. How can you talk when we're trying to move?
>
> DEB: How can you just go about moving without any feelings?

Now, the same impasse in terms of what's going on with each of them:

> DEB: *(being hit by the sadness of it all)* It's sad to say good-bye to this old house.
>
> RICHIE: *(excited, trying to stay "up")* Yeah, but think about where we're going!
>
> *(Deb slows down and stops, then begins crying.)*
>
> RICHIE: *(feeling a bit of dread, having a sense that everything's about to fall apart and become unmanageable)* Uh-oh.
>
> DEB: *(yearning to make connection in the moment)* Please, Richie, can we talk?
>
> RICHIE: *(more dread, in conflict with finishing the task at hand)* Not now, we've got to finish this.
>
> DEB: *(more yearning, a little panicked; needing to process what's going on; she feels she's losing him, everything is turning gray)* I really need to talk. I need to know where you are.
>
> RICHIE: *(irritated at being distracted from the task, at being asked to identify and respond with feeling to one thing when his whole mind is focused on another, on accomplishing a long, tiring, difficult event in their lives)* I'm right here. Moving. How can you talk when we're trying to move?
>
> DEB: *(irritated, amazed at the gap between them)* How can you just go about moving without any feelings?
>
> *(They put the box in the car and drive away in hostile silence.)*

The problem is not in Deb or Richie. Both are relatively healthy people, trying to handle an emotional event in their lives. The impasse is in the "we," in the way in which they are meeting, in the way Deb's feelings affect the relational space, and how that space then affects Richie. As they get further disconnected, they become more polarized, by the end each seeing—and saying accusatorily—that the problem is in "you." "I" am okay, "you" are the problem.

The product/process impasse both at home and at work can be ferocious and hard to break through. Not only are the deep feelings of dread and yearning acting like an engine under the thoughts and actions, but the two different pathways of relational development of boys and girls are clearly at work.

When a man is in this impasse, you can almost see, in the man, the boy needing above all else to be competent. He has always been more valued for being competent at doing things and producing things, mostly by himself and for himself. Connection is sacrificed for competence, for being a doer, a producer. Connection is sensed as a hindrance to getting things done, things *you* want or have to do.

And you can almost see, in the woman, the girl. She has always been valued for weaving a net of connections among her playmates, who then may join her in accomplishing a goal. Sometimes, given the girls' relational pathway, the goal feels less important than the connections (which always imply process), if getting to the goal appears to threaten the connections.

Work with boys and girls on the playground shows that if there's a dispute about the game they are playing, boys will often follow the rules and complete the game at the expense of the relationships with each other; girls will often change the rules or even end the game to preserve the process—and movement—of relationships.[8]

In dialogues with eighth-graders, when we asked about boy–boy friendships and girl–girl friendships, we saw a similar thing: boys' friendships are clustered around *doing* similar things, girls' around the *qualities* of the person and of the relationship. When one boy find a different interest, the friendship may end; girls' friendships end more because of unresolvable conflicts in the relationships or the addition of a new relationship.

> My friendship with Matt ended—he got into hockey and I was
> into basketball. So I started playing basketball and found other
> friends.

(Again, one of the main questions women have of men in gender dialogues is, "What goes on in men's friendships with men?—what's the depth of intimacy between men?")

For girls it's different:

> My friendship with Lily ended and I was, like, devastated! I cried and cried! And I still had to be with her on the soccer team!

Another girl, a fourth-grader, told us with pride that her soccer team had done "great"—it had a record of 1–0–6: 1 win, no losses, and 6 ties! Winning counted less than playing with her friends.

Changing the Oil in the Truck: An Impasse of Few Words

Kay and John are in their early thirties. Both have demanding jobs and live a busy, active life. Since they hardly see each other during the week, they have promised each other that weekends would be sacred for them to be together. And yet just about every weekend John, a do-it-yourselfer, has a project around the house that seems to keep him from being with Kay. On this particular Saturday, he's changing the oil in his truck. First, their words:

KAY: *(coming into the garage)* What are you doing?

JOHN: Nothing much. Just changing the oil.

KAY: Anything I can do to help?

JOHN: I don't think so, no.

KAY: Oh, okay. *(hesitates before leaving)*

JOHN: No sweat, hon, I'll finish up here. Go do something *you* want to do.

Kay goes back into the house; John bashes at the truck. And now, their thoughts:

John is under the truck, thinking, "*Here I am again, engaged in yet another 'flailing around' in the endless weekend war on household, lawn, and automotive decay, defying the change of seasons; I hate this.*"

KAY: *(comes out of the house, feeling lonely, wanting to be with him)* What are you doing?

JOHN: *(thinking, thank God I can at least do this with the truck; I need to change the gas and air filters too, and replace the heater before winter, and touch up those rust spots and wax it for the first time in two years; it needs to go into the shop too—another five hundred bucks—for the things I can't do myself; maybe we can still go hiking later in the day; maybe I can patch that leak in the roof right after lunch; I really hate this, and now she's gonna interrupt? pleasantly)* Nothing much. Just changing the oil.

KAY: *(irritated because this happens every weekend; why does he always think up projects that take forever? why can't he pay someone to do this? why can't we just have fun on the weekend? maybe we could work together; maybe we could switch jobs—I hate being in the house alone)* Anything I can do to help?

JOHN: *(she doesn't know how to do these things; besides, my knuckles are bleeding and I'm in grease up to my elbows; even I don't want to be here but it's got to be done; at least I feel like I'm accomplishing something; it'll take longer if I include her)* I don't think so, no.

KAY: *(he just wants me to go away)* Oh, okay. *(she hesitates)*

JOHN: *(shit, now I'm in it; I wish I could just get up and hug her, but I gotta finish this, and then I can hug her)* No sweat, hon, I'll finish up here. Go do something *you* want to do.

Kay, sad and hopeless, turns and goes back into the house.

John, sad to see her go, goes on flailing at car engine furiously.

This sad result comes about despite both the man's and the woman's intention to be connected. It's as if all the values and learnings of the man keep him under the car when he senses that he might feel better with her, and yet he can't see any way that he can "do" both. All of her learnings keep her from somehow, with him, finding her voice to declare that being with him right then—even in the garage or under the car—is what is best not only for her and the relationship but also for him in the relationship—the "you" in the "we." He sees the situation more as an "I" versus "we" or an "I" versus "you." His goal is to finish the job and *then* be ready to get together with her (he may not be aware that that time may never come, or that the disconnection from this impasse will prevent a good connection later); her sense is that the process has been mutilated, and recovery won't be easy. Both are left with sadness and with images of other times in this and other relationships when the other person doesn't seem to understand what is really going on—or other times when, despite what "I" really want, I destroy it.

There's another invisible difference between men and women that plays a large part in the product/process impasse.

The Continuity of Connection

Women in our culture are the caretakers or "holders" of the relationship. They most often are the ones who are valued for and responsible for keeping things running, noticing the qualities of the connection at any particular time but also keeping track of the connections *over* time. They remember when the kids need to get shoes, or dental work, when the parents' or friend's anniversary is, and what calls—or, now, e-mails—are overdue. As one man, a government lawyer said: "She's the Secretary of Health and Human Services."

This comes up in questions men and women ask of each other in dialogue:

WOMAN: How come you don't remember yesterday's conversations?

MAN: How come you never forget?

MAN: Why is there no time limit—or amnesty—on remembering bad things done by men, or sons?

WOMAN: What breaks the continuity between one day and the next? That is, why is today's conversation so unrelated to yesterday's?

WOMAN: How can you go to bed, even during a crisis, and sleep, and then when you wake up your computer screen is blank? Like everything has been dumped in the trash, while mine is full of icons and text?

MAN: Why can't you just delete?

WOMAN: That feels like stopping in the middle of a sentence. It's totally disorienting.

WOMAN: How can we understand men's lack of interest in details, or in the ongoing feeling of others, in how we get where we're going? What's with the 'bottom-line' mentality?

MAN: Why are women so *obsessed* with the details? You get lost in the details.

WOMAN: Why are men's eyes so much on the horizon, as opposed to the here and now?

MAN: Maybe we're always watching for danger. It's our job to protect you.

WOMAN: But the real danger to us is here, in the relationship.

Humor is often helpful to frame impasses and invisibilities. In terms of this gender difference in the continuity connection, occasionally in a dialogue we might say—only half facetiously—that there is one state-ment no man in the history of civilization has ever made to a woman:

"I was thinking about what we were talking about yesterday."

This is met with the laughter of recognition. Women, valued in the cul-ture for their involvement in the growth of others, for the growth of the relationship with others, and for "faith in the process"—have learned that one of the most important ingredients for this is to maintain the *continu-ity of connection* over time. What happened earlier in the day or yesterday or last week or month or year is important to and part of what is happen-ing right now.

Often this continuity and simultaneity is constantly visible to women; it is virtually invisible to men. Invisible to one gender, it produces much suffering. When men forget, or wipe the slate clean overnight, women get angry; part of the anger is from having to carry the connection by themselves. Another part is from feeling that this task is "pathologized," as in the following:

The "Leaving-the-Party Syndrome"

MAN: What's with the departure syndrome?

WOMAN: What's the "departure syndrome"?

MAN: Why does it take women so long to leave a party? We men just say, okay, let's go, bye-bye, but you take twenty minutes or more to leave a party, saying good-bye, all of that.

WOMAN: You don't understand—we have to kind of practice leav-ing, so we go a little away and then come back, and we check in with each person and on each relationship, where everyone is on things, whether everybody's okay on what we've said, and then we make sure where and when we'll be in touch again—that all takes some time. It's a process of disengaging without discon-necting.

MAN: Unbelievable. I never realized any of this! It's so complicated.

WOMAN: And you make it into a neurotic thing? Calling it a "syn-drome"? Maybe the real neurotic thing is *not* to take the time to say good-bye and make sure the connections are all okay. Maybe you're the ones with the "abrupt departure syndrome," and that our way of saying good-bye, keeping everyone and the relationships with everyone in mind, leaving while still being connected, really, is a healthier way of doing it. You don't real-

ize the work we put into this! It's like you're blind to it! Why do
you resent it? We keep things going!

This is not only an example of the invisibility to men of the continuity of connection but also how, from the perspective of the dominant
group (which is in charge of deciding what is diagnosed as "pathological"), different or other behavior can be called "sick." Diagnosis of psychological states throughout history has been value-ridden, culturally
determined, and gender-biased.[9] The subordinate groups often can see
more clearly some of the things the dominant group is not seeing, not
only what is invisible about the subordinate groups but about the dominant group itself.

In the following impasse, even the definition of reality is at stake. A
man and a woman are sitting in their living room on an autumn night.

WOMAN: I feel cold.
MAN: It's not cold.

Where is the reality here? Is it determined by who has control of the
thermostat? How does who controls the thermostat get decided? Is the
reality what a person feels or what the temperature is? How do the
heating bills figure into this? Or the possibility of putting on a sweater?
Can the man and woman go further in this process, or does it become a
power struggle? Does it ever get put into the terms of who defines reality, or is it just that "she's always cold," and "he's insensitive to my
needs"? Again, power is an issue here.

In one of the dialogues, a male lawyer took issue with the idea that
gender makes any difference in what goes on in the courtroom:

When I'm arguing a case against a woman lawyer, I don't see
her as a woman or treat her as a woman, I just see her and treat
her as a lawyer.

Of course the thrust of his argument, of the equality of lawyers
before the law, is admirable. It is an attempt to deal justly with bias. He
is saying that he tries to treat every person as an individual, not defined
by any group. And yet he isn't seeing what he isn't seeing: she, as a
member of the subordinate group—here, women—*is* impacted by all
the perceptions in the courtroom about that group. She cannot help but
feel and be affected by such perceptions, to which he either is blind or
dismisses as irrelevant. But the experience of the subordinate group can-

not be dismissed or remain invisible if mutuality is ever to be achieved. The truly just solution is an "and" solution: to view her both as a lawyer *and* as a woman. His awareness of the "woman" part of her lawyering could bring new awareness to the issue, which might even result in a fuller reality and lead the way to greater justice, and perhaps even more shared power within the courtroom and outside.

As one white man in dialogue with women implored: "If you see me as a white man, you don't really see me. I'm an individual. You can't define me by any group."

Yet his impact in society and on relationships is determined partly by the color of his skin and his being a man, among other things. This impact may not be visible to him, but it may be visible to women, non-white racial groups, and to nondominant men.

And so one reason that it may be hard for men to engage in a relational process that gets to product is that the issue "who has the power here?" is always present, perhaps less visible to the men than to the women. Women's power in that impasse—their ease at responding with feeling and their quickness in going back and forth verbally with others as an ongoing activity—and its effect on men may not be clearly visible to women either. Let us turn to the final category of impasse, around power.

The Power-Over/Power-With Impasse

Power relations in the larger culture shape any particular relationship between men and women. We have seen how, in early development, the introduction of difference can result in comparison between boys and girls, and how comparison can come to imply "better than" and "worse than" and easily be defined by who has power over whom.

In the most general terms, the power-over/power-with impasse often gets played out along gender lines (although, of course, there are many exceptions and gender reversals): many men experience conflict as a threat or an attempt at control and rely on rules of an "up/down" pecking order to settle the issue and avoid harm or violence; some women want everyone's voice to be heard and attended to, some retreat from what seem like definitive stands or assertions that may provoke conflict, and some clearly identify with power-over structures. Institutional power in the public arenas of our culture is almost entirely power-over—hierarchical structures with clear rules and definitions of who has power over whom. Disputes often are settled by defined argument—debate, not dialogue—and reliance on authority. These societal structures impact all of us, leaving their imprint on men and women both. Power-with models in the culture are rarer and seen more in the domestic or private domain, although they are appearing more and more in traditional institutions as healthy and profitable alternatives. In power-with systems power is shared among diverse equals, dialogue is valued more than debate,[10] and process is crucial to handling conflict. One of the striking examples of a power-with model today is Alcoholics Anonymous and other twelve-step programs, which are organizations totally without hierarchical structures; mutual-help programs.[11]

One example of the power-over/power-with impasse comes from a couple in their late twenties, Kate and Mitch, as they are trying to decide where to go out to dinner to celebrate their second anniversary. First, just their words:

KATE: Where shall we go to dinner?

MITCH: Let's go to Miguel's.

KATE: How 'bout Pintemento?

MITCH: Okay, let's go to Pintemento.

KATE: *(after a pause)* But it sounded like you wanted to go to Miguel's.

MITCH: No, no, it's okay—let's go where *you* want to go.

KATE: But I want to go where *you* want to go too.

MITCH: *(silence)*

KATE: Why *don't* you want to go to Pintemento?

MITCH: I just want to decide.

KATE: But we *are* deciding.

MITCH: We're not getting anywhere. *(tensely)* Let's just make a decision.

KATE: *(screaming)* Why are you yelling at me? *(starts to cry)*

MITCH: *(screaming)* I'm not yelling!

Note that they start in the "we" and end up in the "I"/"you." What's going on in each of them as they are going through this?

KATE: Where shall we go to dinner?

MITCH: Let's go to Miguel's.

KATE: *(throwing another alternative into the pot, enjoying the idea that alternatives will bring about discussion; trying to scope him out and find out what he really wants)* How 'bout Pintemento?

MITCH: (*she wants to go there, we'll go there; it doesn't matter that much to me and I want her to be happy*) Okay, let's go to Pintemento.

KATE: (*feeling good at how this is going, and wanting to engage him emotionally in the decision; pauses; but now wanting to make sure that it will really be okay with him to go to her choice, not wanting to take the power of choosing alone, so she feels she'd better give him a chance to throw this back and forth a little more, so they can share the decision making and the power*) But it sounded like you wanted to go to Miguel's.

MITCH: (*wait a second—I thought I agreed; why is she confusing things like this? I said what I wanted, she said what she wanted; now she doesn't want what she said she wanted? let's get some clarity here; take yourself out of it; give her the power to decide*) No, no, it's okay—let's go where *you* want to go.

KATE: (*I don't want to be the authority here; how come you're giving me what I want and it doesn't feel like what I really want? we both have to live with the choice; I want to decide* together, *and that may mean going where* he *really wants to go*) But I want to go where *you* want to go too.

MITCH: (*why are we into this again?; she's looking at me expectantly; dread is rising fast; I can't stand these drawn-out discussions about trivial stuff that doesn't matter, really; but if I go into this and say all this I'll get killed and it'll ruin everything; better say nothing*) (Silence.)

KATE: (*now what? why won't he answer; maybe he really doesn't want to go to Pintemento but really wants to go to Miguel's and is just giving in and I'll pay for it later; I better keep trying or we'll be nowhere*) Why *don't* you want to go to Pintemento?

MITCH: (*focusing on getting to the "product"; taking charge*) I just want to decide.

KATE: (*how thick can he be? wanting to stay in the process with him, so that the power here is shared; my sense of things falling apart is growing, and my urgency to stay in connection, to keep the continuity of connection with him on this special occasion, is rising*) But we *are* deciding.

MITCH: (*irritated at this whole thing; everything has gotten so complicated about a simple decision; it's now a power struggle and I'm not even sure what the struggle is about; angrily*) We're not getting anywhere. *(more tensely)* I don't care! Let's just make a decision!

KATE: *(screaming)* Why are you yelling at me? *(starts to cry)*

MITCH: *(screaming)* I'm not yelling!

Note again how each is entrenched in the "I" and the "you," despite the fact that they started the conversation in the "we."

While there are elements of dread, yearning, product, and process here, what are the ways in which power is being played out?

Two different models of power are at work.

Mitch brings real strength to the discussion—his clarity in making a decision in his "bottom-line" or "cut-to-the-chase" thinking and his flexibility. He tries to preempt conflict by making the decision, even if it means he goes to a place that he might not like as well. He may think that if he gives in to where she wants to go, he'll get something in return later, like watching the football game the next afternoon. He puts the conversation about dinner into the larger picture as he sees it, denying that it's of much real importance compared to other things in his life and not wanting to spend a lot of time in the process. He sees the importance of making the decision, but he may not see the importance to her of being together with her in *how* they decide (or even of how they decide how to decide). He tries to take himself out of the conflict, not sharing his thinking about the process with her. This can be a power-over tactic too, in fact making himself the more powerful one outside the discussion. (For example, if a person has authority in a system, complete with corner office and title in a corporation, some of the more authoritarian or dominant use of power can be exerted through silence in the face of a subordinate's request for engagement.)

In this example, Mitch feels that if he goes into the process with her it could result in a fight. Finally, Mitch believes in rules: you weigh the alternatives and you make a decision according to the rule of who cares more about this particular choice, and he doesn't care all that much about this one. His view of the power situation does not encompass hers; he is unaware that the issue here is her wanting to be with him in a deep way or her fear that "winning" can endanger the relationship.

Kate is working in a whole different way. Her strengths and priorities are more relational, being with him in connection, and she tends to try and avoid conflict by focusing on him. The process of being with him in making the decision is central to her, "foreplay" for the whole celebratory evening. She wants them *both* to decide not only on the restaurant but on what really matters; that is, she wants him to join her in making the choice of restaurant as well as making the choice of *how* they choose. Kate wants to create a shared-power system, not only hearing his voice but hearing his response to her voice, so that out of this the choice of where they go will emerge. But Kate too may be unaware of her power in the situation: how powerful, to Mitch, is her yearning, her anger, her tears, her emotional-verbal skill, and her willingness to stay in the process to see things through. Kate and Mitch are both trying to prevent conflict and separation, but that is what ultimately happens.

The result is a power struggle. The relationship suffers. It's not going to be a happy anniversary.

This impasse, ending in "you" and "I" and no "we," suddenly fills the whole relationship, making everything more difficult, at least for a while. When a relationship is working well, people can make decisions without this struggle. The reason it blows up here is because in their disconnection their whole relationship, and its entire history, gets played out in this one interaction.

In more general terms, when power is challenged, violence may result. Judith Herman has written about violence as a power-control tactic, which breaks through when men feel their dominance or power threatened. In *Trauma and Recovery*[12] she calls this "the combat neurosis of the sex war." In our dialogues, once the men and women are feeling more connected, questions can be addressed about how men feel about other men's violence and the impact of threat of violence on their own relationships. Children feel this too. A ninth-grade boy said, "I'm male, I'm almost a man, but I don't want to be like the men I see in the movies or on TV. Arnold Schwarzenegger is not who I want to be."

Often men are unaware of how threatening they, as a group, are to women. The moments when this becomes visible can be dramatic. One man, in response to a question from the women in the dialogue, told the group this story:

> I was at my health club, walking toward the whirlpool, wearing only my swimsuit. I didn't think anyone else was around. But then I saw that a woman was sitting in the whirlpool, her back toward me. As I approached, she turned, saw me, and froze. Her face was filled with fear. The sight of a half-naked man approaching had terrified her. I sensed for the first time the

depth of women's fear of men's violence in the culture. I'll never forget the look in her eyes. Never.

Men also begin to discuss how powerless they feel about preventing violence and why they try to dissociate and disidentify with other men. They even begin to talk about how they could feel more able to speak out about violence if they felt more connected to other like-minded men.[13]

Mitch, in the impasse, tries to be preemptive in dealing with the conflict by giving her what she wants. He's trying to be a good guy, moving things along by declaring, by himself, a clear choice. His action is reminiscent of a question that arises at the beginning of the gender dialogues: "Who goes first?"

"Who Goes First?"

As described briefly in the example of our first gender dialogue—as well as in the dialogue with four-year-olds at a preschool—the question of who goes first always arises as the men and women face each other across the room. Let us look at this more closely in terms of power.

We suggest that the group begin by reading the answers without our saying who should start. In the ensuing silence, the women make eye contact with each other and with us, nod to each other and gesture, but say nothing. The men watch them and us. Time seems to drag. Finally one man speaks up:

"Oh-*kay,* I guess I'll go ahead. Our group put down that women are nurturant, emotional, caretakers—"

We interrupt. "How did you decide to go first?"

Startled, he says, "I . . . I just figured that no one was saying anything, so I'd get things moving. Why are you asking me?"

"Yeah," says another man, "why are you putting him on the spot?"

We ask the women what they feel about this situation. They glance at each other, and then one woman speaks up: "It's very familiar. In big meetings, men always take over."

"But none of you were saying anything," says a man. "We were just sitting here wasting time. Nothing was getting done. And now he tries to help us to get something going, and he gets criticized for it."

"We weren't doing 'nothing,'" says another woman. "We were working out who would go first. You went too fast."

"How were you working it out?" asks a man. "You weren't saying anything."

"We were," says a woman. "I looked at her, and she looked over there. We were trying to get consensus on whether we should go first. If we had more time, we would know not only who would answer first in our group but who would go second and third—the whole thing."

"How are we supposed to know that?" another man asks.

The dialogue stops. The group is stuck, disconnected across gender. The silence turns hostile. Tension builds.

We ask whether this situation is reflected in their daily lives. With passion, the women start to talk about how, in meetings where men are present—at work, in schools, churches, other institutions—men often take the lead.

"Exactly," says the man who spoke first. "I was showing leadership skills. We men get a lot of criticism for taking the lead."

"That's so," says a woman, "and we women have to take responsibility for it, too. It's not just you men taking power by going first, setting the agenda, but we let you have the power by not saying anything."

"In fact," says another woman, "it's our way of retaining some power, by seeing what a man will do before we commit ourselves to an opinion."

"It's easier for us to build on what you said than to initiate," says another woman. "We connect by responding. To you and to one another. Like right now."

"Jesus!" a man says, exasperated. "You're making way too big a deal of this! He just went first."

"You sound like my ex-husband," says a woman. "'Oversensitive,' he always called me. Drove me crazy. Whenever I had a strong feeling about something, he'd say I was making a big deal of nothing. It got so I called it 'big-dealism.'" The women laugh. "But it was sad, because I always believed him, believed that it was true."

"It's so clear, isn't it?" one asks, "that it was his way of diminishing you and trying to keep control of you?"

Other women nod.

Another tense silence. This time, however, we have a clear sense that the group is not so much stuck as on the verge of moving toward something new: the men are more engaged, and the women are noticing their engagement.

Finally, the man who went first says, "My God, I never realized this was so *complicated!* I've always felt that women's anger at men's power was off base. Men feel like women have all the power in relationships. Dread is all about the fear of losing our power."

Another man said, "Women's emotions feel so powerful and threatening to me, I never know when I'm walking into a minefield, when I'm going to set off a land mine."

The man who went first spoke again: "I would never have guessed that my going first had such an impact on you!" He considers, and then goes on: "So you women are using your power in different ways?"

"It's a different kind of power," a woman says.

Women too fall into disconnecting patterns in this situation, by avoidance of direct conflict or waiting to respond to the men. Sometimes there's manipulation, akin to what we saw in the four-year-old girls chanting "Boys go first!" As mentioned before, women's relational curiosity can be a power tactic too.

The only mutual solution to "Who goes first" in a gender dialogue came in a first-grade class in a public school, when the boys and girls faced each other on opposite sides of the room:

"Let's flip a coin!" a boy said.

"Yeah," said a girl, "and the winner gets to choose who goes first."

They flipped a coin. The girls won. The girls looked at each other, and then one girl said, "Huddle! Huddle!" The girls huddled.

The boys were left looking at the girls huddling. The boys had nothing to do. One boy shouted, "Huddle! Huddle!" The boys huddled, even though they had nothing to huddle about.

The girls broke from their huddle, faced the boys, and said, "Boys go first!"

The Expense to Men of Traditional Forms of Power

In the dialogues, women often ask men: "Why do you hang on to your power at the expense of your health and your relationships?"

Other variants of this are:

Why do you perpetuate the system when you often see it as harmful to you?

What is the burden of needing to be successful?

Why do men follow leaders?

What's with the competence thing?

What triggers in you the pressure to have the answer—or the final answer?

Why don't men account for the violence toward other men, women, and children?

Why are men so violent? Why do boys beat each other up?

What's it like to be the dominant one?

What's it like to be feared?

Why is control so important?

Why do men put sports and careers before relationships?

And there is always the series of questions about men imagining their power being lost by being in relationship:

Why do you see difference as threatening?

Why do men perceive disagreement as a threat?

Why does approval have so much impact on our relationship with you?

Why does agreement from other men seem necessary for men's sense of loyalty, being heard, and connection?

Why's it so hard for men to understand—and respect—or try out a different emotional style?

A variant on this theme—how power is expressed in relationships—comes up time and again in dialogues with boys and girls, especially sixth- to eighth-graders. Girls ask:

Why do you act one way when you're alone with me, and completely different toward me when you're with your guy friends?

Questions about men's power, dominance, violence, and authority in the culture are always asked by the women in the dialogues. When men feel more connected to women as the dialogues progress, men will ask women more about their experience of being "one-down," or subordinate:

What does it feel like to be oppressed?

What is it like to earn sixty-seven cents on the dollar?

I'm not a murderer or rapist—I've never mistreated women in my life—why am I held responsible for the barbarians of my gender?

And what can I do about it?

The men ask questions about the women's relational and emotional powers:

> What's it like to feel so deeply?
> What's it like to have the power to give birth?
> How can you be so patient with children?
> How do you remember everything people say?
> How can you feel so much for someone without losing yourself?

As the invisibilities to each gender of the other gender's different kinds of power become visible, real connections start to be made. The examples of the thermostat, the whirlpool, the "Who goes first" discussion—these are real "eye openers" to the men and women involved.

Gradually we learned to navigate the wilds of these three relational impasses. We came away with a strong feeling that any solutions to these impasses that used the self/other model—seeing the problem in each person (whether in the person's "neurosis," "need," "instinct," "family history" or "planetary preference") and seeing the solution in fixing each person and then putting the two together—were not helpful. These were individual solutions, based on the priority of the individual and the focus of change on the individual.

The alternative we'd seen was simple: the solutions for breaking through an impasse were connection solutions, based on the priority of the connection between men and women. As both men and women begin to see and to be moved deeply by each other's experience, the expansion into the mutual "we" is enhanced.

In the dialogues, as men and women try to talk about the nuances of power and move beyond power struggles, moving from trying to control the other person to having an impact on how things might go for both persons, a new kind of power emerges. This we call the power of mutual connection, or the power of the "we."

4

Getting to "We"

"How can I think about the 'we' when I'm thinking about the 'me'?"

—A MAN, TO HIS WIFE

"But I can't think about myself without thinking about us."

—HIS WIFE, RESPONDING

In our first five years of gender dialogues we went far and wide, building on our experiences, exploring, experimenting, modifying, and discovering. From a New England psychological association to a *Fortune* 100 corporation's executive summit in Colorado, from the Holy Redeemer Church on the Lower East Side of New York to a world-renowned addiction treatment center in California, from a private boarding school in Rhode Island to a therapy center in Istanbul and the psychiatric department of Hunan Medical Center in China, and from four-year-olds in a Massachusetts preschool to senior citizens in Miami, we worked with the same three questions and used the same form of dialogue: first, in separate men's and women's groups, then with men and women together, facing each other in dialogue.

Invariably we saw the same thing: exploring differences in dialogue creates good connections.

In every group we worked with we saw some shift toward mutuality. People left the dialogue in a more connected place than when they entered. They were not only more connected with each other but also motivated to build connections to others in their lives (including, if they hadn't attended the dialogues with them, their spouses).

Our excitement with helping men and women move toward mutual understanding encouraged us to take the next step. We were ready to see how this Connection Model, and the data on invisibilities and impasses between men and women, could be applied to individual couples in couples therapy.

Our First Couple: Tom and Ann

When a couple walks into the office, they are in distress, and the "we"—their relationship—is frazzled or torn or deeply wounded. This is as palpable as the color of their clothes or the expression in their eyes. The first couple with whom we tried the Connection Model we'll call Tom and Ann. I (Sam) did the therapy alone, in consultation with Janet.

Tom and Ann came into the office so angry at each other and so discouraged about their marriage that they could not even look at each other. Both face me. Tom is a tall, athletic-looking WASP of thirty-eight, with graying blond hair and horn-rimmed glasses. He is a manager at a small computer software company. Ann is a youthful-looking, dark-haired Jewish woman with intense dark eyes, a doctor specializing in women's health issues. Both wear suits. They have two teenage sons. Immediately they start talking about the faults of the other person, referring to each other in the third-person pronoun:

TOM: Nothing I do is enough for her.

ANN: I'm tired of taking care of this relationship.

TOM: She's so demanding! Oversensitive. I try and try—nothing works!

ANN: He's so closed, he never talks. If we start to have a discussion
that involves feelings, he changes the subject or gets angry and
walks out. I feel shut out and alone. I told him that unless he
came to couples therapy the marriage is over.

TOM: Nothing I do is enough. I even went into individual therapy
for her—to try to work on myself.

They fall silent. The relationship is stuck. I get a sense that this is the
endpoint of an impasse, the result of many painful attempts to connect.
I feel for them.

A traditional couples therapy approach might be to try to have each
person stay in the "I"—first person—rather than the "you"—second
person. This couple, however, wasn't even in the second person, but the
third—"he" and "she," what we call "the third-person accusatory." My
initial attempts to get them to stay in the "I"—making statements such
as "I feel" or "I think"—fail miserably:

TOM: I feel that she always makes me feel like a failure.

ANN: I feel that he's treating me like his mother!

I could follow up on "mother," which might lead to a significant
family history. With the Connection Model, however, the first priority is
the quality of their connection, which is always in the present moment.
So I actively try to shift the paradigm away from self and/or other to the
relationship. There are three reasons for this: first, to see what the relationship in fact is, its potential and its history as each of them sees it;
second, to shift away from the idea of "psychopathology" residing in
one or the other; and finally, to see if this paradigm shift might help
move things in the present moment.

Introducing the Relationship, the "We"

With a sense of concern, I say that they are stuck, in an impasse, not
able to move. This stuckness is not the result of a "sickness" in him or
her, not the fault of either, but rather a difficulty in how they are meeting. I introduce the idea that in addition to "self" and "other," maybe
we can also look at "the relationship," almost as a thing or being, with
qualities, a past, and quite possibly a future. I ask what they can say
about the relationship.

TOM: What relationship? There's no relationship here.

ANN: (*starts to cry*) It feels dead. Boring and dead. So different
from where we began.

This may not seem like much, but in fact it is a relational statement,
the first time that either has used the "we" and referred to "it," the relationship. I say, "I know it seems pretty hopeless right now, but maybe
you can describe what the relationship was like when you met."

ANN: He was different—so open and trustable—

I interrupt: "Sorry, I didn't mean to ask about him. I meant the relationship."

This surprises them. For the first time they look at each other. They begin
to talk, more and more animatedly, about how the relationship in the past
was—Ann's words—"safe and loving, a lot of trust, and we used to be
really free, do the wildest things—go to concerts, go dancing." Tom talks
about how he was attracted to Ann's depth of feeling, and how, wanting to
impress her on their first date, he got tickets to Symphony Hall, only to find
that it was Barbershop Quartet Night. Now there is a palpable shift in the
room. Making eye contact, they laugh. They are talking about the past history of the relationship, but they are not in the past. They are in the present
moment, making contact, in connection. There is a real sense of things
coming unstuck, things moving. What is moving is the relationship. I begin
to sense the potential, the energy of their relationship.

Now that they are beginning to connect, I try to build more relational awareness. I ask them to do a "qualities of relationship" exercise:
each will try to come up with images of the *color* of the relationship, the
texture, the *sound,* the *animal.* This exercise jolts them out of their
habitual thoughts and feelings—which usually focus on themselves or
the other person—into the realm of the imagination, focused around
the "we." We go through their answers.

Color:

ANN: Red, cool blue.
TOM: Black, purple.

Texture:

ANN: Lumpy, mud.
TOM: It started out sandpapery, now it's smooth.

Sound:

ANN: Ocean.
TOM: Distant rain.

Animal:

ANN: Cat.
TOM: Tiger.

As they go through this, they laugh and are intrigued with the images. I point out the real similarities in their images, as well as the clear differences. I say that the shift back—smooth to sandpapery—will happen again and that the problem isn't the shift, or the conflict, but how to be in creative movement rather than in deadness, stuck.

ANN: I guess we really don't know each other.
I: I have a sense that you really do know each other pretty well.
    What you don't know right now is how to move in relationship.

The session ends with my affirming that there is in fact a relationship here, a "we" with a history. Ann says that she knows it, but that Tom often seems to forget. Coming back from a business trip recently, he hung up his coat on the rack at the door and walked past her to the answering machine without even saying hello. I suggest that they can try to be creative—even playful—about working together on the relationship. For instance, they might try putting up a sign over the coat rack:

DANGER—WATCH OUT FOR THE RELATIONSHIP!

They laugh. To a certain extent, we are now all on the same side, working together for the sake of the relationship. I feel empathy with the pain in each of them and with the way they are connecting and disconnecting. I say:

"You're both very vulnerable right now, and the relationship is vulnerable too. It's important that each of you take care right now not to do more harm, not to hurt each other or the relationship any further."

They sense my concern, agree, and ask how they can do that. I suggest two tools they can use. One is the *check-out;* when in a fight one person wants or needs to stop, feeling the relationship moving in a negative direction, he or she says so, but then has to say when he or she will bring the subject up again in a reasonable time frame, and then must do so. The other is the *check-in:* either can call for a "check-in," which consists of each person telling what he or she is feeling in themselves and in the relationship; the other listens, without asking for elaboration, just saying, "I hear you." The check-in is a simple but powerful way to make a connection in the moment. Again, it jolts each person out of the habitual thoughts and feelings determined by past experiences in this relationship as well as in others. I ask if they'd like to try a check-in right now, suggesting they look at each other as they do it.

> TOM: (*looking at Ann directly*) I'm afraid to say anything because we might start up again. I feel shell-shocked.
> ANN: I feel you're really trying, Tom, but . . .
> I: Can you just stay with your own experience for now?
> ANN: (*pause*) I feel kind of lost, and scared to trust you again. But I hear you, Tom.
> TOM: And I hear you.

These *authentic* statements from each to the other cause a palpable shift.

Finally I suggest that before the next session they try to write a *relational purpose statement.* Together, on one sheet of paper, they would write down what they see as the purpose of the relationship, what the purpose of their "we" is, why they are together, what brought them together, and what they want to be or do together in the future. This is a way of seeing whether or not a couple shares the same fundamental worldview and values—what underlies the relationship, even with all the pain and struggle—on which much can be built. We've found that how far a couple gets on this shared project predicts fairly reliably how the therapy will go.

As they are leaving, Tom says, "Thanks, you brought back the idea that there is a relationship here, and that it does have some good to it."

> ANN: Yes, it helps to keep the focus on the relationship, not just on him.
> I: Yes, and right now each of you have to take care of it.
> TOM: (*joking, with a poignant truthfulness*) So it'll take care of *me!*

They leave sensing that together we three have broken through an impasse, that a first step has been taken, and that they are moving again, in however tenuous a connection—which builds greater faith that movement is possible. Not only they, but I too, have already gotten to know their "we." We've seen the pain and poignancy, the frayed hope, the wonderful humor that has sustained them through difficult times, and even the sense that it is a "we" that is capable of very big dips but has lots of energy for rapid movement. "It," the "relationship," has been quite clearly on display. As I, and they, saw the "we" more clearly, the light of the "we" illuminated the individuals, so that I and they saw Tom and Ann more clearly too.

They leave with a sense of greater *relational resilience*[1]—the energy available to them for change, a sense of the resources of the relationship. They also have a sense of *relational presence*—their feeling connection in the moment and feeling someone else really with them and with their relationship. This helps *them* to have a sense of the reality of the relationship, too, and its potential. A seed has been planted that they *can* act together to move to greater connection. This we call *relational empowerment*—locating the power or capacity to act *in the relationship*. This empowerment is built on mutual responsibility: "We got into this together, we have to find our way through it together, to something new."

Relationships have a history, a memory, and a purpose that either supports growth or keeps it stuck and fragile. For Tom and Ann, even this brief shift to the "we" suggests that the relationship is beginning to heal.

The second session starts with Ann and Tom saying that things are better but still difficult. Both felt that getting in touch with the history of the relationship had been useful, but as they'd started to work on a relational purpose statement, they'd gotten into an impasse:

TOM: We started out well enough, and decided that one purpose was "to provide a loving environment for the growth and protection of our children, and ourselves." That was easy. But then she wanted more, and got into her "we're not close enough" issue—

ANN: Wait a sec—I didn't say "not enough"—I just want it better.

TOM: You're insatiable—as you said—"the sky's the limit."

ANN: What's wrong with that?

TOM: There's no limit to the sky! Nothing's ever good enough.

ANN: You just want to stay stuck in the mud—as if mud's good enough!

I stop the process. To them the discussion may have seemed bad, but I was delighted. In the first session, they were totally stuck in an impasse, not even looking at each other. Now they are in an impasse, but engaged, on a growing edge, trying to move. There's more to work with. They are actively struggling with each other. And they actually had started to work on their relational purpose statement. I begin to like them much more.

Now that they are connecting, I have room to work empathically with each of them and with their relationship. I am being a bridge for each of them to mutual empathy. I acknowledge that this can be really hard work and that both of them are trying their best. I add that it's not unusual for impasses to come up around trying to do the purpose statement. I ask them to tell me more about what happened.

It turned out that their relational styles in doing this were very different. She wanted to toss things around in dialogue and then write something down at the end; he wanted them each to make a list and then put them together. He'd felt lost in her "looseness," and she'd felt shut out by his "structure." He'd stormed out and then come back, ready to work on it again. She said she couldn't work on it until they processed their fight. He said he didn't want to waste any more time on the fight but wanted to get down to the task. They got nowhere. Each was trying to connect in his or her own way, each feeling that the other was in the way.

Introducing Gender Difference

I talk about their experience as another example of a relational impasse—one we have labeled the product/process impasse—and point out that it is not unusual for men and women to split along these lines. I say to Tom:

"In these kinds of situations, we men often seem to get all hung up on getting it done, getting to the bottom line, 'fixing it,' and don't pay attention to the process—which is her style. You know what I mean?"

TOM: Do I ever! I want to fix it, get it done. And, as she says to me, "Don't just do something, stand there!" (*they laugh*) First, her process around writing this drives me nuts, and then, we have to process that process! I had to fix both! But what you're saying, then, is that the only way to fix it is to stop trying to fix it? (*more laughter*)

I: (*to Ann*) From my experience, women often want to think in dialogue to get clearer. And men have a difficult time believing that such a process can actually get anywhere, right?

ANN: In fact, it works better!

I am thus able to reframe their impasse in terms of how what each of them is doing is influenced by the different ways each *gender* has learned to move in relationship.

The problem isn't difference itself; it's not being able to see difference clearly and without judgment, to work with and move with difference, in relationship. Engagement around difference moves a couple from self-centered or other-centered perceptions to a greater awareness of both people and the potential richness of the relationship. Information from the other person and from the relationship expands the knowledge of yourself.[2]

In fact, a disconnection can be a gift because it can be a symptom of a small impasse you may not see. It can signal a need to attend to something in the relationship. When caught up in the disconnection, either person can find it hard to see that the experience of disconnecting can lead to a clearer focus on the relationship and movement toward a better connection. In the disconnection is the potential for growth if the couple can stay in the "we" throughout. When a relationship *is* working well, this is the underlying process. Frequently it is imperceptible.

Disconnections in daily life are inevitable and frequent. No one gets it right the first time, or every time. The key is to shift away from the vicious cycle of a disconnection leading to a worse disconnection leading to an impasse. The shift is toward disconnection leading to a better—that is, more mutual— connection. This shift may involve what Jean Baker Miller has called "waging good conflict"[3]: initiating it, staying with it, and letting go of it—when appropriate—while maintaining connection.

Picking up on my statement that men are taught to fix things, Tom talks about his work—he's a manager of several people—and about his family. He's the only son of a distant, reserved father and a lonely, depressed mother. I spend time exploring his family history, knowing that Ann senses what I'm doing—making an empathic connection with Tom by taking a "we men" stance toward his vulnerabilities. I ask Ann about her listening to Tom.

ANN: I feel touched, but I feel angry too, about—
TOM: Oh, Jesus! I'm spilling my guts here.
I: Can *you* listen to her anger, Tom? (*to Ann*) It sounds like there's also a lot of pain behind that anger.
ANN: Yes. I guess I'm angry that he won't talk like that to *me,* when I need it so much.

I'm trying, here, to move toward each person's experience, to "hold" the pain each feels and the pain in the relationship, helping them to do the same. We go on to look at his pain at feeling controlled by her and her anger at being seen as a monster trying to control him: his dread, her anger. We get into Ann's family history as well, especially her identification with her own father's experience of her mother as controlling and intrusive, which she is afraid of repeating in her marriage. Both Tom and Ann can feel for and with each other's pain in their families of origin and can begin to see the power of their current relationship to either crystallize the wounds or offer some healing. When their connection is "held," each can begin to work with these feelings about early connections. (Traditional therapy sometimes moves in the other direction: only after individual work or work on "family of origin" issues has succeeded can couples therapy be undertaken.)

From our gender dialogues I know that other important invisibilities based on gender are operating here: the different emotional time scales of many men and women, the different abilities to focus on many things at a time (women) and one thing at a time (men), the different awareness of the relational context, the different ways many men and women express anger and reframe anger in terms of who is hurt or what is wrong in the relationship, the different relational curiosities, the different attention to maintaining the continuity of connection, and, of course, the differences in power both within and outside the couple.

For instance, Tom was slower to describe his emotional state, something both of them had to take into account. If Ann felt that Tom was trying to let her in—and let her see his internal struggle to do so, rather than he merely avoiding it or seeing her as a monster—she could relax and even enjoy this shared process of finding a resonant frequency of emotional dialogue.

Difference can be a blessing to a relationship. Learning to work on difference of gender helped Ann and Tom learn to use difference in general, for instance, around different attitudes toward illness. Tom was something of a hypochondriac, convinced that he had a hearing problem; Ann was a stoic, refusing to go to the doctor even when she contracted walking pneumonia. Each one's attitude could be of great use to the other; Ann could provide a reality check for Tom's ears, Tom could get Ann to the doctor when her fever hit 102.

A crucial question for couples to ask, especially in moments of stress and disconnection, is: "In this moment, are our differences adding or subtracting?" That is, "How are we working with our differences? How could we use them for the benefit of each other and the benefit of the relationship?"

Introducing the Language of Connection and Disconnection

By the end of the second session I am moved by how much they have moved, and I tell them that. To give words to what they've done, I mention the notion of connection and disconnection:

"Our priority has to be connecting. If we're not in connection, there's room for all kinds of trouble to creep in—the past, accusations about family (you're just like your father, you're just like your mother), gender stereotypes (you're like all men, you're like all women) and ethnic issues (you're like all WASPS, or Jews, etc.). If we're in connection, we can talk respectfully about any of these differences without stereotyping. Today, by hanging out through this disconnection, you've managed to make an even better connection. Doesn't it feel that way right now?"

ANN: Yes. In the middle of a fight, I lose sight of Tom as a whole
person, and of the whole history of the relationship. He seems
so diminished—like my father.
TOM: And *you* get bigger—like my *mother*. (*they laugh*)

I mention the idea of the *continuity of connection*—an awareness that the relationship continues to exist even when they are apart or feeling disconnected—and that gender differences may affect their sense of the importance of continuity. Check-ins can be helpful in maintaining continuity. A check-in, via a phone call at work, is a way of "taking the temperature" of the relationship at any moment. It is a way of staying in the "we" even when there's no time or energy to go into anything further. Brevity may be hard to manage, and harder for the woman. As one woman put it: "Sometimes we have to be careful not to let our check-ins degenerate into conversations."

The shared ability to decide when to have the longer conversation is crucial.

Finally, I ask if they'd like to take another shot right now at writing a relational purpose statement. They come up with the idea of writing in dialogue, a line from him, then her. They have fun writing several lines and end with:

ANN: To provide a safe and nourishing environment for each other.

TOM: And—wait for it!—for the relationship!

Our culture emphasizes trying to negotiate and compromise to "agree to disagree," or "get to 'yes,'" where each individual gets something of what he or she wants. These are basically "I/you" stances and can lead to stuck places. We are talking about something different. It is not a matter of Tom or Ann "getting what they want" but rather enlarging who they each are in the relationship. The "agree to disagree" model can be hell for spouses and families, leaving the *relationship* stuck and with no room to grow. It's like getting what you want while staying on your own planet of choice.

We're talking about something else. It's not that Tom and Ann compromise and Tom wins and Ann wins; it's that they *create* something greater than either of them, greater than the sum of their parts: they create a "we," which then makes each of them more themselves. If the "we" wins, each doesn't so much "win" as *grow*. Something new can happen. Creating this over and over also builds trust and confidence, not only in the individuals but in the relationship.

For several weeks things went better. Tom and Ann were cooperating around the house and getting their differences to add, especially with their teenage sons: "We're trying to find out how the 'we' will draw the line with them, together." They started to use the language of connection with each other. ("Our connection right now is strong, or fragile, or warm.") Being in better connection, they could go back over the hard things in the relationship. Humor, which had first drawn them together, made a huge, delightful comeback. Tom talking about "the big D—Dread," saying, "Look out—here comes another dread attack!" Humor, it became apparent, was one of the great resources of their relationship.

TOM: All this talk about the importance of relationship is getting to me. Annie, if you could have on your tombstone "SHE WAS SUPERB AT RELATIONSHIPS," would that be enough?

ANN: Absolutely! Although I'd also like a second line. And maybe a third too—something like—"AND SHE PITCHED IN THE WORLD SERIES."

TOM: Can you understand that I can't even *imagine* that that would be enough? For me it would seem a humiliation—a failure—and I feel *ashamed* to say it.

Session Five

Reframing Autonomy

The fifth session started as a disaster. Ann and Tom came in angry and discouraged, again unable even to look at each other, back in the third-person accusatory: "he said"/"she said." Nothing I tried helped. The issue was money for a vacation, a fight about Tom being too tight, Ann too extravagant. In a deadlock such as this, attention must be paid first not to the specific issue but to the state of the connection. I ask, "Where's the 'we'? What does the 'we' need now?"

> TOM: *(exploding)* The "we"? How the hell can I think about the "we" when I'm thinking about the "me"? Jesus Christ Almighty!
>
> ANN: *(angrily)* But I can't think of myself *without* thinking about us. I can understand what you're doing, asking about the "we," and that may be okay for him, but I'm frightened by the "we." My whole life has been in the "we." When I hear you ask me about the "we" now, a red flag goes up—I'm going to lose the "I." In fact, I don't feel you really understand it from a woman's point of view—what that's like. Maybe we should go to a female couples therapist.
>
> I: I can see how, as a man, I might have some trouble seeing it from your side, but can you try to tell me about it?
>
> ANN: I'm frightened that my concerns will get lost in my work on the "we," that if I'm empathic to him, I'll accommodate to him, and I'll lose. You're asking me to settle for too little.

I respond to her concerns, saying, "It's important for you to keep speaking up whenever you feel that concern about what you need here. All of us need to pay attention to that. Mutual connection requires all of us to be honest and willing to confront the truth. We're all on the side of not settling for less."

> ANN: I'm not so sure Tom is.
>
> TOM: If you're so good at this, why can't you stop me from feeling dread?
>
> ANN: I'm not an expert in this stuff either. I feel helpless too, and I'm tired of taking care of you.
>
> TOM: Look—I've just got to work on my *own* stuff, get my own

crap together first, that's all. Maybe then I can get into this, not before.

This is such a dramatic change from our previous sessions that a lightbulb goes on. I ask about his own therapy with a well-known Self psychologist. It turns out that his therapist has been on vacation for five weeks—ever since we'd started meeting—but had come back last week. Tom had had an intense session focused on his own childhood relationship with his parents, and ever since had withdrawn from his relationship with Ann.

Individual therapy of one or both members of a couple who are also in couples therapy can be extremely useful if it works toward enhancing relationship. Most of the time it does. However, Tom's stance in the couples therapy is not unique. A more self-centered individual psychotherapy may accentuate, codify, and entrench self-centeredness. It may help a man become familiar with every nook and cranny of himself but leave him with a profound unfamiliarity with the pathways of mutual relationship. An inflated, narcissistic self creates disconnection.

Couples therapy, with the frank, clear presence of a relationship in the room, may make it easier to work on men's relational skills, bringing male strengths into relationship. It can ultimately teach men mutual empathy and movement through and toward connection. In couples therapy, men may more easily move, first, from the "self" to the "we." The "we" may be safer to explore than the "other." Once in the "we," a man may then be able to ask about differences, about the "other," and then by facing these differences move toward mutuality, with empathy.

And so now with Tom I say: "I can really feel for you, knowing something of the pain of your past. I guess you feel that if you go into this relationship fully, you'll be less yourself?"

TOM: Less, hell—lose myself completely—she's so controlling!
I: I know you feel that way. But haven't you had the experience in the last few weeks, when you've been in a real connection with Ann, you've been *more* yourself? More alive, more full of zest, you can go out and do things better?

Tom thinks it over, sighs, and, sadly, says, "Yes, that's true."

I: So what keeps you from being in good connection with her?
TOM: I'm afraid—if I go into something with her, I'll get lost—she

sees it as "the sky's the limit," and I see it as "the tip of the iceberg and something big is under there!" I'd gotten so I kept
everything secret from her, trying to do everything alone. You
only achieve things alone. Like climbing Mount Everest.

ANN: *(moved)* Honey, no one ever climbs Mount Everest alone.
    (Tom smiles)

I: Maybe the healing for you can be right here in this relationship.
    Maybe you should focus on where you are in this relationship
    here and now.

ANN: I want to help, Tom.

TOM: I thought you said you were tired of helping.

ANN: If you're open to me, if we do it together, I won't be tired.
    You don't have to do it alone.

For the first time in years Tom starts to cry. He reaches for Ann's
hand and says, "I don't know if I can do it."

We three sit for a while without saying anything. The room feels less
quiet than still. Peaceful, the peacefulness of shared sorrow. Without any
of us saying it, we all understand that something has happened. I sense
this to be the beginning of what we call their shift toward mutuality.

Holding the "We" Through a Disconnection

At the start of the next session Tom and Ann come in hand in hand.
Something has changed.

They describe what they call "a breakthrough." One ominously cold
night during the week, as they were walking up to their house, they got
into a terrible argument and found themselves standing in the freezing
cold outside the door. Each of them felt defeated. Neither knew what to
say anymore. They stood there just outside their door, in stillness, for a
few moments. Both knew that they could easily go through the door
and move into separation and maybe lose the relationship for good.
Neither moved to open the door. Silently, together, they refused to go
through the door and into loneliness. They had come to the edge of the
habitual, and at that instant there was nothing else to take its place.

And then something happened. Both could describe it, but neither
could explain it. It wasn't either of them having an "insight," a new
perception about himself or herself. In fact, they describe it to me as the
opposite: a sense, in Tom's words, that "we'd gone as far as we could by

ourselves, and something else had to happen, and that something else was just, I don't know, just being there together, in the cold."

Ann adds, "That's what I felt—just being there together, defeated. And then . . . quietly, in a sad, but *new* way, we were in the 'we.'"

"We were really together," Tom says, "we found each other in a new way, a way I never felt with you before. It's like it wasn't under my control or your control, it just was a new way of feeling together, and, for me, about you. It wasn't mystical, it was humble, tangible, concrete, like you could almost touch it. I guess the best way of putting it is what we've been talking about here: we were deeply in the 'we.'"

Listening to this I am touched. Tom, Ann, and I sense that this was a signature moment that will have lasting effects. The old protective ways had failed; they had to let go of trying to make anything happen and had surrendered, together, to whatever was going to happen. They were letting go together. They had seen together the futility of the old ways, and having been offered the hope of a new way, were able to move toward the new together. And the shift had not first happened in either person; the first shift had been in, and to, the we. Being together in that mutual way then made each person feel more whole, and real, and more fully themselves.

This sets the stage for learning to "hold the 'we' through a disconnection." It is one of the determining factors in couples either growing or withering. Those who grow learn to hold the "we" through the disconnections, and thus create better connections; those who don't grow lose a sense of the "we" during a disconnection and fragment into isolated selves, more disconnection, and impasse. On the one hand there is movement toward mutuality; on the other, toward isolation.

After this, Tom and Ann really began to move, with a growing sense that, simply put, "we're in it together." My first priority—and theirs—was "holding the relationship," at times lightly, at times with gravity, with and for each other. We "hold" the sense that there *is* an enduring connection, much as we "hold" the relationship with a child, where the connection is always in movement yet never totally out of our awareness. Even when the person is distant or a disconnection is evident, the sense of connection or at least the faith in the connection remains. A sense of good connection can be "held" when people are thousands of miles apart; it may be lost when people are in the same room, or bed. And in terms of conflict, holding the we may sometimes mean going into the conflict, sometimes letting go of it for a time and coming back to it later.

In our culture this "holding" has been women's work; in the couples therapy I help Tom and Ann to see it and refer to it as "our" work. There are a gender differences in this "holding." Sometimes it seems to Ann that Tom loses the sense of the we *in the moment.* She wants him to hold this with her, since she feels she carries it alone. To Tom it seems like Ann loses her faith in the we *over the long term*—during emotional ups and downs and periods of difficulty. He wants her to hold it with him over the long term, which may be easier for him, a man, as—in the words of women in a dialogue—"the stabilizer of the relationship." *Meeting each other where each has felt alone,* not simply relying on these differences, makes it "our" work.

Mutuality is in that "our." Getting to "we" allows "us" to hold the connection. We "hold" the connection when other forces within each person alone or in the world would stretch it or tear it apart, when the incredible stress that couples live with today taxes the connection, or when clouds of fear, anger, hurt, irritability, or boredom cover over the connection.

How does holding the we help Tom and Ann move toward mutuality?

Mutuality grows through two voices in real dialogue. When both Tom and Ann feel seen and heard by each other, both feel moved by each other, and both feel they have impact on each other and on the movement of the "we." We call this mutual empathy.[4] When we "hold" the connection, each person's contribution moves things forward and each person is changed through this process. From the spindle of mutuality comes the "we." Each person then feels seen and heard and moved by the other—each person *senses the other feeling seen and heard and moved*—and something new happens. Something creative happens.

Tom—and many other men—often feels locked into silence in the relationship, trapped between his dread of connecting and his fear of losing her, disconnecting. Afraid that "something might happen," Tom defends the status quo with Ann. Unfortunately, Tom—and many other men—are less skilled at anticipating relational events, so that it is only after things are lost or crippled that men wake up and want to change. Men often seem to have to flee, damage, or destroy a relationship with a woman in order to really *feel* what they have to lose, to realize that they want what they are fleeing. Men's being stuck between the dread of connection and fear of loss, and being afraid of engaging in the uncharted movement of relationship, may have much to do with men's difficulty in both anticipating and recollecting relational events.

Ann—and many other women—more easily initiates relational movement. (She may sometimes focus too intently on "the other.") Ann, seeing Tom move from a self-centered perspective and start to come alive
more mutually, is able to bring herself more fully into the relationship.
Ann is trying to stay with her own experience and still hold an empathic
connection to Tom, without taking care of him or of the relationship.
Women often feel frustration and despair at what is possible in relationship with men, and are tired of taking care of men, doing all the work of
relating. Women may first need to feel men moving toward them, start to
listen and respond, before feeling able to listen and fully respond to men
from a more mutual place. Ann and many other women have traditionally "held the 'we'" at the expense of their own voices and need men to
share the "holding" with them. If the movement of men toward mutuality is from "me" to "we" to "you," the movement toward mutuality for
women is different: not so much the either/or conception of getting from
"me" to "we" but rather the more "and" conception—that the start of
relational movement creates a more shared "we," which continues to be
built with the man as they "hold" it together. At every moment in the
process the woman's "I" voice is strengthened as this sense of shared
"holding" too is strengthened.

With Tom, I am trying to help him move away from a self-centered
way of seeing, opening up the idea that he can attend to the "we" and
to the *different* experience of Ann (and others in his life) without judgment or comparison, that he can impact the relationship with Ann—
and be impacted by it—without losing himself. I am less concerned with
Tom's male "role" and "identity"—which are already sharply defined—
than with Tom's male "relational" skills—which are largely devalued
and undefined. All of my muscle has to be applied to shifting the
momentum away from Tom's "self" to Tom's "connections." I hold the
faith that if the quality of Tom's connections is healthy, we won't have
to worry about his "self." In a natural movement, his strengths will be
brought into relationship with Ann in an even fuller way. Tom will feel
more competent and powerful in this relationship.

With Ann, I am trying to help her do less of the relational work for
the couple, understand men's experience of dread, emotional timing,
and talk, and help keep the focus on her own experience as well. I help
her to represent *her* experience in conflict, to say what she feels and
what she wants, to hold her ground when she feels strongly about
something, and to feel that less energy is needed for defending herself

and more energy for change and growth. Ann is feeling more held in the "we" and more in touch with her own feelings as well as Tom's. Given Ann's vigilance about the connection and about the other person—Tom—I use all of my muscle to shift the momentum back to herself in that connection. My faith is that if she feels Tom "holding" the we *with* her—especially through disconnections—she will be more herself and more powerful and effective in the relationship.

Working together toward mutual, Tom and Ann and I are always moving in three ways: from "self/other" to the "we"; from "I, Tom" to "we men" and "I, Ann" to "we women"; and from connection to disconnection to reconnection (from impasse to breakthrough).

Emphasizing the importance of taking mutual responsibility for the "we" can be a new and fresh level of thinking for us all. "I" statements—"I think X" or "I feel Y"—are of course encouraged, but it's not enough to "get your feelings out." This has to be done with an awareness of the effect on the other person and on the relationship. "I" statements made with awareness of the relational context and an intention to build connection move Tom and Ann to greater clarity and authenticity; "I" statements made without this awareness and intention solidify their impasses.

As in the gender dialogues, only after this shift toward mutual begins to occur are Tom and Ann able to talk about the most difficult subjects. They can now go back over the issues that led to their impasses—money, illness, religion, ethnicity, children, family—with a fresh sense of attending, responding, ruthlessly encountering the psychological facts from this new place of shared meaning. It is amazing how the same questions that had brought hostile silence now bring animated discussion. Dread and yearning and anger can be addressed unflinchingly. Humor is much in evidence, humor not as Freud's weird "sublimated aggression" but in the service of connection.

As with the men in the dialogues, Tom started to feel competent at relationship, at—his words—"doing empathy well."

Ann responded, "I always knew the potential was there."

Tom and Ann became increasingly able to "hold the 'we'" between our sessions. They were mindful of the "we" that was bigger than both of them, a "we" with a vital history and future. We scheduled sessions less frequently—about once a month—and even though from time to time they would call me up in a crisis, these seemed to be more a healthy sign of their new life out on the growing edge of the relationship than a failure to maintain the growing "we." I helped them to reframe impasses to keep them moving forward. Let us mention a few of these reframings.

Reframing Depression

When they come in, Ann says she has been feeling down the past few weeks. We talk about it. Tom, frustrated and worried, asks me: "Do you think she needs a little Prozac?"

Given what Ann has described, I see no sign of an organic depression, and so I brave going against the immense cultural forces acting on us doctors and say, "I don't think so."

"How about a little Zoloft," he asks.

"How about a little reframing?" I answer. I help them to look at Ann's "depression" as a sign of movement in the relationship. It turns out that Ann, more connected to Tom, was becoming more aware of how different it was for her to share her sadness and vulnerability. She was having a lot of feelings about missing one of their boys, who had left for a few months to live with a family in Europe.

TOM: But when she gets this depressed, how do I know when I should just let her cry, and when I should try to do something about it?

I: You could *ask* her. Why not ask her where she is, how you can help?

Tom does so.

Ann doesn't respond.

I ask, "What keeps you from responding, Ann?"

ANN: I stop myself, like I feel dread too. It's still easier to go with what I'd gotten used to doing, talking to my friends instead of Tom. I want to tell him, but I still don't trust his response—I've been left so many times.

I: All of us have to hold what's new in the relationship now. Maybe right now the way out of this depression is through the relationship, letting Tom be with you in your sadness?

This helps. Men often have a hard time *asking* about another's experience. When Tom is able to ask about and to stay with her sad feelings,

Ann is able to move through her sadness in a more connected, less depressed way. Miller and Stiver suggest this important distinction between depression and sadness: when sadness cannot move in relationship, through the process of mutual empathy, depression results.[5]

An alternative way of looking at "depression" is this relational way. If we look back at the "five good things" that result from a good connection, and then take the opposite of each, we see a definition of depression based on disconnection: less zest or energy, less knowledge of self and others, less sense of self-worth, less power to take action, and a desire for less connection (or more isolation). The implication is that these depressive qualities come from disconnections; the movement out of depression may come not through any kind of self-centered analysis (or pills, which can sometimes be more isolating) but through good connection.

Reframing Dependence and Independence

They call me up in crisis. Awakening that morning they had felt close and made love, and then Tom, obsessed with a deal at work, had rushed to get out of the house and hadn't said good-bye. He was driving their son to school when the car phone rang. It was Ann, feeling very hurt that he had just left without even saying good-bye. They come to meet with me that evening.

TOM: Here we go! Whatever I do, it's not enough. You always want more.

ANN: I don't think it's too much to ask you, especially after being so connected, in sex, to say good-bye.

TOM: There's no room for me to just be myself in this relationship. You're so damn dependent on me, and you want to make me just as dependent on you. All day long you've been bugging me, calling me, interrupting meetings, and it's kept me from really focusing on my work.

I: Let's try to reframe this. Tom, what would've happened if you had just stayed in connection and said good-bye this morning?

TOM: She wouldn't be bugging me.

I: So you'd have *more* freedom, not less?

TOM: (*thinking it over*) You got me. But that's so damn hard for me to stay with. It's such a huge job!

I: Maybe not. It wouldn't have been such a big deal just to say good-bye—and that would have altered the whole day. We men have this mental image that to deal with a woman's feeling is an immense thing, but it's not.

TOM: (*smiling*) You mean the real iceberg is in *my* head? (*we all laugh*)

The false dichotomy of dependence/independence causes much grief in couples. Relationship is not a zero-sum game. If Ann feels Tom is attending to the relationship, she can attend to other things. She feels less anxiety if she's not watching all the time, thinking all the time, in her words, "If I focus outside this relationship—on my work, on my self—it and he will disappear." She feels more able to initiate things and have her own life. It's not her "learning to be more independent,"[6] it's both of them learning to hold the connection and having the faith that the connection will sustain and hold each of them in their own lives and creativity. Her calling Tom on the car phone was something new—she never would have done that in the past. As she put it: "I'm not settling for less anymore, and *we're* not either."

Nurturing the "We" in the Face of Stress and Obsession

A number of months later, they call again. Tom had become obsessed with a stressful work situation. All he could talk about was his work, and he recognized, as did she, that he didn't want to be this way. He felt totally stressed out, out of control. Ann too, under the stress of her job and family responsibilities, was fed up. She was refusing to listen to "Tom on his work" anymore.

They come in, and this time Ann suggests, humorously:

"How 'bout a little Prozac for Tom? I hear it's quite good for obsessive-compulsive too."

As we work, I try to reframe Tom's obsession in terms of relationship, that is, that the way out is not in medication nor in analyzing the obsession but rather by moving more fully into relationship. Any obsession is a turning away from living in connection. I suggest that by making the relationship the priority, Tom might let go of his obsession with work. Ann agrees, saying that if she felt connected to Tom, she would be glad to listen to his talk about work:

"If *you're* interesting, your work is interesting to me."

It turns out that a particular "danger time" is when both Tom and Ann come home from work. As with many other couples we have worked with, this often breaks down along gender lines: Ann wants to transition by being with Tom; Tom wants to transition by being with the newspaper. We talk specifically about ways to make the transition from work to home—how to reconnect after a long hard day. (These and other relational steps will be discussed in the next chapter.)

A month later, in what will turn out to be their last session with me, Tom and Ann describe how reframing the obsession had helped and look back with me on what had happened to get them moving, together, again:

TOM: I'm pretty much over my dread now. I can attend to *her* experience, and ask about it. I feel more able to nurture the relationship now.

ANN: It's amazing—I feel listened to now. Not that there aren't troubles—last week we got into a hassle—he was at work and kept me waiting for hours—I started to get angry, but then I wasn't all that mad, because I figured that *we* got into this, how are *we* going to get out of it. The incredible thing is that I feel that his empathy all of a sudden has me thinking: "Hmm, what has *my* part been in not having been present in this relationship in the past? Maybe *I* haven't been initiating enough here. Not that I'm a victim, but rather what part have I played in this? I could be more active and initiating, yes."

TOM: When we're in conflict, I feel I can *do* it now, that my whole ego isn't on the line. In the past, I felt that I had to have the right answer, that what I did was a reflection on what I was worth— now I know that's got nothing to do with it, in terms of Ann. I can let go of my self-centered thinking about this, by asking about her experience. (*to Ann, looking directly at her*) I used to think you were so damn oversensitive—now I see that your sensitivity is so useful to me and to the relationship.

ANN: Neither of us has to do it alone. It's like an incredible gift to feel we can begin to explore what we can do together.

TOM: *Begin?!* Uh-oh. Here we go!

ANN: The sky's the limit.

They call me up a year later, to the day, to tell me they're doing well.

.   .   .

Tom and Ann experienced an extremely positive outcome of using this way of working. We don't want to imply, though, that every couple can go through a process that results in this same form of mutual connecting. All of us, including Tom and Ann, are at best always moving *toward* mutuality. The disconnections are always there; it's a question of how we handle them, how much energy we have for "keeping on keeping on." People are at various stages of readiness to use this way of looking at things.

Often it is hard. Moving toward mutual is not a linear process. Steps forward make it seem like the couple is charmed and strong and full of vitality. But steps back to what seem like habitual limitations feel discouraging. It's not ever-upward wonderful. Change is always changing. There are always new edges and challenges.

For growth to continue it has to be nurtured. Tom and Ann were lucky to have resources of all kinds to do this—money, time, therapy, flexible jobs. For many couples it is much more difficult. Trying to find a "we" when resources are limited, in the stresses of daily life—two jobs, the torture of the workplace, the speed on the highway and the information superhighway, the fact that many of the more privileged of us can't let our children just "go out and play" anymore but have to drive them to their "activities" and "lessons"—all these make it difficult to care and nurture the relationship, no matter how firm the intention. One of the most obvious and neglected suggestions for couples is to cut the stresses as much as possible. Few of us do this easily. New approaches to stress reduction and simplification of our lives are urgently needed. Couples sometimes can find ways to support each other in finding an alternative lifestyle and stress reduction.

All of us are impacted by the institutional fragmentation and violence of contemporary society and the profound isolation and lack of community so many couples suffer. In addition, for those more outside the mainstream, the scarcity of economic resources and the impact of social oppression in the form of racism, classism, ageism, heterosexism, and so on takes an enormous toll on couples. For example, Hopson and Hopson describe the history of slavery and the racism central to the experience of African American men and women as having enormous impact on current relationships between black men and women.[7] No discussion of particular relationships can exist outside of such a contextual framework.

Many men and women stay together despite a frayed and tenuous "we." Sometimes they may not have the resources to support splitting up. Sometimes particular parts of their lives as a couple lend themselves to nurturing the "we," such as "who we are in our careers" or "who we are with our children." These "partial we's" can go a long way in helping each person and their children live a fulfilling life.

And we are not talking about every couple staying together. A couple may conclude that there is no viable "we." If so, the Connection Model may help them separate without as much blame and guilt. One young couple came to us for therapy wondering if they should get married. They had been dating for several years, but they were locked into a painful conflict that made it impossible for them to move together or apart. After a few sessions, helping them to focus on whether or not there was a "we" that was alive and growing, that nurtured each of them, and that was in movement toward more mutuality, they decided, together, that there wasn't. In the last session the young woman said:

"You know, I don't hate him, I hate the *relationship* with him." It was a sad moment, but an authentic and compassionate one. They parted with much sorrow, but without overwhelming suffering.

If children are involved when a couple gets divorced, the quality of the remaining connection between the man and woman becomes ever more important. Many reports have shown that the degree of harm to children depends a great deal on the quality of the relationship between the ex-spouses. Using the Connection Model, it may be possible to disengage from a couple relationship, separate and divorce, without a total disconnect. Although it is difficult, some couples manage to hold a more or less mutual connection around their children, even when they are legally and formally disengaged from each other.

One of the problems for couples is the images we all have of an "ideal relationship." Sometimes other couples seem to have it all together, all figured out. They seem happy. Comparison with such "perfect" couples often makes it more difficult to work on our own relationships. And yet we all know "perfect couples" who suddenly one day, to our surprise, split up. What really goes on in a couple relationship is often pretty well hidden from others.

The norm of "the nuclear family" is a stress in itself. We as individual couples are often isolated from what's really going on in other couples, even our close friends. Rarely are there opportunities for honest sharing of the truth of our couples relationships with anyone except therapists. Thus we are deprived of the opportunity to grow in connection with other couples.

And so at the same time we were bringing the Connection Model to individual couples in therapy, we also began working with several couples at once, in groups.

5

How Couples Grow

STEPS FOR CREATING HEALTHY CONNECTIONS

"Your holding your relationship helps us to hold ours."

—ONE MAN OF A COUPLE, TO ANOTHER MAN
OF A COUPLE, IN DIALOGUE

"Us too."

—THE OTHER MAN, IN RESPONSE

Couples in our culture have few opportunities to share their authentic experience with other couples. Social gatherings or community events are not places where couples can discuss their struggles. It is rare for couples to see other couples working on problems, the couple's "we"—strengths and weaknesses—fully on view.

If individuals suffer when they are isolated, couples suffer too. Would it be beneficial, we wondered, if—much as individuals had moved from "I"/"you" to "we"—individual couples could move from "we as a couple" to "we couples"? Could one couple benefit from seeing the qualities of the connection at the heart of another couple? Would one couple's "we" be familiar to other couples' "we's"? Would there be a "click" of recognition not only with the connections but with the disconnections? Most important, would seeing one couple's *ways* of breaking through impasses and growing in connection help another couple find its own way?

Several years ago we began leading weekend workshops for couples. By now we have data from over two hundred couples. Men and women from eighteen to eighty have come to the workshops, in couples that have existed only a year and as long as fifty years. We have worked with the "we's" at virtually every stage of evolution and devolution, from the infatuation of first love facing the commitment of marriage, through the drama of the middle years—sometimes grand opera, sometimes *Godot*—to the deep joy and measured sorrow of retirement and old age. When these different life stages are represented in the same group, it can be rich and enlivening for all.

We will briefly describe our first couples workshop, then draw on our experience with all the couples we have worked with to offer steps for creating healing connections. We have offered couples the opportunity to contribute their unique resources of struggle and reward for inclusion in this book. We feel privileged to share their voices here.

Couples in Dialogue

We advertised for eight couples to participate in a weekend workshop, at the heart of which was a daylong gender dialogue. The couples who responded ranged in age from late twenties to seventies; most were white, middle and working class, and of varied ethnic backgrounds. All the couples identified themselves as heterosexual. Most were living in New England. Some came to Boston from northern Vermont, Maine, New York, and as far away as Illinois and Virginia.

We started out as with the gender dialogues—a Friday night session and all day Saturday. We then sent the couples home on Saturday night with "homework," to report back to the group on Sunday afternoon, leaving Sunday morning for them to prepare, together. We met a month later to share their ongoing work with the whole group. Our hope was to start a process that would "carry," so that couples, on their own, would continue to work together on the relationship and find processes that would sustain their growth in connection. It was somewhat of an experiment: to see if men and women who lived together, day in day out, could continue to build on what they had learned with us.

Most of the eight couples in this first group were doing well and had come to the group to learn more; some were in trouble, two were on the verge of breakup, feeling they had already "failed" at various kinds of couples therapy. From the beginning the couples groups had a particularly intimate feeling. We needed a larger space than our offices provided, so we met in the living room of our home. This further empowered the group by creating less professional "distance" as we became more open and visible to the group members. We have continued, in our work together, to be as transparent about our own differences and struggles as would be helpful to the other couples.

On Friday evening we gathered in our living room and began introductions. Usually, in workshops, one person introduces him or herself to the group; occasionally a person will introduce his or her partner or spouse. Using the Connection Model, we asked the couples to introduce "the relationship" to the group. We gave them ten minutes to prepare what they, as a couple, would say. They seemed surprised, then pleased. As they talked, some of the couples were quietly serious, others laughed. The shift toward the "we" in each couple had begun.

For the purpose of this chapter, we will describe three of the couples in the first group. They span a range of ages, and their relationships span different stages.

The Young Creators: Donna and Stan

Donna and Stan, in their early thirties and living in New Haven, have had a difficult time since the birth of their son, Sam, two years ago. The child was not planned, and they had married because of the pregnancy. Both are highly creative. Stan is a struggling writer of novels and plays, a short hefty blond man of German heritage; Donna wants to do documentary films but currently is working as a freelance industrial film editor; she is tall, dark, and thin, and is from a South American family who migrated to the United States two generations ago. They both come from working-class families. They constantly discuss separating.

Each had been in several disastrous relationships, and neither wanted to get involved with anyone at the time they met. And then one night they were both attending a concert alone and happened to start talking at intermission. They liked each other—their frankness and vulnerability, their different ethnicities and temperaments (he stolid, she stormy), and above all the sardonic worldview they were surprised to find they shared. They soon started dating and began a passionate affair.

They introduced their relationship to the group as follows:

> Two wolves living in a cave with a cub. We act like it's a ferocious situation, always hyper-careful because we could tear each other apart. But deep down we know it's fragile, gentle, easily hurt. It's like a storm taking a destructive path, completely out of control.

The Midlife Moderns: Suzanne and Giff

Suzanne and Giff, in their mid-forties and living in New Hampshire, are in the gender maelstrom of twin teenage girls and two sons in elementary school. They had been introduced by their families as teenagers, fell in love, and married at twenty-five. Suzanne, a petite soft-spoken redhead from a French Canadian Catholic background, works in an architect's office and is the first of her family to go to college; Giff is old New England Episcopalian, thin, wiry, energetic. A management consultant, he is overworking his way up the firm's ladder. Giff has had a problem with alcohol but has been sober on his own for four years. Suzanne has gotten more and more successful, with many promotions, and is currently managing a large and successful office, with more design contracts than she can handle. When they went away to college and came back that first Thanksgiving and spent it together with their families, they realized they loved each other and started dating long distance. Their relationship spans thirty years, in marriage for almost twenty. They described their relationship to the group:

> It's been reliable and *there,* like the sky or maybe the moon. But it's clouded over, hard to see. Too many conflicting obligations—kids, work. No time for us. We've been in parallel play. Something is rumbling—like an earthquake is coming. Or maybe its just a midlife crisis.

The Innocent Elders: Esther and Irv

Irv and Esther, both in their late sixties, both with rounded edges and gray hair—"grandparenty," they call themselves—are on the verge of retiring, Esther from social work, Irv from gynecology. Their three children are grown, and they are expecting their first grandchild. Both are Jewish, the second generation born in America, the first to make it to professional life. They had grown up in New York City, moved out to the suburbs, and have been spending more and more time at a second house in Vermont where they hope to retire. They have come to the couples group because they have not been able to handle a recent scare: Irv was diagnosed with a serious heart condition. Esther was frightened at the way Irv closed off to her during the healing process; Irv felt that she didn't let him alone to heal. They had met in New York City in the 1950s when they both worked at the same hospital. For each it was the first serious relationship. It grew on shared values and visions at a measured pace. They have been married over forty years. Their relationship?

> "Very old and solid—like a deep river or a porcupine. A long history of doing things a certain way, so now it's hard to move."

As we all listened to the eight couples' descriptions, there was a sense of recognition and interest.

After this exercise, we described the Connection Model, using their descriptions as examples of how couples can shift out of the "I"/"you" to the "we" of the couple. After discussing this shift, we asked them to do a final exercise as a couple before we ended for the evening, something we called The Qualities of the Relationship. Each person of the couple, separately, writes down his or her answer to the questions we posed: What is the texture of the relationship? The color? The climate? The sound? The movie? What animal is a metaphor for the relationship? After writing them down separately, the couples had a chance to share these and discuss their images with each other.

	DONNA	STAN
Texture:	rough, with spikes	steel polish and jagged
Color:	orange and black	flame
Climate:	rainy	stormy

Sound:	a Beethoven mass	silence—can be solitude, can be prison-cell solitary confinement
Movie:	*Shock Corridor*	*Citizen Kane*
Animal:	armadillo	a pigeon swarm—nice, but can turn violent

	SUZANNE	GIFF
Texture:	furry brown, but with spikes	a chop on water, smooth but dangerous to go out on
Color:	tropical blue-green	slate-grey
Sound:	noisy, then as soundless as fresh snow	giggly laughter, like at a cocktail party—people noise
Climate:	Gulf of Mexico—warm, but with hurricanes	Nantucket—great summers, bad winters
Movie:	*Baghdad Cafe*	*Dr. Zhivago*
Animal:	a horse—power and strength	two dogs—rambunctious—but too big to handle, like our two Goldens

	ESTHER	IRV
Texture:	a lot of velvet, but snags	rough cloth
Color:	purple	black
Sound:	Wagner—great moments, terrible half hours	soft chattering, insistent
Climate:	cloudy—floating around	always a sense of the calm before the storm
Movie:	*Fiddler on the Roof*	*Fiddler on the Roof*
Animal:	a fish—a flounder	a shark

As each couple presented their work to the group, there was some laughter but silences too, as the dangerousness of some of the images was evident. We noted the marked similarities in each couple—especially in the couples who had been together for a longer time. The differences, too, were of note—often surprising to one of the members of the couple. It was reassuring how easily each man and woman had been able to describe these qualities of the connection. It meant that each person had a vivid, ongoing awareness of the "we."

We sent them home for the night. Some walked out holding hands. All but Donna and Stan were talking to each other.

The next morning everyone was on time and seemed eager to get to work. We explained the importance of the gender dialogue in building a base for further work as couples. We moved right into separate gender groups, the men with Sam in the kitchen, the women with Janet in the living room. (It is interesting that when we divide men and women into groups, the men tend to be the ones to leave and come back; the women stay put. We have to be careful to vary this.) We then further divided each gender group into two groups of four. Each small group would meet for thirty minutes and assign a reporter to write down the group's consensus answers to our three questions. The men and women immediately started talking, relieved to be with their own gender. Serious and productive conversation ensued, the men talking about how good it felt to talk about themselves and their relationships with their partners, their fathers, and their children, the women talking about how much they missed the opportunity to get together like this in women's groups. After they had come up with the small-group answers, the men met as a group with Sam, the women with Janet, to talk about their answers and prepare for the dialogue.

Next we brought the men and women back together, having them sit in their same-gender groups facing each other on opposite sides of the living room. Janet sat with the women, Sam with the men.

Here it was: eight husbands facing eight wives across the room. The stakes were high.

Much of what happened in this gender dialogue with couples was similar to what we had seen over the years with mostly uncoupled men and women. However there were some differences.

Because each couple had an ongoing "we," with a history, a present, and probably a future, the men and women were more careful. No one wanted to risk the fate of the "we" in front of others. The public image of the couple was to be protected. As Donna said about Stan, "I hate this feeling, but I have to be vigilant and careful he doesn't hurt himself, or others. I'm trying to let go of this, Stan, it drives me crazy!"

Stan answered, "Me too."

In a sense, each member of the couple was quite aware of the relationship, and despite choosing to work on it, would be holding the "frame" of "let's not let us get hurt too badly in front of other people." This meant that initially the fire of anger and conflict that we had seen in other dialogues was missing. It also meant more depth of shared feeling, of frustration, sadness, loss—and more shared humor and loyalty.

The men went first, reading their answers to question one, naming "three strengths women bring to relationship." The answers were much the same as in the other dialogues:

> Motherhood; the desire and concern for relationships; intuition; creating community; maintaining connection between two people; more in touch with their feelings and talk; ability to do more than one thing at a time.

The women felt seen and acknowledged for their strengths but wanted to be sure the men knew how impossible and exhausting it felt to "carry" these activities alone. They also wanted to hear the men name and value their competence at their more nontraditional activities in the world.

The couples' discussion then picked up on one strength of women: the ability to do more than one thing at a time—"She can work on a task and maintain the connection at the same time; if I'm working on something and she comes in, it's an intrusion."

> GIFF: Making the switch from business to relationship is like bringing the car down from high speed to a dead stop, like having to put in another engine. She wants to talk about us, and I start to feel there's something wrong with me, I start to feel incompetent, and that Suzanne has the upper hand. I don't want to be wrong, I want to retreat, get my ducks in order—and then, when she asks me again to talk, I want to say, hey wait a second. I just don't have the emotional skills to be in that conversation right now.
>
> SUZANNE: I don't mind waiting for you to find the right moment, but that moment never comes, and you never come back, it gets

buried. So I struggle to keep it moving, trust that it will keep moving, but I get into this eggshell thing—walking on eggshells around the house. I rehearse this over and over, how to talk with him, and he feels he's on eggshells too. It just blows up. I don't have this kind of feeling in connection with women.

IRV: But I feel like there'll be no end—you'll want to do this end-lessly!

SUZANNE: If we do connect, we can get through it and get on with other things.

ESTHER: I don't feel there's a right or wrong answer. It's not repeti-tive, it's refining, finding the consensus or understanding. You see it as having a right answer. For me—for women, I think— "right" is "authentic." Stay connected to me, and when it's "right," it just flows.

DONNA: Exactly. Creativity is not a right or wrong answer, it's being *in it* with me!

This ongoing dialogue created the sense that the couples were able to bring much of their history and experience into the dialogue and that they were beginning to trust the group. The issues—compartmentalization of work and relationship, dread and yearning, the process of creativity ver-sus "getting" somewhere—were familiar. But the work was at a deeper level because of the couples' years of working on the issues in the past.

In their answers to question one, women showed much appreciation for the strengths the men did bring to the couple's relationship, includ-ing adventurousness and passion, ability to stay focused, steadiness, and solidness. The focus turned to the double standard of what women want from men: on the one hand, vulnerability, on the other, invulnera-bility in the world.

STAN: When I'm gentle and vulnerable, it freaks Donna out. You women need to make up your mind what you want.

ESTHER: It's true, we give men a double message, be strong and be vulnerable—but don't scare me. I do get scared when Irv is vul-nerable, but I still want it.

SUZANNE: For women, vulnerability helps us to connect with one another. I never see his vulnerability as a weakness. I *love* him vulnerable.

DONNA: Motherhood is one of our strengths, and it's the greatest vulnerability. I love Stan the most when he's his most vulnerable, when I see him really open to his love for other people, and for our son, Sam.

Women's question two for their husbands focused on two areas:

What does your silence really mean?
How can we reach you and know what goes on inside of you?

The men talked about silence being a sign of dread, a defense against not knowing the answer, or sometimes even a power strategy.

GIFF: No answer is better than what will come if I do answer.

STAN: Right. If we're not fighting and our son is happy—it doesn't get any better than that. I don't want to risk talking.

DONNA: Stan has three states: the horrible, the silent, and the nice. That's our big problem: he wants it "nice," I want it "real."

ESTHER: My fantasy is that it wouldn't bother Irv if he didn't talk for a year.

IRV: Try five.

STAN: Would you settle for a month?

The group laughed. The men and women were starting to relax and have some fun.

DONNA: It got so bad, I'd ask Stan at random: "Anything you want to *tell* me? Like you've lost your job? You're having an affair? You're working for the FBI? I'm throwing the field open—you can say *anything* to me, okay?"

STAN: My worst nightmare.

ESTHER: Four years ago Irv got more quiet, he got more silent. At sixty-five he'd been diagnosed with heart disease. Just when I needed to talk about it more, he talked less.

This shifted the group to a shared sense of what it would mean to lose the other person of the couple—something everyone could identify with. It was much on everyone's mind—and rarely acknowledged to each other. People talked about their losses. The connections deepened. Again we saw some of the same differences, and the invisibilities: dread, the relational context, relational curiosity, different relational timing, and the others.

But the couples were connected by their sharing these differences, and the work was quickly deeper, more intense, profound, and easier than in a group of uncoupled men and women. Every answer, every comment, was offered in the context of men or women in general but was given added power by the specific man or woman—and the specific couple relationship—in the room. There was a constant back and forth between what "men" and "women" are like and what "Donna" and "Stan" and "Irv" and "Esther" and "Suzanne" and "Giff" were like. The group differences added to the individual and vice versa. Individual voices that expressed exceptions to the group gender differences under discussion enlarged the discussions not as challenges but by adding complexity and mystery. Out of it came the feeling that the "we," the "relationship," was a vital, alive thing or process, at the heart of every couple that struggles and not all that dissimilar from that of other couples.

The men then read the women their answers to question two:

> Why can't you have more patience about our need to be alone?
> What are you searching for and what makes you feel whole in a relationship?
> Why do you need so much connection?

DONNA: You might as well ask why we need so much to breathe.

SUZANNE: If I'm not connected, I'm suffocating.

ESTHER: For us, connection is not such a big deal as for you. For men, it's a whole big involved thing, something you have to do. It's not a "do," it's a "be."

DONNA: Marriage sometimes is the worst of both worlds—both dealing with another person and feeling alone. I feel like saying something—hey, you want some low-maintenance girlfriend, go find one. I keep wondering if I'm better off alone.

SUZANNE: The lonely togetherness is the worst.

ESTHER: Irv doesn't want to share his sorrow. In almost forty years I saw Irv cry once.

DONNA: Stan's tears are so important—a real gift. They help me feel him, and then I feel connected.

As the group went on, there was the shift toward mutuality we had noticed in other dialogues. With the couples, it happened quickly and provided the underpinning for important issues to be talked about attentively. At one point Donna said:

> It feels so good to see Stan over there flanked by all the other men! I wish he had other men in his life who deeply supported

him! I really appreciate that he's getting supported here in this
work, in this alternative view: that we really *can* connect.

STAN: When we first sat down, all of you women looked so fierce.
Now, you look friendly.

SUZANNE: So who changed?

At the end of the dialogue time, we asked the men and women to
read their answers to question three: "What do you most want the
other gender group to understand about you?" The women's answers:

How much we need to be heard. We want to be in mutual,
authentic partnership. We need you to share—in order to have
emotional and sexual intimacy. We don't mean to be interview-
ing you or interrogating you; we want you to feel our attention
as an invitation, not a criticism. We're interested in relational
connection, not just emotional connection. If we're emotional, it
doesn't mean we don't have a good point.

The men's answers:

To appreciate what it means to be a whole man in this world.
We're passionate about things and have feelings and we talk
about things which *cause* feelings. We do care about relationships—just as much as you do. If we're quiet it doesn't mean we
don't care.

We sat together as a group for a few moments. No one wanted to
break the spell of the silence. It was a silence of having walked through
something together, faced hard questions—health, loss, sorrow, anger—
and come away not so much with answers as with a sense of shared
faith in asking, answering, looking together.

"Thank you," Janet said.

Members of the group echoed this.

We all knew that the gender dialogue had helped each couple see the
other couples' "we" in plain view and addressed in respectful dialogue.
We turned to the final part of the weekend: sending the couples home
with homework. We suggested that each couple do three things:

1. Write a relational purpose statement. Since we believe that relationships do have purposes, writing them down is helpful. Together, on
a single sheet of paper, write down the purpose of the relationship.

This can be its goals, visions, values, the questions the relationship asks, whatever.

2. Write out an example of the particular impasse that you as a couple get into. We explained the notion of "relational impasse," pointed out some of the impasses the group had gotten into, and then suggested that on a sheet of paper, each couple write out in a column going down the left-hand side of the page the lines of dialogue of one of their own typical impasses. In a second column, write out, for each line of dialogue, what is going on in the man; in a third column, what is going on in the woman; and in a final column, what is going on in the relationship, the "we." (See figures later in the chapter.)

3. Choose a project that you would like to do together and begin it.

With assurances that they would keep in touch over the month, they left.

We were left cleaning up the empty coffee cups and residual snacks, hardly noticing what we were doing as we talked. We were excited and satisfied at how well it had gone. How would it "hold"? Could they sustain the momentum of the group? We knew how difficult it was for couples to have time for anything in the chaotic, fragmented world of working and children and modern life. Would they have time and energy for this? Where, if anywhere, would this go?

A month later we found out, in a somewhat embarrassing way: several of the couples showed up at our door a half hour early, and we were not ready—still cleaning the house, putting away our daughter's toys, and late for our bagel run. The rest of the couples were on time and glad to see each other. A few, it turned out, had been in touch with each other over the month. In fact, Suzanne and Giff (from New Hampshire) had had the idea with Irv and Esther (from New York) of a kind of buddy system, each of them "checking in" from time to time— especially at times of impasse—each member of the two couples on a separate phone or speakerphone.

The couples greeted each other as old friends who had shared an important experience in the past. Without exception, they seemed lighter, more alive. We went around the room for a check-in on the state of the "we." Each couple had done well. They had done their relational purpose statements, their impasses, planned their project. As they started to describe their work, their enthusiasm for the results was palpable. As we listened, we felt moved. The couples were grateful and hopeful. Why? In its simplest form, put in the words of Giff, to Irv and Esther:

"Your holding your relationship helped us to hold ours."

"Us, too," said Irv in reply.

We had taken it on faith that if we were able to help men and women in couples create and sustain a "we," each person of the couple would feel enlivened, empowered, enriched. The sixteen people here confirmed what we had seen happen over and over again: when connection is strengthened in the couple, the man and woman feel more themselves, not less.

We spent the Sunday afternoon sharing the "homework." At the end, all eight couples said they wanted to continue to meet. We set up monthly meetings, which kept on for almost two years. All but one couple did extremely well.

Four Steps Toward Connection

From this workshop and from many other dialogues with individual couples, groups of couples, and unrelated men and women—we have come up with four general steps to describe how men and women can create good connections.

Building "we" awareness.

Building "man" and "woman" awareness.

Learning to talk "connect" and "disconnect."

Nourishing and empowering the "we."

Each step contains parts of the others. The separations are artificial. Some specific suggestions within the steps have already been described; they will be mentioned here more succinctly.

These steps and suggestions help many couples, though it is not always clear how or why. Our experience is that if a couple follows these suggestions, "keeping on keeping on" with the faith that mutual connection is possible, change can occur. Often it is a subtle process beyond intent or will-power: while we can *do* the steps—and *while* we are doing the steps—connection *happens*.

Alcohol and other drugs mostly act as barriers to authentic connection—often while giving the illusion of connection. Usage of alcohol and other drugs clouds the effectiveness of these steps. If substance abuse exists in a relationship, recovery is absolutely the first priority for healthy growth to occur.

We have recorded here some highly successful outcomes of both members of couples working *together* in these processes. Many couples may not quickly experience such positive results, and we would invite you together to seek out support—in therapy, couples groups, or working with other couples. Small changes can have major effects over time; persistence and support are key. It is essential that one person *not carry the work alone*. For those trying to discern the degree of nonmutuality or abuse in a relationship we hope that the recognition of the necessity of working in the "we" can be helpful in taking steps to change or disengage from such a relationship.

Building "We" Awareness

This is an essential step for any couple. Given the "self/other" shape of the cultural mind-set, it may take a good deal of our focused attention to shift toward an alternative view, placing the "we" at the center of our lives. How do couples build the "we"?

1. Describing the qualities of the relationship in its birth and infancy, and its milestones

Every relationship has a birthdate, infancy, developmental passages and milestones, and a present. The "we" has a life of its own. Even the most unhappy couple can recall with a measure of pleasure and excitement how it all began. Here are some examples from this first couples group.

> *Donna and Stan, the Young Creators*
> When we first met and for a time after, the relationship was passionate, risk-taking, funny, open, honest, fearless in facing feelings. We always engaged in crazy artistic intellectual fireworks. The current milestone was the unplanned pregnancy and then Sam. Everything changed. The "we" has been severed, pushed to the side, bruised and neglected.

Suzanne and Giff, the Midlife Moderns
The relationship was full of trust—absolute trust of each other—with a deep sense of knowing each other, honest and authentic, with shared histories and deep caring for each other's families. It was filled with a steady commitment to helping each other live his or her dream and having children together. As the kids grew and the work got tougher, the "we" got frayed. The big milestone for the "we" was when Suzanne realized that Giff was interested in another woman. Nothing happened, but we didn't really attend to it and now we're in jeopardy.

Irv and Esther, the Innocent Elders
The relationship at first was solid and calm—especially given the yelling and screaming in both of our families—humorous, sincere, trusting, affectionate, and reassuring. It was wonderful to have someone we each trusted to go to the magnificent cultural events in New York City at that time. Milestones? The normal progression of life, very much what normal men and women of our generation did. The big current jolt was Irv's heart condition, and the "we" hasn't been able to handle it, really. It's like a constant jarring noise in the background. We can't find a way to turn it down between us.

2. Describing the current relationship

Together, write down the description of the "we" now. The descriptions the three couples presented to the group are typical. Images of nature are often used, as if in the human imagination the relationship is some being, alive in the natural world. Several other couples in the group reflected this:

A couple in their twenties, with a baby:

It's like reed grass, rub it one way it's fine, but the other way it cuts. You never know which way it's going to go. It's very young, really, like a fawn, a lot of innocence, great potential. We're exhausted and anxious, and the focus is on the baby not on us.

A couple in their late thirties, with three adolescents:

> It used to feel like an eagle we saw when we were on vacation in the Dakotas—it soars beautifully, but it has claws out ready to pounce. Now it's like a suspicious EKG—all erratic highs and lows, rarely in the middle. It's reactive to the kids' energies, made worse by all their teenage stuff.

A couple in their seventies:

> It's a rock, solid, smooth on the outside, that is on one side, but the other side is rough and sharp. Or it's like a house that has weathered a lot of storms—half a century of storms—filled with great moments and with losses—our parents, our friends, the fear of losing each other. A lot of fear, but some grace, too, in the "we" right now.

These descriptions tell a great deal. If a man and a woman in a relationship are asked to find and describe the "we," they will soon discover whether or not there is a "we." If there is, they may use these suggestions to start to move together toward a healthy, mutual place, and the prognosis for the couple is good. If not, they may disengage in a connected process, sparing each other horrible suffering. Sometimes couples do not move but stay locked in nonmutual, barren relationships. For example, one couple could not come up with a shared image.

The wife said, "We're like two branches of a tree, growing separately. I realize that the other branch is there, but I don't really see the trunk at all."

The husband said, "Our relationship is like an electric razor, which you plug in to a battery pack to recharge. Then you go off and come back when it's ready to use. Sometimes you come back and its dead."

It is clear from this how painfully disconnected they were.

3. What qualities does the relationship have now?

Once we shift from looking at the world in terms of self/other to looking at the connection between us, we open the pathway to talk about the *qualities* of those connections. Not just the person, but the relationship with the person. This "qualities of relationship" exercise, in which each person separately writes down the qualities of the "we"—color, texture, climate, sound, animal, and so on—and then shares them, gives a sense of how similar and different the view of the relationship is to each member of the couple. This can also be completed by the couple for the start of the relationship, during milestones, or into the future.

4. Writing a relational inventory: exploring differences

One of the most helpful steps for couples is to find a way to "look together" at the we. One way to do this is to take an inventory of the relationship.

Make two columns on a sheet of paper, one for the strengths and resources of the relationship, the other for vulnerabilities or weak areas. A nonjudgmental discussion of strengths and weaknesses can help build awareness of the we. For example, one couple described their strengths as coparents and partners in the tasks of daily living. They assessed their weak areas in the honest sharing of angry feelings, the ability to play, and taking interesting vacations together. This inventory supports the growth of mutual responsibility for building healthy connection and shifts the focus of difficulties away from either person alone.

The relational inventory also calls for couples to look together at their differences. We have suggested that the question of how differences impact relationships is crucial. First the couple can describe their differences, without judgment, and then look at how and when these differences "add"—that is, enhance their relationship. Finally, the couple can assess how and when the differences interfere with connection and even create impasses. Couples can easily identify crucial differences in their relationship: cultural, religious, sleep/waking cycles, standards of neatness, priorities, and so on. The ability to use differences to support the we and to encourage growth in each person is of great importance in building growth-fostering connections.

5. The future "we"—writing a relational purpose statement together

Whether we have been brought together by seeming chance, fate, or design, many of us have a faith or belief that our continuing to be together has some purpose. It is more than instinctual drives, habit, or just personal gratification that keeps us together. In our hearts, and often unarticulated, we hold a vision of the "we." Some commitment or shared value forms the basis for the relationship.

A relational purpose statement is a way of articulating that vision. We suggest to couples that on a single piece of paper, finding a way to

write together, they describe the purpose of the relationship: What are
we together *for?*

This is difficult to do, but in therapy and in couples groups we have
found that, if a couple can't set the time aside to get to this, or doesn't
value this enough to complete it in some form or other, it does not bode
well for the ongoing relationship. Couples who complete this statement
tend to do well.

Once a purpose statement is written down, it can serve as a future
reference and reminder of why a couple is together, particularly at those
times when it doesn't seem at all clear. The opposite of "awareness,"
after all, is not ignorance but "forgetfulness." In the storm of life and
relationship it is easy to forget the larger purpose, and helpful to have it
written down.

Here are the relational purpose statements the three couples presented when they came back that Sunday a month later:

Donna and Stan:
To create. To support each of us to create our own art, and for
both of us to create our "we," now our three-way "we" with
Sam, together. To keep connected to the higher purpose that
brought us together, the incredible passion we had, to *live* that
fully so there are no regrets or resentments later.

Suzanne and Giff:
To raise children and ourselves in a safe, nurturing environment
where everyone can thrive and develop their potential. We want to
instill and teach, by example, the values of understanding, compassion, generosity, and peace. As a couple we want to foster each
other's interests, at work and at home, and to learn to play better.
We want to help each other grow emotionally and as a couple, to
be friends and share the joys of our interests, of life and loving and
of participating with our children as we all pass through the stages
of life together. We have a deep love for nature and the outdoors
which we enjoy together and are committed to protect.

Esther and Irv:
To see each other through this grieving process—for our parents, for
Irv's health—to be with each other through whatever happens from
now on, to take the best care possible of each other—and of the relationship, to be there for our children and our grandchildren, and to
live the reality of how much we love each other, growing from that

first moment we talked on the surgical ward at Lenox Hill Hospital, all those years ago. To learn to celebrate our journey together!

6. "Where's the 'we'?" Taking mutual responsibility for the relationship

The issue here is to transform the care and feeding of the "we" from one member—often the woman—or no one, to both members of the couple. Moving from guilt to joint responsibility is extremely liberating, and especially important for women, who are often burdened with the caretaking of the "we." When attention is paid, together, to the "we," each person can feel supported and more free to try out new ways of moving in the relationship. The language of "we" is helpful here. Again, as one man said, "We're hanging out in the disconnection here, trying to find a way back into connection."

One couple described how they managed anxiety about money. He would deny the precarious state of their finances; every month she would open the bills and go into a panic. He learned to have the presence of mind to remind her, "We do it together." Both his denial and her anxiety were lessened as, sitting side by side, they went through what they had to do.

Each person is responsible for their own behavior and words but also responsible to each other and *to the relationship.* When you're angry, and speak angrily, it's important to be aware of the effect of the anger not only on yourself and on the other person but *on the relationship.* Anger can be a constricting and constricted state that gives neither the angry person nor the partner much room to move. It has "impasse" written all over it—in some ways, all impasses contain anger. If the relational way is to open up the space for the relationship—and both participants in it—to move, it is helpful to reframe anger in a relational way, as described earlier, as a symptom of someone being hurt or something being wrong in the relationship.[1] This opens up room to move.

The same can be said of other feeling states: sadness, guilt, shame, and so on. Couples need to hold the awareness and ask of themselves and each other: What is the effect of what I'm feeling, saying, doing on the other and on the "we"?

Mutual responsibility is the key to working through impasse. As a couple (or a group) struggles to understand and move together through an impasse, the relationship grows toward relational resilience (the shared energy to move) and relational empowerment (the shared ability to act). These qualities reside not just in the individual but actually in the "we." They arise not in "I" or "you" but in our *process of connecting.*

What must also be determined is which member of the couple will take responsibility for initiating these exercises. (Who, in fact, will take responsibility for taking responsibility?) Usually the woman will say, "All right, we're supposed to write our purpose statement," or "What is your idea of the 'we'?" This one-sided responsibility is a source of much resentment and anger in couples. To avoid this nonmutuality it may also be helpful to do an inventory of who takes responsibility for what in the relationship, then list the areas of mutual responsibility: what do we, together, take responsibility for? How do we decide together what each of us is responsible for?

Finally, it can help a lot to shift particular gender-role-assigned responsibilities for a period of time (she takes out the garbage; he makes sure the child care is arranged), to "put yourself in the other person's shoes." This may help shift the burdens from responsibilities "assigned" unconsciously by gender role to responsibilities that enlarge each person by creating a mutually responsible "we."

In summary, the most crucial questions that a couple can ask in times of disconnection or impasse are:

"Where's the 'we' right now? And what does it need?"

This is about *locating the "we."* It is at the beginning of a disconnection that the man and woman of a couple will start to retreat to the "I" and the "you"—especially into the deadly "you." Those are the decisive times. It is just those times that, if either or both can have the presence of mind to ask "Where is the 'we' right now?" that the situation can turn around, from a disconnect to a connect. If not, the connection starts knotting up into an impasse.

For example, Stan, when he felt the relationship was keeping him from his creative work, sometimes would explode: "You're driving me crazy! In order to get anything accomplished, I've got to get out of here!"

Donna, fearing he'd never come back, would say, "You care more about your own work than about Sam and me."

They continued in the "I"/"you" accusatory mode. Stan stormed out.

If they had had a previous agreement—and some practice—at those kinds of moments one of them could have said, "Hold it—where's the 'we' right now? What does it need?" Stan might have said: "I think what the 'we' needs right now is for me to go off for a while—I'll be back later to help cook dinner, okay?" Donna might have said, "Okay, if we can talk after dinner." Stan might have agreed. It could have been a *mutual* decision, a mutual awareness of each person's wishes, framed in terms of the relationship. Even disengaging—moving apart in time and space—they might have still felt connected.

Another example: when Giff came home from a weeklong business trip, he was anxious to see Suzanne and hoped to have a romantic homecoming. But when he saw her, he was preoccupied and for some reason didn't act warmly toward her. She too was excited to see him, but when he walked in, something happened (perhaps yearning meeting dread). She felt his reserve, and she too felt the difficulty of making connection. Each held back, and each blamed the other, silently. The conversation that ensued was mainly about "you" and "I"—there was no mention of "we." If either of them at that difficult transitional moment had been able to bring out the relational presence and say, "Wait a second. First things first. Where are *we* right now?" it might have provided connecting momentum and saved them a lot of grief. This requires attention. As Giff said, quoting a "rule" he'd learned in business: "You only coast one way—down." Relationship is movement: if you're not moving together, you're moving apart.

7. Mutual impact on the "we"

Control in relationship is deadly; impact is stimulating. Men in couples often feel they are being controlled; women may feel a lack of control. Impasses are often put in terms of control or power struggles.

The alternative idea is impact, or mutual impact. This can be helpful in guiding movement out of power or control struggles. When each person feels that he or she is having an *impact* on the relationship, movement is from power-over to power-with. Gendered experiences of power must be explored in couples. Men need to acknowledge the contrast between their enormous power in the world and their feelings of impotence in relationships. Women often need to reconcile their feelings of powerlessness in the world with the man's experience of their real power in relationship. When men can see this not as power *over* them but as mutual and beneficial influence, power *with* them, it may help greatly. Power struggles may lessen. Some questions that address the issue of power include: "How do I negatively (and positively) impact the 'we'? How do I allow myself to be impacted by the 'we'? When do I not?"

Mutual power lies in moving the other person and being moved by the other person. Power is not like a little battery within each person—*power arises in the connecting.* This we have called "mutual empowerment." After a healthy connection with someone, *each* feels more empowered, and the couple itself is empowered. The great potential for a man and woman in a couple is the way that their differences, shifting to "we," can add. That addition, that being greater than the sum of the parts, is an example of the power of mutuality.

8. What's the growing edge of the "we"?

Anything that grows has an edge. Relationships are always moving, and attention to the edge of that movement of growth can be helpful. It is extremely helpful to become aware of and to articulate the growing edge.

> *Donna and Stan:* Our growing edge is like walking a dangerous tightrope, where we feel we are either being heard or being abandoned.

> *Suzanne and Giff:* Our growing edge is learning to push the envelope of the past, letting go of old ideas about who we are.

> *Irv and Esther:* Our growing edge is finding new roles for each of us in retirement.

Building "Man" and "Woman" Awareness

This connection step focuses on building an awareness of the impact of gender on connections. How do couples build gender awareness?

1. Diagram your individual vision of the "I," the "you," and the "we"

Over time, we have discovered that men and women envision the "we" quite differently. That is, there is a gendered "we."

Each member of the couple can draw a diagram of the "I" the "you," and the "we." This is what the three couples drew:

DONNA & STAN

Stan: Donna:

THE "WE"

THE "WE"

SUZANNE & GIFF

Giff:

Suzanne:

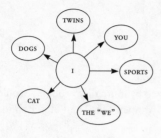

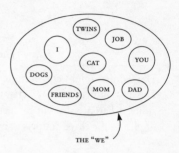

IRV & ESTHER

Irv:

Esther:

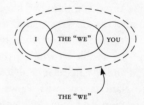

(seeing what Irv was drawing, Esther merely put the - - - of the "we" around it all.)

For many women, the "we" is built on a sense of mutuality and relational movement—of how two voices in dialogue move together, the "we" being greater than the sum of its parts. Inclusivity is the theme. The "we" does not extend out from the self, nor is it the overlap between two selves, but *includes* the self.

For many men, the notion of the "we" seems to be more of a "thing," with properties and qualities, even with boundaries of what is "inside" and "outside." It may also be an extension of a man's "self" boundary, which aligns and defines the "we" in terms of "me." This can be a kind of merger or power trip, the man's view dominating the woman's, as when a wife tells a friend, "We vote Republican." Or it can be a "we" that has a firm boundary of "it's us against them," like a team always in a game against another team.

The old and traditional 1950s notion of the "we" of the couple as drawn by the man might be:

The "We"

The woman might corroborate his vision.

The new, millennial "we" characterized by mutuality probably would be quite differently drawn by men and women both, and closer to the examples of the three couples above.

2. Stage your own gender dialogue and go over the gender invisibilities that arise

Each of you in private writes down your answers about your partner to the three questions we have used in the dialogues. Face each other and read the answers, then respond.

Try to determine whether the gender issues each of you brings to the "we" are visible to your partner. Go through the list—male relational dread and female relational yearning, relational context, relational timing, relational curiosity, views of power, attention to the continuity of connection, and men's hidden internal experience. Are these present in your relationship? Try on each of these for *each* person. For example, look for dread in the woman's experience, and yearning in the man's.

Are there other differences between you that are invisible to one or the other?

For example, if differences in relational curiosity or relational timing become more visible, try together to act with an awareness of these differences. We have found that for a couple to name these differences is helpful. Naming may lead to the couple working together to bring the differences into the relationship. For instance, either of you might suggest that the man *ask* about the woman's experience, or suggest that the man might need more time than the woman to respond to a question or a statement and that her *holding off* from asking for a moment might help. It's not the woman's responsibility alone to "hold off," or the man's alone to "ask." Many women are frustrated with the role of "waiting for men to respond," and many men are frustrated with the role of "talking" or "asking." The responsibility has to rest in the "we." Both the man and the woman are responsible for being aware of these different invisibilities, making these suggestions, and trying to apply them.

3. Diagram your own relational impasse

As we have seen, every couple gets stuck in certain habitual places that could result in major disconnections. We have found it helpful to ask couples to draw a diagram of their impasse, in the particular form shown here. Choose a habitual dialogue between you that results in an impasse and write it in the left-hand column. Then, in one column write down what is going on in the woman's mind as the dialogue proceeds, in the next column what is going on in the man's mind, and in the final column, together, write down what is going on in the relationship.

It can be helpful to "name" your own impasse or to work with the general category of impasse, dread/yearning, product/process, and power-over/power-with.

What this exercise does for a couple is to allow each person to name his and her own experience, to see what is actually going on in the other's experience, and to work together to see what is actually going on in the "we"—again, fostering "we" awareness. Both are learning to take the perspective of the "we."

The next piece of work together will be to take the same dialogue and write, together, a "breakthrough" of the same impasse.

What follows is how the three couples diagrammed the three kinds of impasses.

Suzanne and Giff, the midlife moderns, came in with a diagram of the dread/yearning impasse. It had arisen as they were driving back from the couples workshop. (See p. 144.)

Irv and Esther, the innocent elders, brought a product/process impasse back to the group. It came up as they were sitting at breakfast, around the issue of whether or not they should move permanently to their summer place in Vermont. (See p. 145.)

Donna and Stan, the young creators, came back to the couples group with a diagram of an impasse that combined all three general elements. They called it: "The Amtrak Impasse: Power, Dread, Yearning, and Trains." They had been off on a family vacation and were coming home by train. They were being met at the Amtrak station by Stan's parents, a couple with a distant, rather silent and suppressed relationship. Stan and Donna get off the train and try to manage their many bags, while at

THE DREAD/YEARNING IMPASSE

The Habitual Interaction	The Woman	The Man	The Relationship
Silence. Driving back from the workshop.	Good feelings.	Physical closeness.	Some connection. A fragile "we."
Woman: I'm glad we went. How did you feel about it? I really need to talk.	Wanting to enhance the connection (get closer by sharing feelings.) Worried about his reaction.	Alarm goes off. Oh God!—she got me! Starting to feel tension.	Tremor.
Man: It was good. But I need to be quiet.	Hopeful, then sudden escalation of hopelessness.	Hope this satisfies her for a while.	Rupture.
Silence.	Anxiety. What's wrong with him? Why did I push him to go to the workshop?	Growing sense of dread, rising from the gut.	Starting to move away, apart.
Woman: I know you're trying but I feel nailed shut.	Frustrated, angry, but trying again to connect. It's dangerous to get my hopes up.	Guilt—I should be able to do better than this. Moving away emotionally.	Feelings are polarized.
Man: And I feel you're trying to pry me open! (pause)	Energy thwarted. Sinking into despair.	Anger—I never do enough! I can't stand this again!	Angry disconnect.
Man: Sorry, you can talk if you want to.	No way I'll be like his mother, talking with no one listening.	Shame and guilt; try to patch it up or else it will be hell for days!	Attempt at truce.
Woman: No, I don't want to talk if it's not a joint discussion.	Despair; longing to connect. He has no clue who I am. Hopeless about workshop.	Despair, but a little relief. She's not happy, but at least I'll have quiet.	A quality of despair.
Silence. They drive toward home.	Hopelessness. The future looks bleak. We're not going to make it. I always wind up alone. What's wrong with me?	We're doomed. I'm not fit to be with anyone. Maybe I'll be better alone.	A disconnect. Impasse.

PRODUCT/PROCESS IMPASSE

The Habitual Interaction	The Woman	The Man	The Relationship
Silence. Sitting at breakfast.	Feeling edgy about failing to address an important issue. The "elephant in the room."	Not feeling anything in particular.	Some connection. A fragile "we."
Woman: Let's talk again about moving to Vermont.	Wanting to enter the process, but worried.	A jolt. Not this again!	A shake-up.
Man: I like it where we are, but if you really want to move I'll do it. Fine.	Wait—don't put it on me. Let's talk.	Tired of this issue. Need to get to bottom of it. If I disengage, I might get what I want by default—whatever *that* is.	Introduction of differences.
Woman: I don't want you to just *do* it, I want to *discuss* it!	Why can't he just go back and forth *with* me?	Uh-oh! I'm going to get lost in her endless drama.	Movement in opposite directions.
Man: I am discussing it!	Feeling rebuked, shut out, isolated.	Anger at these interminable conversations without decisions and actions.	Connection exploded by feelings.
Woman: With *feeling.* I want you to talk as if you *care.*	Yearning to connect, trying to be clear about what she needs.	Dread, rising. Who do you think you are? She's gotten just like her mother.	"I/you" split. Stereotyping.
Man: If I get into my feelings, you'll just get angry and we'll *never* make a decision!	Hopelessness—he's never going to change. He's more and more like his father.	Exasperation. Lashing out with critical anger and cynicism.	Isolation.
Woman: I can't decide on something so important without listening to my feelings.	Angry. Giving up. Trying to stay with what she believes in—alone.	Angry. Giving up. Thinking of moving, by myself, to Boca Raton.	Disconnection and impasse.
Man: You are driving me crazy! We never get anywhere!	Feeling crazy—angry.	You are crazy.	Accusation and rage. Total impasse.

the same time needing to greet Stan's parents and take care of their son, Sam. It is Christmastime. The station is crowded and chaotic. (See p. 147.)

4. Use "relational principles" to diagram a breakthrough of your impasse

We have found that it is helpful for couples to have a few relational principles to rely on in trying to break out of impasses. In diagramming a breakthrough of your impasse, use the same habitual dialogue, but this time start from the right-hand column: "Relational Principles." Use the following principles to rethink and then rewrite the dialogue to make it a dialogue of connecting. An impasse is a relentless downward spiral. Breaking the momentum and creating something new can be done in an infinite number of ways.

A FEW RELATIONAL PRINCIPLES

Relational shift. This is the movement from a focus on "I" or "you" to the focus on "we," to what is happening in the movement of relationship. The stance is one of looking at this together, side by side, and admitting that "we're in this together (more than anyone else in the world my partner and I are in this pain together); and what are we going to do about it?" It's a realization that there is more value in a confluence of both perceptions than of either alone—more value than either "fighting it out" or "agreeing to disagree."

Recognition and naming. You have to go through the interaction enough times to realize that it is an impasse. For example, most couples, if encouraged to, can recognize the beginnings of their own variation of these habitual destructive spirals. Recognizing and then naming them, out loud—"Here we go, this is our thing again, our 'moving to Vermont' impasse"—can be a healthy first step.

Early intervention. As soon as one person or the other recognizes or feels something is going wrong, it is important to name it immediately, to do something different, to shift the momentum away from the habitual interaction, the old destructive pathway or loop.

Connectors. Here are some examples: speaking; making "I" statements with an awareness of their effect on the "you" and the "we"; putting feelings into words; respectful listening; offer-

POWER-OVER/POWER-WITH IMPASSE *(with Elements of Dread/Yearning and Product/Process)*

The Habitual Interaction	The Woman	The Man	The Relationship
At train station. Met by man's parents. Man gets a redcap.	Relaxed.	Competent.	Bambi.
Woman: Stan, please keep your eye on the bags. (goes to parents)	Anxious.	I have to think about her anxiety *and* the bags.	Bambi meets Godzilla.
Man: (silence) (waves at her)	Angry.	I'm thinking—"My father's watching." Back off. Try to control image in front of parents.	Disconnecting.
Woman: Where's Sam's backpack? A bag is missing.	Pissed off, disappointed, self-righteous despite myself.	Don't want to act *like* them. Embarrassed and wondering, "Why are we together?"	Danger.
Man: Why is that *my* fault? (5-year-old Sam starts to cry)	More defensive.	Defensive—angry.	Polarized into "I" vs. "You."
Woman: I told you so.	Very angry. He's not sharing the loss and sorrow. He blames redcap.	Angry at her and at myself.	At odds.
Man: Oh—so you're right again! Like always?	Angry at myself for being with this man at all.	Thinking about leaving her for good.	Psychosis rising.
Woman: Yeah—always! (lapse into silence)	I wonder how I can work and raise Sam by myself, and how to get his brother's stuff out of the house too. How can I hurt him?	Who gets the house, the car, the cats?	Total disconnect. Total loss for both.
Man: (Silence. 5-year-old cries)			

ing direct requests and direct responses. Connectors allow participants to stay in the flow of the relationship and expand their sense of mutuality.

Staying with differences and conflict. Emphasize the absolute importance of staying engaged.

Creativity in action. This includes a searching for, and an openness to, new solutions, risk-taking, vulnerability, tolerating ambiguity, and patience, as well as being in process, trying new approaches, expanding beyond self-interest, and maintaining a sense of humor about it all.

Letting go and coming back. When something has moved or shifted, acknowledge that taking a break my be helpful, and may in fact move the process along further.

Appreciate small changes. Small changes actually create momentum for major movements toward mutuality; change may occur in small steps over long periods of time.

Here are the diagrams for the breakthroughs of the three previous impasses.

DREAD/YEARNING BREAKTHROUGH

The Habitual Interaction	The Woman	The Man	The Relationship
Silence. Driving back from the workshop.	Good feelings.	Physical closeness.	Some connection. A fragile "we."
Woman: I'm glad we went. How did you feel about it? I really need to talk.	"I feel close to you. Can we talk?"		"I" statement. Asking directly. Shift to the "we."
Man: It was good. But I need to be quiet.		"Uh-oh. Here we go. I feel good too, but if we talk I'm worried we'll spoil it. Let's not go down that path."	Recognition/Naming. Shift to the "we." Early intervention. Connector: putting feeling into words.
Silence.			
Woman: I know you want silence, but I feel nailed shut.	"Are you willing to try? I'd really like it. I really need to."		Staying with difference and conflict. Creativity in action: risk-taking, vulnerability.
Man: And I feel you're trying to pry me open! (pause)		"Give me a minute to decide. God, we are so different."	Creativity—search for new solutions. Staying with difference and conflict.
Man: Sorry, you can talk if you want to.			
Woman: No, I don't want to talk if it's not a joint discussion.	(with humor) "Dread, eh? Okay. Just don't go away. Stay *with* me."	(with humor) "I'm right here! It's so peaceful for me, not talking. But it *is* lonely." (pause)	Staying with difference. Connector: putting feeling into words. Creativity: patience.
Silence. They drive toward home.		"Okay. Let's go for it. How did you feel about the group?"	Risk-taking. Play, humor. Recognizing and staying with difference.
			Relational curiosity.

PRODUCT/PROCESS BREAKTHROUGH

The Habitual Interaction	The Woman	The Man	The Relationship
Silence. Sitting at breakfast.	Feeling edgy about failing to address an important issue. The "elephant in the room."	Not feeling anything in particular.	Some connection. A fragile "we."
Woman: Let's talk again about moving to Vermont.	"Okay, now I know this is loaded, but is there a way we can talk about money?"		"I" statement, and shift to "we." Early intervention. Acknowledge differences.
Man: I like it where we are, but if you really want to move I'll do it. Fine.		"Yeah, it is tough! Give me a minute, then we'll try."	Putting feelings into words. Shift to "we." Recognize difference in timing.
Woman: I don't want you to just do it, I want to discuss it!	"If we're in it together, you can take all the time in the world. Or at least a minute."		Acknowledge how hard it is—gender difference. In the "we." Humor.
Man: I am discussing it!		"And if I start to go away, I mean emotionally, we can hang in?"	Creativity. Authenticity. In the "we."
Woman: With feeling. I want you to talk as if you care.	"Okay. And if I get angry, you won't go away?"		Authenticity. Connecting, with feeling. Staying with difference.
Man: If I get into my feelings, you'll just get angry and we'll never make a decision!		"I'm here."	Connecting, with feeling. Holding the "we."
Woman: I can't decide on something so important without listening to my feelings.			
Man: You are driving me crazy! We never get anywhere!			

POWER-OVER/POWER-WITH BREAKTHROUGH

The Habitual Interaction	The Woman	The Man	The Relationship
At train station. Met by man's parents. Man gets a redcap.	Relaxed.	Competent.	Bambi.
Woman: Stan, please keep your eye on the bags. (goes to parents)	"Okay. We're exhausted, hassled—and there are your parents. We've got a tough one here. Let's stick together."		Recognition/Naming. Shift to "we." Early intervention.
Man: (silence) (waves at her)	(goes to parents, comes back)	(waves to parents) "If we're gonna get killed, let's die together."	In the "we." Acknowledging feeling.
Woman: (coming back) Where's Sam's backpack? A bag is missing.	"We lost Sam's backpack."		Staying in the "we."
Man: Why is that *my* fault? (5-year-old Sam starts to cry)		"Shit. I'm sorry. It's my fault."	"I"-statement, with awareness of the "we."
Woman: I told you so.	"*Our* fault. This is a mad-house. Let's find it."		In the "we."
Man: Oh—so you're right again! Like always?		"I love you!"	"Bambi" falls in love!
Woman: Yeah—always! (lapse into silence)	(hugs him) "Let's look for the backpack and then go face the music!"		Better connection.
Man: (Silence. 5-year-old cries)			

Learning to Talk "Connect" and "Disconnect"

Moving Through Disconnection to Better Connection

This group of suggestions is about learning a new language and process. Couples may find it helpful to learn the language of "connection" and "disconnection," placing connection, rather than self or other, at the heart of experience. Men and women often begin to say things like, "Our connection was good today," or, "I feel a disconnect with you right now." This shift can help move disconnections toward better connections and was very much in evidence after a few sessions in the couples therapy with Tom and Ann.

1. Recognize that "connection comes first"

The natural tendency when trouble about a particular issue arises is to focus on the issue, and on the individuals. We have found, though, that the first priority has to be to focus on the connection.

If a couple is in connection, anything can be talked about well; if a couple is in disconnection, nothing can. Talking without connection is as much an impasse as frozen silence.

The shift from a language of self to a language of connection pushes the logic of our language in what may seem paradoxical ways. As one couple put it: "We've learned that for one of us to say 'We're disconnected' is a connecting thing to say."

Another couple said: "It's so much easier when one of us says, 'We're in a disconnect.' What we used to say is 'You're being a jerk,' or 'I feel neglected.' To use the word 'disconnect' changes everything! We can start to talk about 'it,' not about 'me' or 'you.'"

2. Identify difficult transitions that threaten the "we"

In simple terms, relationship has three phases of transition: moving into connection (getting engaged), holding the connection, and disengaging (but not necessarily disconnecting). All couples face times that threaten connection. For some, it is the transition from the end of the workday to the beginning of time together at home. This often is worse for men than for women coming home from work, as some women compartmentalize work and home less than men do. For others it is

Sunday nights, as they prepare for another week at work. Holidays, anniversaries, visits to extended families in distant locales—all of these can make the relationship more vulnerable. As one couple said:

"We have to treat the relationship with kid gloves at those times, or it'll really get hurt."

Quite deliberately, they have learned to say "it" or "we" will get hurt, not just "I" or "you."

The transitions around sexuality for a couple may also be especially vulnerable times. These will be discussed in the next chapter.

3. Hold the "we" through the disconnection

In the hard times, when disconnections appear and start to take on that monstrous quality that will lead to an impasse or worse, the potential for real growth is greatest. To maximize this potential and not fall prey to the old patterns, couples need to "hold the 'we' through the disconnection." At these vital moments of possible growth a couple can move from the aloneness of their differences to *being with each other in* their differences. Shared attention to being with each other in this way can lead to differences adding and a sense of real mutuality.

Holding the "we" through the disconnect does not mean abandoning the "I" or "you"; rather, each person can be more him or herself by being held in relationship. Remarkable change can come about by not losing sight of the relationship when every force of culture and gender conditioning is pulling each person to abandon the "we" for the "I" or "you." Again, it's not just what you do, it's what you do *next,* while holding the continuity of the connection, that matters a great deal. Staying engaged allows each person the freedom to take risks, make mistakes, and repair and go forward. To feel the feelings together and do absolutely nothing—no "fixing" them, no "analysis" of them, no "Xanaxing" them or "Zolofting" them—invites a certain kind of shared understanding. A shared sense of sorrow may even appear, and this shared experience of sorrow and empathy for each other and for the relationship can lead to a healing of a couple's wounds. It is mutual empathy, in bloom. Beyond strategy or thought, something happens.

The couple moves through disconnection to better connection.

The experience of one couple's holding the "we" through a disconnection can be useful to another couple. This is what happened with Suzanne and Giff and Irv and Esther in the couples group. They hooked up as "buddy" couples—like the "buddy system" we learned as kids. We have found that couples can easily identify with other couples, and we've heard again and again a version of the comment, "Your holding your connection helps us to hold ours."

The potential in this couple-with-couple mutual connection is enormous. It is based on the idea of "identify, don't compare" and on the process of learning *with*. An ideal way for couples to do this is in couples groups.

4. Check in

"Checking in" is a way of maintaining the continuity of connection. In general men during the day stay in touch with the relationship less frequently than do women. A check-in is, at any time, "taking the pulse" of the relationship. Either member of a couple can call for a check-in. The first person says, briefly, where he or she "is" in thought or feeling about the other person and about the relationship. The other says only "I hear you," then responds in kind. The first person says, "I hear you," and that's it. Calling during the workday can be especially helpful. And even to say, "I don't know at this moment where I am or what I'm thinking or feeling about the relationship" is a way of maintaining connection.

5. Check out

"Checking out" is a way of preventing destructive disconnection. If things are getting too heated or nonproductive, either person can call for a check-out. "I'm checking out" means that I'm stopping this conversation, this interaction, and leaving. However, if I check out, I am responsible for bringing the issue back up in a reasonable period of time, anywhere from five minutes to the next morning, but no more than twenty-four hours.

This captures the relational principles of "early intervention" and "letting go and coming back." It's crucial, in the words of one couple, "not to let the impasse last." This is like the traditional, "Never go to bed angry." If "checking out" can be discussed at the time, it can be a couple learning how to let go together. If only one person of the couple feels that the "we" is at risk, he or she may need to talk a little—go back and forth a few times—to reach some decision about how to disengage and when to reengage. This allows for disengagement without disconnection.

6. The twenty-minute rule

If a couple is struggling with a difficult ongoing subject—for instance, infertility—often the woman feels "we never talk about it," while the man often feels "that's all we ever talk about." It can be helpful to initiate the twenty-minute rule[2]: every day we will put aside twenty minutes to talk about the issue, no more, no less. That way the woman knows that she will have a chance each day to get his focused attention on her concerns, and the man knows that the time for discussion is limited and when it will be over. If a couple continually gets into an argument about a particular subject, it may be helpful to split the time into two ten-minute sections, where each person talks without interruption while the other listens. Interactive dialogue at such times may be too dangerous, but attentive listening might help.

7. Reframe common dilemmas in terms of the "we"

Reframing has been described in the therapy with Tom and Ann. Depression, obsession, autonomy, dependence, grief, trust, control, connections with children and parents—when these feelings or issues arise, rather than seeing them as residing within the individual, try to reframe them in terms of the "we."

A common issue for a couple is depression. While some people are biologically depressed and need medication, often "depression" and other psychological "syndromes" may at heart be signs that something is wrong in the relationship. Even with a biochemically depressed person on medication, shifting the focus to the priority of the relationship and not locating *all* the problem in the depressed person can be helpful. We saw one older couple from Arizona, the husband a minister and the wife a teacher. The wife had been depressed on and off for many years, and her husband had been a terrific help to her in dealing with this. But when the children moved out, the strain became too great, and they got more disconnected. She then went out and started buying expensive cats, to his chagrin. Not only did he not like cats, he couldn't afford the thousands of dollars spent on exotic Persians and Russian blues.

When they were up to sixteen cats, they entered therapy. Using the relational model, they were able to shift the focus away from either one of them to the "we." They reframed "her" depression in terms of "our coming to terms with the loss of having the kids living with us." More importantly, it was not "her" recovery that became the focus but "our new connection." Before long the cat count decreased to twelve, and finally to two. It was a fourteen-cat cure.

8. Bring your "outside" creativity into the relationship

Creativity has traditionally been recognized as something developed outside of relationships, in art, literature, or science. Often these are seen as solitary and individual pursuits. But relationship is a creative process. The importance of creativity has not yet been fully recognized in the study of human relationships. It has been affirmed primarily in the arts and sciences—traditional male realms—and not yet in daily life and relationships, where women's creativity has often gone unrecognized.

The processes that foster growth-enhancing connections have much in common with what have been called "creative" processes: curiosity, flexibility, spontaneity, freedom of movement, patience, persistence, humility, playfulness, humor, intuition, risk-taking, trying out new perspectives and configurations, paradoxical thinking, holding opposites simultaneously, knowing when to hold and when to let go, and openness to change and revision. It can be a new idea to a couple to bring these qualities, which each may have developed outside the relationship, into play to *create* a "we."

Donna and Stan, the filmmaker and writer from the couples group, were remarkably creative outside the relationship. What really helped them as a couple was the suggestion that they learn to bring their individual creative skills into the service of the relationship, the "we." Donna was feeling depressed for several weeks. Stan didn't know what to do. Finally one day he came home, waved two airline tickets at her, and said, "I arranged an extravaganza—a trip to Rome!"

Donna laughed. "I really appreciate that, your trying. But we can't afford it, and I don't really want that. I don't need extravaganzas, all I need is for you to be with me, us together."

They shifted their perspective from the depression being "her" problem—destroying the relationship—to the "we" being "our" way out of her individual depression. They came to realize that at their worst their individual artistic struggles got in the way of each other; at their best their creativity fed the relationship, in turn feeding each of them in their life and their work.

With another couple, both painters, we suggested that they view their relationship as the process of doing a painting together: each would throw paint onto the canvas, freely, with the idea that it wasn't what they each did at the time, it was what they each did—and did together—*next*. It was bringing the process of "revision" or "rewriting" into the realm of relationship.

9. Use humor

To laugh together is both a sign of and a way of connecting. Humor can be disconnecting or connecting, depending on how it is used in relationship.

On the one hand, humor can be a sign, for a man in close relationship with a woman, of rising dread. One major question women ask men is, "Why all the jokes?" Men often will use a joke to disconnect. This deflective process may be invisible to them.

But humor, when it is used with awareness of the "plight" of the couple in a disconnection or an impasse, can be connecting. It can be both a way and a sign of beginning to move out of the stuck place toward mutual connecting. Humor can be found in the worst impasse. Sometimes holding the "we" will allow the man or the woman to step back and laugh about it, breaking the destructive, narrowing, hyperserious spiral. Just as men and women can get stuck with habitual phrases that lead to disconnection, so too can woman and men learn habitual catchphrases that trigger a way out through humor and that add a perspective on how ridiculous the whole thing is. For example, in one of our workshops, a couple found their way together by staying engaged playfully:

MAN: *(having done something disruptive of the relationship)* I'm sorry.

WOMAN: *(silence, angry)*

MAN: I said I'm sorry. I'm sorry I'm sorry I'm sorry!

WOMAN: *(still silent, though a little less angry)*

MAN: *(frustrated, getting angrier himself)* How many more times do I have to say I'm sorry?

WOMAN: *(playfully)* One more.

MAN: I'm sorry.

WOMAN: *(laughing)* "Okay!" *(laughter from both)*

Here, tongue-in-cheek, are three all-purpose catchphrases for men to say to women to help the relationship:

1. I know how you feel and it's *horrible!*
2. I was thinking about what we talked about yesterday.
3. I just called you at work to say I want to talk all night long!

And three catch phrases for women to say to men:

1. I know how you feel and you're *wonderful!*
2. I've been thinking about how terrific you are, all day long.
3. I just called you at work to say I want to make passionate love to you all night long!

Feel free to find other fail-safe humorous phrases of your own.

10. Stay in the present moment, not the past

The critical stumbling block to mutual connection, we have suggested, is the ego. The ego is the sum total of all our millennial and childhood conditioning. The ego is the past.

If the man or woman has been conditioned by their individual, self-centered traditional therapies to delve back into the past to solve a present dilemma, and if this is held tightly in the relationship, the couple is probably doomed. The reduction of the present to the past—the reduction of the present to *anything else* (drugs, theories, the unconscious, instincts, past lives, planets, religious doctrine, and so on)—is doomed to reduce the living, breathing connection that is at the heart of growing in healthy mutuality. A focus on the past is often an escape from the work of connecting, for connecting is always done in the present moment.

What about old grudges and resentments?

These need to be worked through, but the process happens only if the man and woman are in good connection in the here and now. Susan and Fred came to therapy after she found out about his having had an affair. They were angry and humiliated. But even though the affair demanded discussion, connection had to come first. Susan angrily told the story of how she had discovered the affair and wept about having been lied to by the man whom she had met in the innocence of being teenagers together and had trusted for decades. She could not even look at Fred. He too looked away as he talked about how guilty he felt. Their talking about the rage and resentment and shame went nowhere until—making connection around what they had once had (in the past)—they could briefly look at each other and make contact in the present. As they got more connected in the present, they could go back together over the past events. Part of their work was placing a limit on "our" staying in the past tense. What they eventually discovered, after several months of talking and working in therapy, was that the affair was a wake-up call for a deadened marriage. By holding the "we" through the major disconnection they could heal and find the life in a more alive "we" once again. They both worked very hard over a long period to create this new "we."

Nourishing and Empowering the "We"

This step is about "the care and feeding" of the "we." As couples repeatedly move from disconnections to better connections, something new emerges. As a new "we" starts to grow, it has to be nourished and empowered. Through our experience with couples we have become a repository for many kinds of creative suggestions for fostering the growth of the "we," which needs attention, care and concern. While it may seem obvious that relationships need nourishment, it is an elusive obvious. Many of these suggestions are obvious but difficult to do.

1. Time for the "we"

Men and women may have different emotional time scales, and creating productive time for the "we" can be a challenge. The "twenty-minute" rule and ways to maintain connection through the day have already been mentioned. A few examples of ideas couples have come up with:

Setting aside an hour a week to talk about the relationship, or the state of the connection, is invaluable. Start with a check-in, and go from there. This is incredibly difficult to do in families with children, but it is essential in terms of the care and feeding of the "we."

Take time for "us" away from home and children. One couple who had been married for forty years, and who had eight children, had together taken one night every month away from home. Rarely did they miss.

Another couple commuted together, thirty minutes each way. They did this for fifteen years. She knew that she would have his ear; he could be doing something (driving), and being side by side felt easier for him than face-to-face. They used the time to talk, and also to learn things together: they listened to books on tape and language tapes. Over the years, they learned to speak Italian!

2. A place for the "we"

It is helpful to find a place where the "we" can live. Where is the best place for you to make connection? Couples have come up with many different visions, including:

The top step of the cellar stairs. Whenever a particular couple had a need to talk, they would sit on the top step of the cellar stairs with the door closed, escaping from their four children.

A meditation space in the house.

An old family book stand in the hallway, where the "book of the 'we'" (an ongoing record of their notes to each other and about the "we") was placed.

An island in Maine with no phone, electricity, or TV.

"Our" rock or "our tree" or "our street" or "our garden" or "our restaurant."

Nature walk. One couple found it helpful to take a nature walk: on the walk out from home, the woman described exactly what she saw and felt; coming back, the man did the same. A more daring version would be to close your eyes and have the other person lead you and describe to you what they see. This is a wonderful way of learning to appreciate how and what the other "sees" and thus contributes to the relationship.

An airport. We were sitting in an airport waiting for a flight. A day's travel had made us feel disconnected, and we were having trouble getting connected again. Janet asked Sam to describe to her what he saw in each person who walked past. It was fascinating to hear his perceptions—usually present but kept private—and, when it was reversed, for him to hear hers.

3. "We" in action and projects

Physical activity and shared projects can be of great help in the movement of relationship. There's more to creating healthy connection than talk—there's being and doing and creating, together.

Playing together is essential, and couples have talked about getting into a "we" rhythm in canoeing, bicycling, running, singing, acting, playing sports, doing puzzles, or designing gardens.

Learning together: languages, computers—whatever.

Creative projects. Focusing shared attention on a project, where skills add, can bring men and women closer. Co-creativity can be a pathway to growing the "we." Working together—whether it is on a relational purpose statement, on the relationship itself, in prayer or meditation, or in choosing two projects to do together (one from his area of expertise, one from hers)—can be incredibly helpful. Helpful not only in finding a creative and spiritual "we" but in bridging a major disconnect that often exists now in couples between "the relationship" and each person's "work."

In our workshops, couples have chosen many different kinds of projects: one finally finished the photo albums from their wedding four years ago, one planted a memorial garden for a child who had died, one performed a ritual at the ocean for an adoption that had fallen through, and one painted and renovated a new summer cabin together. At first it may be difficult to work together, and impasses may arise. But breaking through an impasse to work and create something is a thrill and achievement. The good feeling and the understanding moves out into other playing fields of the relationship. The projects of the three couples in that first group:

Donna and Stan planned to write and film a movie about the life of their child, Sam.

Suzanne and Giff decided to choose and plant a special sapling to signal the birth of the new in their "we."

Irv and Esther planned to volunteer together at a health clinic for postcardiac surgery.

Action in the world. Many couples find that doing service and volunteering helps to put them in touch with a "we" larger than their own nuclear "we" or family "we." Nourishing others, we are nourished. Many couples put service into their relational purpose statement.

4. Stress reduction and relaxation strategies

The "we" gets stressed and needs ways to relax. Weekly meetings, inquiring about where the stresses are in the we as well as for each person, can be productive. There is a rich and useful literature[3] on relaxation techniques and stress reduction programs, which can be worked together. Daily check-ins may help, as may setting goals month by month. Being together in a less stressed state will open each person to the we and relieve stress in each. Moving from "self-care" to "mutual care" and "care for the we" is the path we are suggesting.

5. Finding "our" spirit

The Oxford English Dictionary suggests that the root of the word *psychology* is the Greek for "a study of the life-breath, the spirit." For most of its history throughout the twentieth century, psychology has determinedly split off from the study of the spirit. In the past decade or two, there has been an attempt by many to find the spiritual momentum at the root of psychological change and growth. It is helpful to access the connection between each one of us—and between the two of us as a couple—and the benevolent forces of the universe that exist outside of one person, and outside of two.

Often couples come to realize that "our" spirit is alive but that it has been buried by the inhospitable life we have been living. A couple relationship is ideal for unearthing the spirit, for what we have called "the third element"—the relationship—is a power greater than the self. It is more than the sum of you and me. It has a life, qualities, a past and a present, and probably a future.

Here are several suggestions for finding "our" spirit:

Talk through a *spiritual history of the "we."* How do you define your spirituality, and what has been your shared spirituality up until now?

Take a *spiritual inventory of the "we"* in the here and now. What are each of your spiritual beliefs right now? What are your shared spiritual beliefs?

It is helpful to work together to find what you might call your spiritual "we." We often have couples write a *spiritual purpose statement* as part of their relational purpose. The growth of relational maturity—of the "we"—is both held in a larger "we" of community and is also a resource for the larger "we.'" Hopson and Hopson[4] write of the political and spiritual dimension of the Afrocentric vision of collectivity that can shape a shared vision for black men and women as they engage together in the struggle for liberation and justice. Carter Heyward adds this theological dimension of mutuality: "as we are formed by mutuality, we become bearers with one another of the justice of God."[5]

6. Connecting through silence, meditation, and prayer

There are many different kinds of silences. Silence can be creative, opening, and releasing; silence can be shutting out, closing off, and hostile.

We suggest that couples set aside time *together* for prayer, silence, and meditation. This can consist merely of sitting in silence together for a few minutes at the beginning and/or end of the day. If one person has a prayer or meditative practice, perhaps the other can learn it and join in. The Buddhist and Vipassana practice of "following the breath" can be not only relaxing but connecting.[6]

Just sitting with another person is a way of connecting. Especially when there are difficult things to discuss, the Quaker practice of "speaking from silence" may be very helpful. If there is a quandary in the couple, one of conflict, sit together for five minutes in silence before speaking. You will find that not only will you be able to speak more authentically and powerfully, but the silence is a way of "hearing each other into speech"—Nelle Morton's wonderful phrase.[7]

One couple came up with the idea that each morning, after sitting together in silence for ten minutes, each person in turn would tell the other his or her "vision of the day." What lay ahead during that day? What were the worries? The challenges? The anticipated joys? *When,* exactly, during the day were these rough spots occurring? (The husband or wife could be thinking of the other partner at this time and "send" care and concern.) Then at the end of the day, each told the other, briefly, how these envisioned moments in fact turned out. This became one of the most connecting practices this couple had ever done.

They and many other couples who practice holding the spiritual "we" often find that healthy growth starts to happen, much as throughout history and across cultures, with attention to the spirit between people, the grace of connection happens.

Donna and Stan, toward the end of the meetings of the couples group, told the rest of us about their developing a shared vision of the spiritual "we":

The "we" is like two ice dancers, a pair in an ice ballet, where when they're together they move together, and even when they're in different parts of the rink they are moving together, knowing where each other is—and where *it* is—the relationship. Each other's movements and the movement of the relationship are affected by each of us, and us by it.

Suzanne and Giff wrote a spiritual purpose statement as follows:

Our Three Questions

One: How do we find an alternative way of living—alternative to the stressful, competitive, fragmented, and violent one around us?

Two: How do we live with compassion in the relationship, and bring compassion out from the relationship to others?

Three: How can we stay committed to learning?

The creative spirit has a long tradition of expression in prayer and meditation. Another suggestion we make to couples is that together they write *their* prayer. Donna and Stan wrote:

Mother, father, god, goddess,
Be with us.
Help us to bring forth
Nurturing and creative energy
Within us, around us, and between us.

They told the group that they say this every morning—or most mornings—after sitting in silence together for twenty minutes. "Actually," Stan said, "it's ten, and sometimes two, depending on when Sam wakes up."

Suzanne and Giff, hearing this in one session, came back a month later with their own morning prayer:

In humility, we call forth the Divinity,
to be with us in living our understanding.

Irv and Esther began lighting the Sabbath candles on Friday nights, saying the Hebrew prayers, rekindling the tradition of their immigrant parents.

. . .

The next chapter focuses on sex. It may seem odd to move from the creative spirit to sexuality, but at best—for both men and women—the spiritual and the sexual are not that far apart.

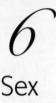

Sex

IN BED WITH THREE IMPASSES

"I need to connect to make love."

—A WOMAN, IN DIALOGUE

"I need to make love to connect."

—HER HUSBAND, IN RESPONSE

If ever men and women needed to be in good connection, it is when they are making love. Self-focus alone rarely leads to satisfying sexual connection; mutual connection can lead to good sex. A couple's sexual relationship is often a casualty of the suffering of disconnection. Frequently it is part of the man's initial focus in the first visit to a couples therapist, while the woman's initial focus often has to do with the emotional connection.

As we have seen, as a man and a woman try to connect, disconnections and then impasses often arise. This is true in sexual connections, where the same three impasses we have already talked about can be seen: dread/yearning, product/process, and power-over/power-with. Our data on sex comes from individual therapy, couples therapy, and couples groups. Talking about sex in groups can be powerful, as men and women take the risk, in front of others, of breaking the prototypical silence about the sexual realm of their relationship. One of the most important aspects of dialogue is to introduce, explicitly, the effect of gender differences on the sexual relationship. Helping men and women use differences to create healthy connections, to become aware of the mutual "we" that fosters the growth of each and both of them, is almost always reflected in their sexual relationship.

It soon becomes clear to the men and women that to do the sexual work together, they have to do the relational work together. They cannot be separated, nor is it necessary to work on one first. Many women often start from this premise, while many men may be more reluctant to admit this. In the couples who start to move sexually, both the man and the woman almost inevitably come to hold the sense of the priority of mutual connection, which encompasses, nourishes, and empowers the blossoming of the sexual.

These couples have taught us to think of sexuality in terms of three movements of the relationship: moving into the sexual, moving through sex, and moving out of the sexual.

Moving into the Sexual

The sexual impasse around the process of engaging, or of moving into explicit sexual connection, is typical—and arises from the differences between men and women physically and emotionally. Men frequently see physical connection as a means to relational connection, and women the reverse. Over time this difference often leads to impasse—less of either kind of connection (sexual or relational), anger, resentment, disappointment or blaming, or giving up on sex and focusing on other areas of the relationship. Reframing these impasses as difficulties around movement into connection may open a couple to new perspectives and sometimes to new ways of moving. The theme is learning to surrender, together, to the shifting worlds of different time frames, emotions, and bodily arousals that have been called "foreplay," and stay together as the movement into sex builds.

In offering an opportunity for deep connection, sexuality stimulates

the longing or yearning for connection. It also stimulates all the protective actions and reactions evolved through past experience of hurt, disappointment, and humiliation in relationships—in this and others.

We have noticed that while many men (and some women) identify with relational dread, many women (and some men) identify with sexual dread, which evokes these protective actions and reactions. Dread/yearning is a major impasse in sexuality. Men's relational dread can arise in the woman's heightened yearning for connection as a prelude to sexuality; women's sexual dread may arise as things get physical. In the movement of getting connected, the difficulties we all have of slowing down, being real, in touch, and connecting come to the fore.

Men and women often split responsibility for different aspects of the relationship. Many women often feel angry and alone in tending to the emotional part of the relationship, where many men feel the responsibility for initiating the sexual part. Again, working toward mutual responsibility is helpful.

Moving Through Sex Together

The different sexual rhythms of men and women make moving together in sexual connection a great challenge. Men's more linear movement and product-performance orientation may collide with women's more process-dialogical way of moving. Women often say that they want to feel that neither partner is leading, but rather that both are in simultaneous movement. Women often avoid any form of initiation that feels like power-over, that is, directly asking the other to follow or focus on her movement. Men may have more difficulty in power-with, in following or being moved or moving with the woman.

One man put it this way: "It's such a shift from the rest of my life where I'm in charge, hyperactive, hyperbusy. Here I'm supposed to slow down and listen to her, attune my movement to hers. I can't do it. I go too fast, and she gets hurt. So I tend to avoid the whole thing."

His wife responded: "I feel I have to get into the present moment, to be here. I need to feel safe, but also *real*. All the feelings I've been avoiding start to rush in: anger at you, things that weren't said, all my pain and disappointment in you and in myself. Tears come. I don't always feel up to it, and I don't feel you want to hear me. I guess I have my own version of dread."

Moving together through sex at its best is both the man and the woman holding the "we" through sexual connection and disconnection. One woman described this as a "sexual dance we do together."

Moving out of the Sexual

The process of disengagement creates a final challenge: once connected, how to disengage without disconnecting. Men are more likely to end more abruptly, moving on to the next thing, which may be sleep or work, even showing impatience or intolerance for sustaining the connection as long as a woman may want. Women often need more movement around separation—like saying good-bye at a party, a more gradual, back-and-forth process. Women may feel a wish to move together through the disengagement from the sexual connection. In both the emotional and physical realms, he leaves, rebuilding his boundaries; she is left, feeling abandoned. They are disengaged and disconnected. The mutual event would be disengagement without disconnection.

Three Couples

We will present three couples who were members of a long-term couples group that focused much of its attention on the sexual arena. These three couples are composites, and their voices represent those of many couples with whom we've worked.

Liz and Paul

An urban couple from Boston in their late thirties, Liz and Paul have been together for eight years, married for five. They have a three-and-a-half-year-old son, Max. Both were married before. Liz is still friends with her ex-husband, while Paul left an unhappy first marriage to be with her. Liz, originally from Seattle, is a beautiful dark-haired woman with fine features and striking light blue eyes. Paul is tall and broad, of Scandinavian ancestry, and describes himself as "very physical." Both give off a sense of earthiness, power, and energy. He is chairman of the geology department at a local community college—which he describes as a very stressful job—she is a designer of jewelry and clothing.

They met in their early thirties and had a passionate love affair with, according to both of them, "absolutely amazing sex, for the first few years." They came to the couples group because, in Liz's words, "things have cooled off almost to nothing since the birth of Max. It's like we're avoiding each other, as if we fear the intensity—when we do get together sexually, it's still intense. Lately the avoidance is increasing. We both wonder 'Why do we stay away from it, if we are so passionate about it?'"

Liz describes herself as very "social," with lots of women friends, and as a "very erotic person." She says, "I want more, I want to explore my sexuality, I'm coming out of these first few years of pregnancy, nursing, the whole intense connection with my baby. I feel so strong in so much of my life now, but so blocked in sex. I can't figure out why. I want to initiate sex, but I can't do it."

Paul, a more introverted person, says, "I mostly withdraw now, from the sexual stuff—occasionally I'll come on really strong. It's all or nothing for me, I don't know how to modulate. I'm always the one who initiates it."

Their "qualities of our relationship" answers?

LIZ: The relationship is like a tiger—moving in the world with strength and confidence, playful but also dangerous; vibrant colors, all shades of reds and oranges.

PAUL: The relationship's climate is autumn, the vibrancy of autumn colors, the temperature's going down, bright sun is pulsating, water is falling over rocks, there's a sense of portent and excitement; the animal is a huge swooping bird.

Sarah and John

A country couple, living on nine acres in Maine. Sarah is in her late thirties, John is five years older. They've been married for ten years, with two boys, nine and six. The whole family, in Sarah's words, "is into outdoors activities—we love to ski and hike—focused on learning about nature through all the seasons of the year—which, in Maine, consist of winter, mud, summer, and a fantastic fall." Sarah, from an old New England family, is a tall, lithe woman with striking red hair and green eyes and a delicate manner. As she says, though, "I know I have a whim of iron. There's been a lot of grief the past two years—I lost both my parents."

Sarah works as a computer consultant to software companies. John, of Scots-English descent, is also a redhead—his red hair more fiery, hers more dark. He works as an entrepreneur, helping small businesses get on their feet. They both work out of the house, though he travels a great deal. They came to the group because, as Sarah says, "We've tried everything, including lots of couples therapy. With our work and our kids, we're still not giving ourselves a chance—we find ourselves, more and more often, treating each other like pieces of furniture."

They agree, as John says, that "the relationship has a lot of unused potential, but we can't seem to get to it. So much has come between us. So many hard feelings. We're growing more and more apart, both emotionally and sexually."

In the sexual arena, Sarah seems to be more interested right now, John is holding back because he says he doesn't believe she can be open. She has a history of sexual violation, something she has worked on with a good therapist and feels is finally healing. She has also been very involved in a support group for help with her grief about her parents' deaths. John, describing himself as becoming "more self-reliant and self-contained," rarely asks for help from anyone, even Sarah.

Their "qualities of the relationship":

> SARAH: The relationship's colors are gray and foggy, and it's like climbing a rock wall, inching up this rock, and there are beautiful colorful flowers wedged in the rock, but we can't really get to them; the animal?—it's a mountain goat which might just make it up the rock face.
>
> JOHN: The relationship is a desert scene with a colorful bouquet of balloons floating up—surprising, with a lot of hidden complexity and intensity; a jack-rabbit.

Alma and Lou

From Rhode Island, both are in their mid-forties and have been married "forever—we were nursery school classmates and high school sweethearts and grew up in the small suburban town where we still live." Both grew up in working-class Italian homes. Alma is tiny and sparky, with dark hair, dark eyes, and is very animated and vibrant—with a soft side that often will move quickly to tears. Lou, overweight, ruddy-faced with thin black hair, jokes that he likes to think of himself as "a real 'Joe Six-pack' kind of guy, not that complicated, I like the simple things in life like a game on TV, a can of beer, hot dogs, and sex

twice a year." He manages a small moving company his father started. They are parents of three teenage girls, eighteen, fifteen, and thirteen.

Both Lou and Alma are of Italian American background. Her family has a high incidence of alcoholism, and she has become a licensed substance-abuse counselor working in the state system. She says, "I'm interested in personal growth, and I've accomplished a lot, on my own, so far." Lou says of himself, "I don't talk much, or expect much. Family is really important to me, I'm a real family kind of guy. I spend a lot of time coaching my girls' soccer teams. I'm very proud of them and their mother."

Alma has insisted they come to the couples group because "with the teenagers in our house we're in deep trouble—we barely talk to each other at all." Lou doesn't have much interest in being in the group, "though she's right about the girls—I mean, I thought marriage was hell? I don't have much hope about men and women getting together. But I guess we're here to prove that even though we come from the smallest state doesn't mean Rhode Island people are really small-minded, y'get me?"

In the past several years they've settled into a pattern of rare sexual encounters, which happen fast and then are over quickly. Alma has said, recently, that she wants more. Often when they start to get sexually involved, she cries, and he gets turned off. She is particularly distressed by his pattern of falling asleep almost immediately after sex.

Their qualities of relationship reflect their shared love of animals:

ALMA: It's a well-traveled paved road, but sometimes you step off and it turns quickly to an unpaved one verging on a jungle path with snakes in the trees; the animal is a tortoise, definitely, in that it's beautiful and reliable, but slow and hard to move.

LOU: It's a mix of different species—dogs and cats—gauze between the two; the animal? a big old dog that sleeps all day but that nobody can mess with—it can be very rough with anybody who gets up close and personal.

Gender Dialogue About Sex

During one of the initial meetings, we posed a question to the men and women:

"What do you most want to understand about the other gender's sexuality?"

We separated the men and women, and in small groups they came up with their answers. Next, facing each other across the room, the dialogue began. The men went first.

Men's Questions About Sex

What turns you on? Do women fake orgasm? Why don't you initiate sex? What's it like to be touched by a man? Is men's sexuality perceived as dangerous? What gets in the way of passionate connection, of which sex is a part? How important is orgasm in terms of lovemaking? How responsible am I, the man, supposed to be, for women's orgasm? Why do you women need an emotional connection in order to feel sexual? Are you interested in breaking out of habits of our sexuality and how do we do it? If women are responsible for relationship, are men responsible for sex life? Is there a gender difference in how important the sexual part of the relationship is? If we can't act like aggressive lusting males, how do we square that with our lovemaking? How do we square our passion with our sensitivity? What is your women's sense of passion? Why do women need to talk before sex? Why do women need to talk after sex? Why do women need to talk *during* sex?

This brought a roar of laughter from the women. The humor released some of the fear and embarrassment. As the dialogue began, we realized how helpful it was to the couple to frame these questions not in terms of each of them personally but in terms of "men" and "women," that is, seeing the effect of gender on sexual relationships. Again, in the dialogue, the men and women spoke up to represent their particular experience, which drew a more nuanced, textured canvas of the gender differences.

The women first responded to one general question the men posed.

"What is the range of sex for women?"

LIZ: Sex can mean anything and everything in the context of relationship. It's the first real interest you get from boys, from men. The problem is, you often *assume* that it means a loving relationship, at first. Later you learn that if your relationship is multidimensional, sex can be multidimensional.

PAUL: For me, physical intimacy is simple; for Liz it's complicated.

LIZ: Not that complicated. To me it seems simple: I need a connection—and then there can be high play, high adventure.

PAUL: See? That's complicated! *(the group laughs)*

LIZ: In adolescence, sex was fun, but kind of limited. Now, if it comes out of connection with you, Paul, I have a huge range. But some things have to be there for me to get involved.

PAUL: By now the framework should be there. You shouldn't make me start it new each time. It's like reinventing the wheel. I've been monogamous all these years, had a child with you—in this fifteen minutes of foreplay do I have to reestablish the perfect connection in order to make love?

JOHN: Yeah—what's supposed to happen in those fifteen minutes?

LIZ: Fifteen minutes? The whole day is foreplay for me.

SARAH: What's not supposed to happen is sex first, closeness second. Talk that makes connection is the best foreplay in the world.

LOU: I feel that men are one down in this, like you're saying there's something wrong with our view but nothing wrong with your view.

LIZ: It does sound that way. But I don't feel I know how to do it either. I know I'm not satisfied with half-sex, settling for too little. We want it all.

OTHER WOMEN: All! All! *(laughter)*

LOU: So you want us to be good little boys—behaving in a certain way?

ALMA: No, we'll meet you halfway.

LOU: Oh, so we'll settle on seven and a half minutes? *(laughter)*

LIZ: It's creating trust and safety in that fifteen minutes. Women have a lot of fear in the bedroom, it's an unsafe situation. Our mothers and grandmothers are there with us. All our past history of abandonment, danger, and violation. *(pause; a quiet, sober moment)*

PAUL: I'm thinking about those impasses we discussed. In those fifteen minutes, there's enough time for all three to come up!

LIZ: Three impasses and the effects of our mothers—

SARAH: And our mother's mothers—

ALMA: And our fathers—and the history of women throughout the ages.

LOU: No wonder it's hell. I thought I was just in bed with *you,* Alma! *(laughter)*

This loosened up the group further. The shared laughter was a sign that the men and women were each identifying with what the others were saying. There was a sense of walking into territory that had always been a mystery, to men about women's sexuality, and to women about men's. The dialogue about the "fifteen-minute factor" was a beginning of understanding. This first connection around sexuality allowed the group to move toward even more serious, sensitive exchanges. The women went on to talk about another of the men's questions:

"What specifically turns women on?"

ALMA: *(playfully)* You think we'd *tell* you? *(laughter)* But seriously, it kind of depends on the feeling of the moment. I'm not like a cookbook with specific instructions—just add this, just pour that.

SARAH: It's not specifically sexual, it's the whole act.

LIZ: If we start to feel shame or blame from you, it turns us off.

SARAH: What's attractive to me is male responsiveness. Your incredible vitality and energy, male energy. It's also frightening.

LIZ: Yes, and I want to feel seen and appreciated, considered—

SARAH: —regarded and respected—

ALMA: —nurtured too—

OTHER WOMEN: Yes. There it is.

MEN, TOGETHER: We got the answer!

WOMEN: Spread the word!

(A lot of laughter.)

PAUL: But how do I *do* that?

LIZ: Why do you make it seem too hard? It seems so simple to me. Foreplay for me is the whole relationship, it's all connected for me, for all of us I think? *(the other women nod, murmur)* If that were understood—

SARAH: There'd be more sex.

PAUL: Okay—so what *makes* you feel considered, regarded, respected?

ALMA: That! Exactly that!

PAUL: That *what*?

SARAH: Your attention to us, your *asking*.

ALMA: The truth is I really don't know what turns me on. I need us to figure that out together.

SARAH: The physical movements in sex are like a dialogue, a conversation with questions and answers, our bodies speaking to each other through slow and deep responsive movement.

LIZ: The images we have of sex have all been painted by men. We're just learning about our own sexuality. And about what's really going on for you. *(to Paul)* If you say *your* truth—whatever it is—I'm not going to leave. *(choked up)* If you tell the truth, that's respecting and honoring me. It's not about bravado or macho or physical prowess. It's about courage, courage to be yourself and to be with me. If you can be brave with me, and I with you, we can go *everywhere!*"

PAUL: But how do I show passion without your feeling I'm being dangerous? How does passion go with sensitivity?

LIZ: I want your passion, Paul, but I want to feel you *with* me. Not just yours, but ours.

PAUL: *(angrily)* How the hell do we do that?

LIZ: *(frustrated, looks away, then says)* There it is. That's us. I try to really open to you and you leave. This is such a treacherous subject, it turns, just like that, to anger and blaming.

JOHN: Us too. I wish Sarah could be more passionate, looser. I always initiate the new things, and I wait around for her to be ready for sex. Worse—I feel responsible for her orgasms. I'm expected to be natural and passionate and yet be aware of her needs, repress my own passion to take care of her needs. When we got married, there was a lot of sex, but now sometimes Sarah experiences the way I touch her as aggressive, and so I stay away from her. I'm angry, and she can feel it. I don't want to not touch for the next forty years. It's like tennis—if someone doesn't like to play tennis, then you get someone else who likes to play. If someone doesn't like touching, you get someone who does. An old girlfriend of mine lives in Europe now, and I always find myself fantasizing about being really passionate with her, and I start to wonder—do I still love her?

The group fell silent. It was a sobering moment. Everyone could sense the sadness at the threat of breaking up. No one said anything for a while. Sarah had tears in her eyes.

JOHN: Sorry. Sorry, Sarah. I guess I'm really frustrated and angry. But I'm here, aren't I? I'm not in Europe.

SARAH: *(wiping her tears)* We're here, yes. And I appreciate that.

The strong feeling was a connecting force in the group. The anger and sadness was an authentic statement of where the couples were. A start had been made on two important issues shaped by gender, that is, shared by the men and shared by the women: how women are turned on by real interest and curiosity and attention (opening a shared dialogue), and how men feel not only physically frustrated but emotionally frustrated when they feel they can't bring their passion directly into the bedroom.

We moved on to the women's questions.

Women's Questions About Sex

What *is* sex? What is the relation between sex and intimacy, sex and sexuality? What do you feel is women's responsibility in sex? How can you help us to know and act on our own sexuality? Do you see that it is difficult for us to stay attuned to our own sexuality? How can men want sex when the relationship is in a terrible place? How does sexuality become so connected to masculinity and self-worth? Why the urgency for sex? Do men like eye contact? History—family, religious, cultural—its impact on sexuality? What is the impact of our personal and collective history of sexual abuse on our sexuality? On yours too? What is the impact of children and mothering on sexuality? And on men's? How do we work with different levels of sexual interest? Timing and approach? Do you understand how much of our sexuality is affected by your acceptance of our bodies? Do you understand how difficult it is for us to accept our own bodies and how much that interferes with sexuality? What do your fantasies mean? What are men's anxieties about women's global sexuality?

The men and women started talking, again, about their "real" sexuality:

"What is sex?"

LIZ: I remember in the past a feeling with Paul that my whole body was alive, through the whole process. It's not linear, where first you do the intimacy, and then the technology—it's both moving together.

PAUL: For us it's different—it's the penis. For Liz, it's intimacy, maybe like what she has with her women friends. If her relationships with women are so great, so wonderful, why doesn't she walk across the line. If you look at your women friends as models, why not have sex with them too?

LIZ: Women-to-women intimacy is erotic, but I don't find it sexy. Sex does requires intimacy, but I want it with *you.*

LOU: If left to my own devices, sex would be straightforward and easy. That alternative don't exist when we're dealing with what you need, your issues.

SARAH: You're talking from a male sexual model: "It's women's problem."

JOHN: You can't just say "It's not that"—you have to say what it *is.*

SARAH: I'd say, "the feeling that we're really in it together, communion."

JOHN: Which is what *you* want.

SARAH: I'm trying to get to what *we* want. We're talking about "love-making," *us* making love, generating love *in this interaction?* We have to do the work, *together,* of breaking down the separateness.

PAUL: Give me a specific.

LIZ: Take my breasts—

LOU: Now? *(laughter)*

LIZ: Paul likes to begin by kissing my breasts; I don't much like it. We don't know what to do with this. I feel like we're right on the edge of an answer, but—

JOHN: Well, call us right up if you find one—I don't care what time of day or night. *(laughter)*

LIZ: I guess I would say hold off on a direct approach. If you approach indirectly, in a spiral movement, instead of a frontal assault, I like it that way. I'm talking about coming in sideways, gently. It's like the movement of a dance.

SARAH: If we move closer, together, I don't feel like my boundaries are being violated, but that we're both opening our boundaries gently, together.

PAUL: Okay. I do understand what you're saying.

SARAH: If I don't feel judged, if you start to explore your own boundaries and your responsiveness too, I feel more safe and comfortable—and really turned on.

ALMA: Did you hear that, Lou?

LOU: I'm writing it on my wrist.

JOHN: But the problem is, that when you are most asking for that is when we men would just as soon drop the whole subject. We don't know how to do that, especially at that moment. It's unfair.

The group fell silent. They were stuck. We suggested, then, that they were talking about both a sexual impasse and a relational one. For men, movement toward sex may bring out women's dread; women's yearning for connection before and during sex may bring about men's dread. Men move away from the relationship; women move away from the sexual. Impasse.

JOHN: So men feel dread in relationship and women feel it in sex?

SARAH: Maybe we should try switching roles?

ALMA: For a week I initiate the sexual, and Lou initiates the relational?

LOU: No way. I'd be dead in three days.

ALMA: You'd get fantastic sex.

LOU: Deal.

PAUL: Maybe we could try keeping track of what it's like for each of us, what it means to be the "holder of the relationship between us and with our child," "or the holder of the sexual relationship." I mean are we saying that, like sex is always in my head, relationship is always in hers?

LIZ: Always. That's what we're saying, yes.

The group was moving now, from accusation and anger and "I" versus "you" positions to a sense of "We're in it together." Their language reflected this; as they talked they used, more and more, the word "we." Given the chance to respond to each other, with the support of their own gender—the men together on one side of the room, the women on the other—they had shifted: first, from seeing the issues as "my neurosis" to "it comes with the territory of being a man or a woman"; and now they had also started to make the shift from opposition to mutuality—the same "shift toward mutual" we had seen in other groups we had worked with. We had a sense that now, in a more mutual connection, they would be able to do some deep work around sexuality.

The group then focused on another of the women's questions:

"How can men separate feelings from actions, like in sex?"

LOU: Easy, I just do it.

PAUL: If the feelings get in the mix you can't get anything done.

LOU: Yeah, we think: "This'll get me into the swamp'n I'll sink."

JOHN: At work we can't get anything done if we focus on how we feel, so at home I won't go into feeling. When we're approaching each other, if I start to feel powerless or incompetent, unable to fix it—fix "us"—I try to ignore the feelings—I know if I go anywhere near them I'm gonna get beaten up—

PAUL: Emotionally I feel like Liz beats me up all the time.

JOHN: It's our lack of confidence in the emotional realm. Our success-failure meter is tipped way down toward failure.

ALMA: I really feel for you guys, I mean how, if a woman feels strongly and says it to you, it trips you up.

JOHN: We're not even *aware* of cutting off strong feelings, we just do it. Especially around sex. Sexual feelings take over.

LOU: Sex helps us to cut off feelings, right? Gets us through that dread. Then we can open up some.

MEN: That's right. Yes.

PAUL: I don't know about that. I'm aware. I see the consequences of cutting off, but I'm still afraid to get into it. I feel something really strongly, but act like I don't. It kills me! I have real trouble trusting my feelings, trusting myself. Trusting Liz. How does trust get built?

LIZ: Through connection, babe. *Alongside* me. I'm not afraid of your intensity or your vulnerability. I love you.

Again the group falls silent, a silence of everybody "getting it." We could feel this sink in, a kind of summary of everything said so far. We were talking about the strong, sacrificed yearnings on the part of the men to be in good mutual connection with others—men and women both; and we were talking about the strong, complicated and often buried and blurred yearnings of the women in the room to be in mutual sexual connection with men. There was a sense that, on a deeper level, we all were sharing the immensity of the loss. The grief was palpable.

LOU: I hate to admit it, but she's right. It's like in my moving business. You can't just *lift* something alone, you gotta get a coupla guys and pay attention and kinda *ease*. Y'get me?

(A pause. Everyone bursts out laughing.)
ALMA: Lou, I think we all do.

The group leaves, with the idea that each couple will try the gender-role switch: women will be responsible for the sexual, men for the relational. They will report back in a month.

Couples Struggling to Find the Sexual "We"

The role switch did not work for any of the couples. As we went over this together a month later, it became clear that the solution to the sexual impasses was not in simply changing individual roles—men taking on emotional connection, women sexual connection—but on finding the "we" that would then allow both men and women to use their individual and culturally shaped strengths *in that "we."*

As we've suggested before in other arenas, the issue and the solution in the sexual arena is less changing "role" than creating "relationship."

For the couples of the group, differences without a sense of the "we" ended up dividing the couples further; differences held in the "we" connected them and allowed each man and woman to be more fully themselves and more in the relationship emotionally and sexually.

The group continued to meet once a month. Gradually as we continued to focus on the sexual aspect of the relationships, there was a strong sense of movement from stuck, difficult, or dangerous places that had long histories, to shared understanding and current action. Each couple—and the group as a whole—was struggling to learn more about the sexual "we."

One key moment that crystallized the shift to mutuality for the couples came in the dialogue around one of the women's questions:

"How can we women talk with you men about our different sexuality without feeling judged?"

Sarah, as spokeswoman, asked this question and elaborated: "So often our ways of being sexual get talked about as pathology."

> ALMA: Sex is not an on-off switch. It's more that we're moving together, with eyes open, taking each other in, kissing, being more present with each other.

SARAH: It can be sexual in a certain way without being genital contact. I can have a rich sex life without genital sex. Men seem to think that that *is* sexuality, as really getting to *it,* and that other things are a transition to *it.* We're saying that sexuality includes more than genital. We're all so programmed to see sex as genital.

LIZ: Even the notion of "foreplay" is a definition of something *before* something that really *is* the play.

JOHN: Yeah, but as soon as you define genital sex as a problem, there's a big problem for men.

SARAH: But it's like once genital sex starts, sensuality gets cut off, like you can't do both.

JOHN: *(sarcastically)* But what we hear is something like, "Can't you guys stop wanting to put that thing in here?"

LIZ: It's a way of touching, kissing without thinking about anything else, or trying to *get* somewhere else—"second base" or "third" and all that. There's a difference in what you radiate through your body.

ALMA: What's men's experience? The link between "lustful" and sexual? Is it purely an "I" and not an "us"? A dominating, objectifying part of it? To us that's terrifying, and disconnecting.

LOU: Our whole lives we've been taught "Slam bam thank you ma'am," and it's *in* me, too, I can't deny it.

SARAH: But there's no "us" there. Just you and what you're doing. What are your fantasies when we're making love?

JOHN: Why is it so terrible if some "I" thoughts intrude? When I was young, it was great, all fun-sex.

SARAH: Fun for whom? Sometimes it wasn't fun for us. A lot of times we had to get high to think that it was fun.

PAUL: Now, I'm almost thinking more about Liz than myself.

LOU: Me too. My mind is on Alma. Otherwise I could just do it alone.

SARAH: It's great to hear that from you! We *want* to hear your experience, be with you, vibrate with you. We just don't *know* in our hearts and our bodies what goes on with you, and we *want* to!

(The women nod and murmur their agreement.)

LIZ: I do feel Paul is tuned in to *me* sometimes, not himself, and I feel the lack of the *we.* It's not "what are we feeling together in the moment?", not just the physical part, not just the genital part, but what *else* is going on in this garden of sexual delights? It's about the *quality* of the connection between us.

PAUL: Yeah, it's true. Good sex comes from good soulful talk.

LIZ: It doesn't have to be intense all the time, it's not always an intense connection, sometimes it's more internal, tingling, light and playful.

PAUL: It's so bizarre—if both of us end up enjoying it, why do we collude in not doing it? Is it inertia? I get up and jet-pack myself for a day at work, and then come home and it's incredibly hard to transition back to that world at all, let alone an intimate sexual thing. All day long I'm the goal-directed, emotionally closed-off good boy at work, how do I transition to the sensitive, open man?

ALMA: It's hard for us too.

SARAH: The hardest thing for us is the transition—how to move into sex together. It's so damn confusing! That's when a lot of difficulties come up—for all of us—isn't it? *(agreement from other couples)*

ALMA: So if we can both own that confusion—it'd go a long way. Instead, I get blamed for being confused, as if he's not, or as if it's not our problem—and our solution. To just be in the confusion and fear together would be great!

PAUL: Agreed. *(Others, too, agree.)* Solving it would be good too.

LIZ: The question is "what is the 'we' in 'We're making love?'" Isn't that what we've gotten to today?

JOHN: Finding the "sexual 'we'?"

(General agreement, a sense of working on things together now.)

ALMA: It's *not* saying you men are wrong in how you think!

LOU: Or you women either.

This brought the group to a new place, an "us." Out of the "good conflict," out of all of us holding the relationships through accusation, polarization, grief, and regret, had come a sense of "we're in it together." Everyone tacitly understood that nobody—neither men nor women—has it right and that there's a lot of isolation, confusion, and a need for compromise and creativity and engagement around difference, to get to "we." We pointed out that now the group was talking incredibly openly about experiences of sexuality between men and women without judgment or "pathologizing." The group was simply hearing the facts of each other's different experience. Without a sense of mutual connection, there's hell when those differences collide, and nothing, especially not the sexual, can be addressed. With good connection, the differences can be used to create a movement toward even greater connection, and anything, even the sexual, can be addressed with respect and interest in the differences, personal and gender.

Toward the end of this meeting we all had a sense that some authentic facts of men and women's sexual experience had been made visible. We had looked squarely at the issues of physical and emotional difference in sex, of transitions into sensuality and sex, of work and home, of past and present—even of foreplay and eye contact. We had moved far beyond stereotypes of "women are not as interested in sex as men" and "men don't want anything else."

As we ended the meeting someone suggested that the next time we met we try having each couple present to the group their own sexual impasse, with the group trying to help solve it. Nervously, but hopefully, everyone agreed. We met one month later.

Sarah and John

SARAH: We say we respect each other and support each other moving forward—we're doing so well individually, but not together. The ideal scenario for me would be just to hang out with each other with sex as part of it, but that doesn't happen very often. We either say we don't have time to make it happen, or we don't want it to happen—because of the intimacy aspect of sex, not because of the physicality. I asked John to stop traveling so much and he asked me, "Are you sure you want to be more available?"—it was a good question. So the impasse has to do with "making the time," and "opening to each other" *sexually.*

JOHN: We have varying degrees of defendedness, with rare abandon, especially when we're away from home. Home is too, I don't know, just too loaded and cluttered. Hanging out together on vacation is easy and flowing. But in my head I'm always going "She's closed off to me I know she's closed off to me." I'm angry she's closed off—if I start touching her I know it will bring up her difficult history of sexual abuse and all that. I want sex, I yearn for the release of sex, the physical closeness. But when she just wants to "hang out" and "talk" about what's coming up for her, I feel deflated. I get into dread and anger and back off.

SARAH: That's our impasse around sex. When I try to get into it my way, he's too angry. We've tried to negotiate—what do I want, what do you want—it doesn't work. Compromise doesn't do it. I can't live with your anger.

JOHN: I feel: "I'm going to get into this and nothing will happen"—and it's very angry-making, and I just freeze. What I've tried to do is just to let go of it all. It's like when I took a mountain climbing course in the Sierras, and I was supposed to let go and float down this long slip-line across a river. I was so scared, and couldn't let go, and couldn't let go—and that's what I have to do here. Let go of sex. Because I'm not going to let this tear us apart.

SARAH: I won't either. But I'm not saying let go, either. *(pause)* Over the years it's gotten more intimate and more difficult. My old ghosts came up and I couldn't get them out of the bedroom. I've worked on this in my therapy. Sometimes making love I'm spacing out—dissociating—and it's hard to hold on to myself, what I want. When I can, it's okay. When John takes the initiative, sometimes I feel I get ambushed.

JOHN: And now I've pulled back and am trying to let go and now that's not okay?

They fell silent. We suggest to them that the sexual "we" has really been injured and maybe they need to get familiar with it again, as they have done earlier with the "relational we." It might help to write down, together, the qualities of the "sexual we." What were the qualities when you first got together, and what are they now?

SARAH: That's a good idea. Just talking about it makes me think we've overestimated how hard this has to be. We can do that, can't we, John?

JOHN: It's hard. My anger and despair comes up when I get into this. I think I can go so far as to think of what each of us does to help the "we"—I mean "the sexual we." I think I have enough humility for that, anyway.

ALMA: If you could each nurture that sexual "we" a little, and not be so critical and hard on it, maybe it would grow. I know, deep down, that that "we" is a healing place.

PAUL: Anger about sex does leak out into other things—dishes on the counter—"this is something Liz's not doing." I lay a guilt trip on her—it's your problem, not my problem. Like you John, I resign myself to all this, I get into "You're forcing me to dis-connect from you, and from myself, and I'm not going to respond anymore." But I'd like to move from that—I'd like to get back our sexual "we." My confusion is that now I'm not willing to let go of that rejected place. When she tries again to make contact, I get confused.

JOHN: It's that moutaineering course again, putting that hook in my harness, looking down that slip-line down that cliff, being scared shitless and then letting go. Now I've got to let go into this.

LOU: Maybe the "sexual we" is a kind of letting go down the cliff *together?*

JOHN: Yeah. I like that.

SARAH: Me too. We *both* are on that line, John—we *both* have to let go. I have to let go of the past, and be more with you in the present, and you have to let go of your anger, and see what happens.

We suggest that the sexual part of the "we" is fragile and vulnerable, just finding its way again, and has to be treated gently and nurtured. There's something sweet and innocent about the sexuality they once had, and now they can allow the "we" to enlarge to hold all of who they are today and what they've been through. The group goes on to suggest that John and Sarah, to keep the continuity, each do a daily "sexual check-in."

There is a sense, in the whole group, of the need to let go of the pri-ority of the self, or of the other, and trust the "we" of the relationship, together. If each couple can hold the relational "we," they can then hold the "sexual we." It will lead to: "Who are we sexually?" and "Who can we be sexually?"

The group then moved on to Liz and Paul.

Liz and Paul

PAUL: *(angrily)* A lack of physical reaction from Liz feels like a lack of emotional reaction. I'd love to have her *respond* to my touch-ing her by opening up.

LIZ: *(hurt, defending herself)* My body is capable of enormous response. I feel okay about my body. Of course, there are things I don't like about it, now. I used to dance and go to nude beaches. I wore clothes that were sexy, but that's not where it is now. I'm a mother, a strong woman. *(Starts to cry.)* I feel I'm out there being strong and beautiful and I get a quick sexual response with no depth and it doesn't move me—it's so sad! I know Paul feels that—he touches me, it doesn't feel right, and I feel if I honestly let you know what I feel that you'll go away.

PAUL: But I'm here. I've shown over the last ten years that I'm not going away.

LIZ: There is a way of listening in the moment—if it gets sticky, you mostly get angry, you don't stay with me. You stop the process, and I feel you just want to get to genital sex itself. It's hard to describe how I want to move but I think if we danced together I could show you.

PAUL: I can listen only so much, and then I start to feel there's no room for *me* to move and that's when I feel really aggressive.

LIZ: For me it's a feeling of *wanting to be met*—danced with—that brings out my sensuality, my sexual energy. If you would just say or show me, "Let me see that part of you," it'd be great, I'd feel I'm being met and I'd bring forth everything. And part of that is my dissatisfaction—not dissatisfaction with you but with how we are connecting.

PAUL: Then part of what needs to happen I just can't do. This vulnerability of being there with Liz in the moment, not getting defensive, waiting for her. It's hard for me to *join* that dance, that process. Even when I try, try hard, I still seem to mess it up. Work is intense, and not going well, and the transition to home is a bitch. On the way home the other day I drove past this flower shop and went back and bought Liz some roses, but as I got closer to home I got more and more resentful somehow. When I walked in I just said, kind of angrily, "Here!" and handed the roses to Liz.

LIZ: He threw the flowers at me. I said, "What's wrong with you?"

PAUL: I screamed, "I'm *trying!*" I'm struggling with power—whose needs are met in bed—sometimes I feel jealous of the baby. I get into "I'm gonna work on this for you because it's real important to you, Liz," but then I feel locked out. I feel like I won't give to you unless you give to me.

LIZ: I try to initiate things I want, and you hold yourself back and then suddenly get angry and come in strong.

PAUL: What holds me up is "trust." I left my first marriage for Liz and I've always felt guilty, like I can't be trusted. Liz wants me to look at her, eye to eye, and I can't. I hate myself sometimes. But we're good parents together—watching each of us as parents is unbelievable! *(He starts to cry.)* I need you to respond to me without acting like you need protection from me or that I'm going to leave you. Like I'm not some kind of monster.

LIZ: When you feel that, you just lash out at me, and I get scared. Why can't you just *tell* me?

PAUL: I don't think "How's this gonna effect her"—I just blow my top.

LIZ: And I hide.

PAUL: Which makes me feel we're getting nowhere. I'm no good, and that makes me *more* angry!

They fall silent. We suggest to them that maybe Paul's lashing out is a way of his trying to stay in the process, trying to bring himself into the "we."

PAUL: Over the years I, no, both of us, Liz, have taken ourselves more and more out of the "we" to protect each other, but that doesn't work.

LIZ: The times I *do* I stick up for myself, and stay present, I feel really strong.

PAUL: And I do applaud that.

LIZ: We're both trying to find a place to come into. But when you talk about the "we," I feel I have to come up with *good* things, not the conflict in the we—but maybe that's not the idea.

We suggest that expressing and holding their differences can lead to healthy conflict and then to better connection, a stronger more vital "we."

LIZ: Maybe we have to let the conflict be part of the sexual dance, without it becoming a dangerous power struggle. If we stayed together in the conflict, maybe we wouldn't have to be so angry, or alone.

PAUL: That sounds really right to me. I want to see it as *our* problem, Liz, bringing all our differences into the mix. I want to be in it with you.

LIZ: *(tenderly)* I hear you. That's exciting to me. I want you to have your freedom in sex too, but without losing touch with me. We women have been taught that men read sex into everything, so you don't dare do *anything*. I want to be daring too. *(playfully)* Believe it or not, Paul, I've wondered what it would be like if I met you at the door totally naked—

PAUL: But you didn't because you thought I'd think you wanted sex? *(Laughter.)*

LOU: If Alma met me naked my first question would be "Okay—where's his car?"

JOHN: Mine would be: "Where's the baby?"

ALMA: Men! Just because a woman is climbing all over you, you think of *sex!* *(laughter)*

Everyone in the room could feel that Liz and Paul had broken through an important impasse for them. They had spoken with strong feelings—anger, sadness, guilt, fear—and the group had helped them do so with an awareness of the "we." The energy of the conflict had led to greater connection. It felt as if they, affirming their desire to work it out *with* each other, could open new doors, use humor, and take risks.

We shifted our attention to the third couple, Lou and Alma.

Alma and Lou

ALMA: Our impasse is how to make time for sex. Life is so busy with three teenage girls, you barely know who you are, much less spare the energy for being with each other.

LOU: When Alma initiates sex I'm almost always glad. But we don't take the time. We rarely go to bed at the same time, and when we do I channel-surf, and Alma reads. Sometimes she rubs my back and that's great. When I'm into it she's okay, but then I fall asleep right after and she gets angry. After sex is no time to talk. I am too exhausted at the end of a day. I've heard everything you women have said but it still feels like making it too complicated. Sex is simple, real simple, and should be.

ALMA: Is it so difficult to find another time when we're not so exhausted, or afterwards to give me a few minutes of holding—not even talking, talking is not what I want at that time. I feel it could be anyone you're having sex with, and you want out, back to your separate corner, as soon as possible.

LOU: I really don't feel you want me either. You're so much happier
with your mother and your friends. You live in another world.
And I'm basically happy alone.

ALMA: But there *are* moments when you reach out, Lou, and I feel
you want to be with me. When I was away last year you wrote
me that beautiful love letter. That's why I wanted to come to this
group. I feel you are so lonely, really, and yet you stay shut off.
Lots of family, lots of work, watching TV, drinking beer—I
worry about that—and not really letting anyone in. I know
you're unhappy and angry at your life, your responsibilities at
home and work, and with your mother. I think you're
depressed. *(To the group)* When I tell him that he really gets
angry and won't talk for days. I think we might be headed for
divorce, not from fire and conflict but from deadness and attri-
tion. I want to stir us up. I don't want to lose you.

LOU: Duty is number one for me. We've been together twenty-two
years and I can't believe it's like we have to keep deciding
whether to be married.

ALMA: I have to share this with you all. Lou's already had a stroke,
and he's only forty-eight. *(Everyone is moved.)* It runs in his
family. He won't even share his feelings about this with me. The
stakes are very high.

LOU: Why do you think I came here? I can't let go, and I don't
know what's going on inside me. The only thing holding me
together lately is duty. What if I wanted to retire or move to
Florida? Would you come with me?

ALMA: If it was right for us, if it came out of a shared decision.
(Tenderly) I'd go anywhere with you.

LOU: This embarrasses me. But I'm going to try. *(Nearly screams)*
Dammit I need you. *(Pause, choked up)* I know what you say,
but I don't believe you really want me.

ALMA: I'm not sure I do, unless you let me in.

LOU: It feels good to just be real. You're an incredibly beautiful
woman and I'm not letting you go. I feel real angry about
things, inside, but I'm afraid to be angry, like it will kill you or
me. But what I hear you saying is that not letting you in is
killing us. Is that it?

ALMA: Yes.

We comment that the two of them getting to the authentic "we" is a relief and opens the possibility of really moving, together.

LOU: I always worry that if we get into deep connection, we're going to talk about heavy stuff—like right now—and that's going to break things apart even worse. But I gotta admit it never seems to, really.

PAUL: But that's the fear—that it'll move things in a direction that *I* don't want. It might move us to San Diego—

ALMA: Right, or move Lou to Florida. *(The group laughs.)*

LOU: But it's good, talking like this. In our lives today we're surrounded by couples getting divorced, and it makes me feel stronger being with others who are working on staying together.

The others agreed. Our Sunday afternoon was over. The sense of mutuality was almost palpable as we said good-bye. Our plan was to continue to meet one full Sunday every month.

Three Couples Transformed

About a year from when we began, we ended. In the last session, after not having met for several months, each couple talked about how things had changed, how much they had moved to mutual, and how much more open and interesting the sexual part of the relationship had become. These are three extremely good results, but they are not that different from what we have seen in other couples groups. Not every couple does this well, nor can we say that these results are permanent. We do believe, however, that such extraordinary movement, under optimal conditions, points the way to how much is truly possible.

Sarah and John

SARAH: It's as if John and I had been in a dark tunnel, and all of a sudden there was a blast of light. We're coming alive individually and together. I don't know how to explain it. We've really had some incredible sex.

JOHN: Sarah and I went for a weekend together to the Cape, and nothing was happening, and I almost started complaining, but I bit my tongue. I knew that if I responded the same way as before, it would be a big mess. So I said to her, not once but a few times, maybe four or five, "I'm committed to doing things differently." By the fifth time around I thought, Hmm, this is getting interesting, my anger is dissipating. And something shifted, and the orgy began. *(laughs)*

SARAH: We've been incredibly open and creative.

JOHN: It's like what we talked about here—I let go and moved *into* the relationship, instead of holding on, or backing away.

SARAH: And you *asked* me: "What would be a better way of our doing this?" You never *asked* me, before. That made an incredible difference.

Liz and Paul

LIZ: *Big* changes. I've felt really with you. Speaking through our bodies. One night I set up the bedroom with music, and candles, and we spent hours together—*and* it was truly an ecstatic sexual experience. It wasn't dependent on what Paul did or didn't do, but what *we* did. He moved in some very different—not antagonistic—ways, and we kept moving in relation to each other, together, sometimes gently, sometimes wild. It was full of who we both are. I couldn't sleep half that night, it's way richer a sexual experience than I've ever had before. I felt a new sexuality within myself and between us. Paul has been really *in it with* me, both of us saying and expressing the tough, straight things in the relationship, and it all kind of clicked. I walked around feeling the heat flowing, flowing all through my body all the next day too. Incredible.

PAUL: *(shyly, smiling)* It's really what I wanted, but different than I would have imagined. It's amazing how small steps have had dramatic effects, like moving through a door, and the world is dramatically different. Since the last meeting, I've had a number of realizations, and none of them have been particularly about sexuality, but about the relationship. It used to be I'd come home from work overwhelmed and Liz would take one look at me and march into the other room. I said to myself, you can get overwhelmed by this or that, or you can just stand up and decide to go into the "we," and march forward toward her. That's what I've been doing. And the other thing I realized: I've got to be on my personal journey to find a community, maybe of men, to help. I'm way too alone. I *admire* her with her friends—which is of course why I was angry before.

Alma and Lou

ALMA: We're doing pretty well. Lots of outside changes too. We're selling our house. Lou's mother died. The new house makes us feel like a chance to start over.

LOU: My mother's death was very powerful, and Alma was really there for me. It's a big burden lifted off of us. The "we" now seems to be very much alive. I'm definitely a convert.

ALMA: Really, we had an amazing moment after the last group. Lou took me away for my birthday and was very tender. I started crying and crying—for us, for his mother, for my family, for all the pain we've been through. I felt terrified that he was going to go away, but he just held me. I said, "I'm so afraid of trusting you" and he said, "I'm just going to hold you till the fear goes away." It was the most loving moment of my life. Neither of us moved for a long time and then we made love. Even if we never have that experience again is has changed everything.

As we went around listening to the rest of the couples in this last meeting, everyone talked about the changes they'd seen in themselves and each other. The tone was grateful, and happy. Everyone had greater hope that change was possible.

SARAH: You know, I feel I really want to go deeper now with all you guys, you seem so beautiful to me. My whole image of men has changed.

ALMA: Looking around at you all, it's like we're each jewels for each other. Seeing each of you struggle with your own relationship has been so incredibly supportive for me and Lou.

PAUL: This group is like a vessel, and we put parts of ourselves and our relationship in this vessel. And as a man I feel I'm not alone in asking the questions I'm asking, I mean with life's struggles. I'm not a terrible person, I'm just me, a man, in a relationship with a woman. It's a relief, very comforting. Very few men I know have had the chance for this depth of expression. There's an incredible honesty here—it's very rare.

JOHN: We've all learned we don't have to run to our corners every time there's conflict or danger.

SARAH: Even when we're in our own worlds, there's a sense of companionship, of the group being with us.

LIZ: We've started making sure our child gets to bed early so we have *our* time. I was always sitting there waiting for Paul to change, and now that he's moved toward me, I'm free to see how far I can move in this dance.

PAUL: In this group I feel not only my own feelings, but other people's. I can see how you other couples do it. I can go beyond just the feeling, like of anger, to being with Liz *in* the anger. If I'm acting like an asshole I can get beyond her accusation that I'm acting like an asshole. It's a big change in how I am in relation to women.

We comment that the worst thing for couples is how they get isolated in the society. This group, as an example of a kind of "couples community," can help break the isolation. Is that what allows such profound movement?

SARAH: Maybe it is. It's so wonderful to be in this new place with John. He's working just as hard, but I'm not as lonely. It's not a matter of how much time, it's a matter of the connection.

JOHN: The quality of connection. Not the quantity.

SARAH: It's just sort of melted away the loneliness I've lived with for so long. It's like we're *seeing together.*

PAUL: On my "lashing out" theme? Now, rather than blaming the person—blaming Liz—I try to name the disconnection, talk about "the disconnect." Doing it that way gets us moving again, out of our impasse. If I say to Liz "I want connection," and she says "I can't listen right now?"—I say "No way, baby, you can't put me off! I want that *connection!*" *(laughter)*

ALMA: Listening to you is like hearing ourselves—these relationships seem so inspired! We all left a lot of baggage behind, there's a lot more there—*we're* a lot more there. Things have gradually been revealed over time, like they've been there all along, but got lost. It feels so much gentler now. I've dropped my levels of judgment of Lou, and the old scripts in my head, which allows him to be the best he can be.

LOU: Which is very terrific. *(laughter)*

JOHN: I feel that now, finally, we can let go. After so many years of holding on to things so tightly, it's great to just let go!

SARAH: There's a sense of forgiveness now, and grace, that we're enough. *(Looking around the room at each couple in turn)* I can feel it in all of us. Thank you all.

Steps Toward Sexual Connection

In the shift toward mutuality of these couples, the movement toward the "sexual we" involves similar steps that help men and women get to the whole "we." Sexual differences, in dialogue, move men and women to create something new, something mutual. This creation may happen quickly and dramatically or slowly and subtly. In the shared creating lies great hope for sexual change, sexual growth in connection, sensuality, and a true love "making." Here are a few brief examples of how couples can try the connection steps from chapter 5 in the sexual realm.

Each of these suggestions can be framed in terms of the movements described at the beginning of this chapter: moving into the sexual, moving through sex together, and moving out of the sexual.

Building "Sexual We" Awareness

1. Describe the sexual qualities of the relationship, in its birth, infancy, milestones, present, and in the future (a sexual relational purpose statement). Discuss and record, together: What is our sexual we? For example, what are the *qualities* (texture, color, climate, sound, animal, film, etc.) of this "sexual we"? What were the qualities in the past? What can we envision in the future?

2. Write a sexual relational inventory: strengths and weaknesses of the sexual relationship.

3. At times of sexual disconnection, ask "Where's the 'sexual we' right now? What does it need?" This is taking mutual responsibility for the sexual relationship.

4. What is our mutual impact on the "sexual we"? Not *only* what "I" see sexually or what "you" see sexually, but can we share the seeing? Can we ask the question, together: What do "we" see sexually?

5. What is the growing edge of our "sexual we"? What is *our* empathic distance from each other, sexually? What is the distance that we *need* to be from each other—emotionally and physically—to hold each other and the relationship empathically?

Building "Man" And "Woman" Sexual Awareness

1. Sexual differences: become aware of and learn more about the emotional, physical, and spiritual differences in sex between you as a man and you as a woman. Let go of judging these differences. Realize these differences are not *only* individual but shaped by being brought up as a man or a woman in your culture. Awareness of the different physiological responses of men and women sexually is always helpful, and such information is widely available.

2. Do a gender dialogue around your sexuality. Ask the three questions: Name three strengths the other person brings to the sexual relationship. What do you most want to understand about the other person's sexuality? What do you most want the other person to understand about yours?

3. How do gender invisibilities play out in sex? For example, the difference in relational timing between many men and women is always active in the sexual connection: men are on a faster biological time, women on a faster emotional one. Talk about timing and other invisibilities based on gender.

4. Learn to bring the "sexual I" into the "sexual we." From the perspective of the we, each person has the opportunity and the challenge to most fully find and express their own sexuality. Sexuality grows as relationship grows. It is not a property of each individual alone, nor unchanging over the life cycle. Rather it is a changing and unfolding expression of both people as they meet in the we.

5. Sexual impasse, sexual breakthrough. Use the diagramming process to understand what's happening in "I," "you," and "us." This will help shift from sexual impasse to breakthrough. See if the three categories—dread/yearning, product/process, power-over/power-with—are helpful in understanding what is happening between you sexually.

Again, awareness of the "fifteen-minute factor" in movement into the "sexual we" is crucial. Both the man and the woman have to carry an awareness of this tender time and share responsibility for it. As with everything in the field of the we, of relationship, merely *naming* it—

both at the time and at other times, in thinking about what happened or could happen in reflection or anticipation—is helpful.

Learning to Talk Sexual "Connect" and Sexual "Disconnect"

Moving Through Disconnection to Better Connection

1. Connection comes first. The priority in any sexual interaction has to be the state of the connection, which also means the state of the disconnection (whichever is easier to address). Using the words "connect" and "disconnect" shifts the paradigm away from "self" or "other" to "self *and* other *and* the connection." In this case, in addition to connection in general, sexual connection can be focused on.

2. Hold the "sexual we" through the disconnection. The important movement in relationship is the movement through disconnection toward reconnection. This movement also characterizes sexual relationships. Disconnects are inevitable; growth of the "we"— and the "sexual we"—happens when both people hold the "we" and are able to move back toward connection when a disconnection occurs.

3. Sexual check-in. Use it to keep the continuity of the sexual relationship during the day, and during sex.

4. Sexual check-out. In times of destructive sexual conflict, one or both of you have the presence of mind to check out and stop it, then to initiate conversations about what happened.

5. The sexual twenty-minute rule and weekly meetings. If you hit a recurrent impasse sexually, agree to talk about it for twenty minutes at a time, no more, no less.

6. Identify difficult transitions that threaten the "sexual we." In addition to the transition into sexuality of "the fifteen-minute factor," each couple has times when any attempt at transition into the sexual is dangerous. For instance, the transition from work to home can be lethal for some couples, for others the transition from kids to bed. Find your own danger times, when the probability of sexual disconnection is highest. Become aware of the differences in engaging, holding, and disengaging.

7. Reframe common sexual dilemmas in terms of the "sexual we." Depression, obsession, dependency, anxiety—these can be reframed in the emotional realm, as described in the previous chapter and in the couples therapy with Tom and Ann, but they can also be reframed in the sexual realm. Try thinking about "sexual obsession" or "sexual depression" in terms not only of the "I" or "you" but of the "we."

8. Bring your outside creativity into the sexual arena.

9. Use humor in sex.

10. Help each other to stay in the present sexual moment, not in the past.

Nourishing and Empowering the Sexual "We"

1. Find special places and times to nourish the "sexual we."

2. Practice stress reduction and relaxation together.

3. Find "our sexual spirituality." Connect sexually through silence, meditation, and prayer. Try moving from sitting in silence together to being sexual together. Where are the links between our spirituality and our sexuality?

4. Seek out a community of couples. Find another couple—or a group of couples—to inquire with. With a special "best friends" couple try the buddy system, checking in as a foursome, talking through your disconnections. It may be very difficult initially to talk about sexuality, but you may be surprised, as the couple-to-couple relationship grows, that these things can be talked about: "How do you get together sexually with the children around all the time?" "Isn't it hell to make the transition from work or putting the kids to bed to being sexual?" "We had a sexual disconnect today—we need some help in talking it through."

.   .   .

Moving from specific work with individual couples to couples working with other couples brings us to the final part of our inquiry: How can this gender dialogue work contribute to building connections in the world? The future is our children. How can we begin to support healthy connections between boys and girls?

7
Boys and Girls Together

HEALING THE RIFT, SAVING OUR FUTURE

"What's with all that sighing and crying?"

— SEVENTH-GRADE BOY, TO GIRLS
IN DIALOGUE

"Why do boys act up in class and beat each other up?"

— SEVENTH-GRADE GIRL, TO BOYS
IN DIALOGUE

We were led to children. By chance or fate, after we had been leading gender dialogues for about seven years we began to be invited into schools. We had been sensitized to gender issues in schools by having a child of our own in preschool. A high school principal who heard Sam lecture about the relational development of boys and men asked if we would bring the dialogue work to her high school students.

Working with these young people we soon saw how the different pathways of boys' and girls' development played out in school settings—

in the classroom and beyond. We now have led gender dialogues—the same three questions, the same dialogue process—in every grade, from preschool through college. From the first school sessions, with eleventh-graders, we felt affirmed in the usefulness of what we were trying to do. As one of the eleventh-grade boys said, "This is the most important thing I've learned in all these years in school. Every student should do this."

A girl told us, "These are the things I've been waiting my whole life to talk about with guys."

The other comment that came out of those first dialogues with high school students was, "It's not enough that *we* do this. If we do it, it's only fair that you get our teachers to do it too. They're our models."

"And," another said, "our parents too."

Whenever possible, we have tried to work with all three groups.

After working with every age and grade, we decided to focus our attention on middle school, grades 6 through 8. We chose this age group—ten to thirteen—to begin more intensive work, based on developmental patterns we have observed.

From preschool until about first grade, boys and girls play together to a certain extent in the classroom, playground, and on play dates. However, starting at about first grade, under the strong cultural forces often transmitted through the family, media, and school, boys start to mock other boys for playing with girls. Cross-gender play and learning become more and more devalued, and eventually, in many case, tail off and then stop.[1] Birthday parties become much more gender segregated. In general, from first or second grade through grade 6, boys and girls separate from each other, boys hanging out with and learning about relationship from boys, girls hanging out with and learning about relationship from girls. They have little experience of real cross-gender relationship that involves learning to work with differences. They play and learn in parallel for several years, not really drawn together again until early adolescence. Rarely does anyone seriously challenge this separation, these missed opportunities to learn from the other gender about the reality of relationship by staying connected across differences. We have called these five or six years "the years of missed chances" for learning about cross-gender relationships.

Of course, there are exceptions to these generalizations. Our hope is to study these exceptions as well as to study the impact of cross-gender sibling relationships on development through these years. We hope to encourage parents, teachers, and all adults who work with children to support healthy cross-gender relationships and to help children resist the messages that divide them. Their relational health as adults, and our future, may be much helped by this encouragement.

In gender dialogues with children up to about sixth grade, many of their responses to the three questions reflect stereotypic images from the popular culture. For example, one question that fourth-grade boys had of girls was, "Why do you wear short skirts and makeup and hang out in bars?"

By tenth or eleventh grade, the responses of students in gender dialogue are more and more like those of adults. They have had more experience in real relationships with the other gender and are somewhat more able to express their perceptions of themselves and relationships as adults do.

In grades 6 through 8—approximately age ten through thirteen—boys and girls are making the transition from a comfortable division and separation from each other to an attempt to move into relationship. We hoped that cultural images of ways of being with each other could be challenged before they solidify. Because during the "years of missed chances" they have not engaged in relational growth together, boys and girls in this age group are mysteries to each other. They have learned different ways of being in relationship, mostly from same-gender experience, and bring these expectations into cross-gender relationships. It is an important time for them to have access to each other and to develop respect and empathy for each other.

In about sixth grade these different ways of being in relationship collide. Many boys still have a yearning for connection—with boys and girls both—that is not yet fully hidden or denied but is going underground. For many girls the vital authentic connection to self and others is being challenged by images and experiences in relationships with boys. They feel these forces not only in the classroom but in the hallways and at the lunch tables, on the sports fields, on the buses, and at home. The following voices of boys and girls from a number of middle schools, public and private, speak to these experiences poignantly and creatively. It is a time full of potential for change.

Middle School Students' Gender Dialogues

Question One: Name three strengths the other gender group brings to relationships.

Girls' Answers

Boys bring different perspectives.
Guys are funny people.
Lighten things up, fun to be around.
Don't stay angry for long.
Muscle strength.
They don't have to take care of themselves as much as girls.
They don't take things so seriously.
Fun to flirt with.
Entertaining.
Romance.
Laughter.
Dreams.
Courage, daring.
Boys are stress relievers.
They motivate us.
Boys can keep secrets.

Boys' answers:

Girls know the homework assignments.
Girls are a different kind of friend.
Good study buds.
More emotional.
Girls know how to sing the blues.
Kinder and more peaceful.
They introduce us to new things.
Girls show their feelings.
Girls bring happiness and comfort.
Girls talk for most of the conversation so we don't have to talk.
They don't have such big egos.
They can compromise better.

Girls are not so involved in physical violence.
They restore us our faults.
They can tell if you're lying—like they can see right through us.
You can be more yourself with girls.

The boys felt happy with the girls' perceptions, though some note that girls don't say much about boys as friends. The girls feel surprised to hear how much the boys value their emotional and relational strengths. They often note that boys don't speak of valuing girls for their intelligence, physical competence, or courage. Both groups begin to see how the same qualities that are strengths are often the ones that create difficulties or about which they feel devalued.

Question Two: What do you most want to understand about the other gender group?

Girls' answers:

Why don't boys cry?
Why do boys beat each other up?
How come you don't talk first?
Why don't you talk much?
Why don't boys talk about anything interesting?
Why do you like bloody, gory things?
Why some boys don't appreciate us?
Why do some boys put girls down?
Why do they think they're so superior to us?
Why do you say such mean things to us, and to each other?
Why do boys hide their feelings?
Why do they only go for looks?
Why do you make fun of smart girls?
Why do they always follow someone?
Why do you act toward us one way when you're alone with us and
    another way when you're with your friends?

Boys' answers:

What do girls do all day?
Why do girls hang back in class?
Why don't you say what you mean?

Why girls are so unpredictable?
Why all the exaggerated mood swings?
Why is everything such an emotional ordeal?
What are you interested in?
Why do girls gossip all the time?
Why they talk more than we do?
Why do they whisper and giggle?
Why they have more get-togethers than boys?
What's with all that sighing and crying?
How do girls show affection so easily?
Why do you have to make things perfect?
What do they really want in boys?
If you say you like the sensitive guys, why do you go for the macho jerks?

Girls' questions to boys center around boys' silence and their hiding feelings. They also ask why boys put girls down and feel or act superior. Finally, they ask about physical violence and what it means. Boys' questions focus on girls' emotionality and their ways of "talking" and showing feelings. Having boys and girls ask each other questions and giving each other the answers, pondering and exploring together, moves them beyond stereotype and judgments. The dialogue provides room for boys and girls whose experience is not the "norm" to give nuance and complexity to the discussion and help move beyond stereotype. It is also valuable for them to see the power of gender in their lives, and how everything cannot be simply attributed to each person's individual experience.

Question Three: What do you most want the other gender group to understand about you?

Girls' answers:

We're not Barbie dolls and anorexic blondes.
We're their equal, we're as good as they are.
Understand the person not the stereotype images.
We're not sex objects.
We're not spineless little wimps—at least not most of the time.
Our friendships are really important to us.
We're not some toy you can push around.

Looks are not everything.
We can fight too—we can be almost as violent as you.
What you say hurts us.
We are as smart and tough as you—but we bruise easily.
Most girls don't take comments on their body features as compliments.
If it were not for women, men wouldn't exist.
Some boys think we're weak, but we're not (sometimes we are).
We do everything! We do most of their work in their lives.
We can do the same things that you can—mostly.
They think everything we do is connected to them, but we're not on
    earth so you can go out with us for your own sake.
I don't whine all the time.
That when we are moody we are not having PMS.
It's okay to be in a bad mood. Sometimes.
Sometimes we just don't want to be with you.

What we hear from the girls is a sense of being treated as lesser, and an attempt to declare their strengths and stand up for themselves. They are calling to the boys' attention—assertively and sometimes angrily—that they can hold their own and are protesting boys' assumptions that they just want to be with guys or are just there to go out with them. (Sometimes they try to defend themselves by identifying with some aspects of boys' roles and behavior, for example by saying, "We can be just as violent as you boys.") The girls are angry and defensive. They feel put down, shamed, and devalued, measuring themselves in the dominant paradigm, but at the same time as they hint at self-doubt, they are fighting back. Listening to the girls, we are moved by how misunderstood they feel, objectified, devalued, and unappreciated. They want boys to "get it." They are fighting the stereotypes of the culture ("We're not sex objects or Barbies"), and they are trying to assert their strengths ("We are sensitive," "Our friendships are really really important to us"). At the same time they already feel the culture labeling many of their strengths weaknesses, pathologizing them as "oversensitive," "weak," "wimps," "emotional ordeals," and overcome by "PMS." They also make clear that they can be hurt.

Notice also how the girls, in answering, are sensitive to the relational context, qualifying what they say with "sometimes," "mostly," and the like. We rarely hear the boys do this.

Boys' answers:

We are a decent group—we're just fooling around when we beat on
  each other and call each other names.
How I think and feel.
Please see who we are inside.
Please see my heart.
We're aggressive because we can't show our feelings any other way.
We act like jerks around you because we're nervous.
We need to learn how to not show pain.
Why we use excessive violence—letting out our emotions, and show-
  ing we're buddies.
We don't hate girls, just some of them sometimes.
We can be good friends with you.
I'm only trying to get attention.
How hard I try to look good.
That we feel we always have to look cool.
Girls are one of our priorities, but not the only one and we have other
  things to take care of.
Even though I act like a pervert, I'm really a nice guy underneath.
We may fool around but we are really nice people.
What we like to do.
What we look for in them.
We are more physical than girls.
Who we are.

The message the boys are sending, loud and clear, to girls is that there
is a side of them that is hidden—the "nice guy," "caring," "vulnerable"
side. Listening to the boys, we are terribly moved by their struggle to
keep alive the yearning for relationship they were born with and for
several years expressed easily. It is painful to hear in these eleven-year-
olds the shame and sorrow and yearning and despair at losing and hiding what they really, deep down, want.

In seventh grade, the boys are still expressing their yearning for connection. That is, one aspect of the relational paradox is already not
being validated in schools and in the wider culture but is so strong in
the boys that they want to make sure that girls know it: their caring and
relational yearning, rather than their self-centered, macho toughness.

Also, the boys want the girls to know that they are "doers," needing
to do more than just be with them.

By high school, the boys will less readily admit to the yearning, relational part. In their experience with relationships, especially with boys but also with girls, they will need to deny and hide their relational yearnings to be "real men" (there may be more pressure on boys to deny this with other boys). This track, as we have seen, generally is not challenged, and often quite implicitly validated, in schools.

Thus, both the boys and the girls are on the crest of a powerful movement toward hiding or distorting part of themselves to adapt to prevailing relational images of who they must be to be "real men" or "popular women." The forces of the "normal" culture are so strong that it is an unusual boy or girl who publicly can resist being affected by these forces. Privately, the pain is evident and can result in the terrors, and, for some, the terrible self-destructive and hurtful actions of teenagers.

"What We Learned": The Middle School Students Reflect

The students mostly enjoyed the gender dialogues. Often during a dialogue, as questions and answers flew back and forth across the room, the attention was acute. It is as if, having moved along separate pathways of development for several years, they now welcomed the chance to break through the mysteries the other gender held for them. As they did this, much in the same way as the adults we've worked with, there was a shift toward mutuality between the boys and girls. They began to seriously consider questions that at first brought sarcasm, defensiveness, and teasing.

The responses of the middle school students to our questions are sophisticated and thoughtful—even wise. We asked one classroom of boys and girls to tell us what they'd learned in the dialogue:

Both boys and girls: Everyone has too many stereotypes.
Girl: Boys didn't know that much about girls.
Girl: Boys have their own personality styles.
Boy: Girls think that we think they are a lower people.
Boy: Some girls are not that different from some boys.
Girl: Some girls think boys think we are just there to be pushed around.
Boy: Some girls aren't weaker than some boys.
Girl: Boys are violent for a reason.

Girl: Boys don't really seem to notice all the physical violence that we see in them.

Girl: There are many things that girls didn't understand about the boys and vice versa.

Boy: Girls stereotype us because they think we stereotype them.

Girl: Guys don't just think of girls all the time.

Girl: Why boys hurt each other sometimes.

Girl: Boys hit each other not by trying to hurt each other but by greeting each other.

Boy: Both genders are equal, but different.

Boy: We really have a lot to learn from each other.

Girl: We can really hurt each other if we don't understand each other.

Finally—as in these last two responses—their responses reflect the movement toward the "we." This is the "mutual we," growing out of dialogue, where authenticity and empathy are born, emerging out of the energy of healthy conflict and confrontation with difference.

When we asked for suggestions on how we could follow up this work, one girl said, emphatically, "Seventh grade is too late. We really could have used this in fourth grade."

Other students agreed. And when we did the dialogue with fourth-graders, a boy told us, "We're too old in fourth grade. You need to do this in kindergarten, before the cooties come in."

"Yeah," said another boy. He paused. "But what *are* cooties anyway?"

As part of our exploration of the world of middle school, we led the same dialogue process with middle school teachers. The following is a composite of teacher responses to question three.

Middle School Teachers' Gender Dialogues

Question Three: What do you most want the other gender group to understand about you?

Women teachers' answers:

Why I think the way I do.

Our emotions.

How hormonal changes affect our moods but don't define us—PMS, pregnancy, menopause, etc. are real physiological conditions.

Our need to be equal in society.

That people's differences don't make either gender weaker or better.

That we process things differently.

We have some of their strengths—sometimes to a greater extent.

Our tuning in to our emotions is a real strength.

Our empathic nature.

I don't want a solution, I want a listener.

Our need to talk things out—it's a strength.

Our need for bath products.

Every mood other than happy is not PMS.

Crying is okay and not necessarily a weakness.

Relationships are not just "women's issues."

Our physiological conditions are not cause for unemployment—or glass ceilings.

Connection is not control.

What we bring to the relationship is just as important as what they bring, i.e., daily efforts at home are as important as monetary contributions.

It's frustrating to hear that they think it's a fifty-fifty relationship when it really isn't.

Note how similar the women's and girls' answers are. While the girls have a sense of doubt—as they are preparing to enter their first relationships with boys—the women have less doubt about what they want and need the men to understand. These adult women, in the validating context of women's groups, can affirm their own ways of being, thinking, and processing, even as they recognize how these have been devalued or pathologized. They can more clearly and articulately speak their truth.

What these women could offer girls in a context of open dialogue is the validation of girls' strengths, their different ways of knowing, their different biologies, and the recognition of and resistance to the cultural forces that pathologize certain qualities of women and women's ways. Women can model for girls the importance of knowing and saying what they want and need in relationship. To do this, the women teachers themselves must be validated in this endeavor by the school system, both by other women in the system and across gender, by men.

Men teachers' answers:

> Physicality—in a group of boys/men we are really physical—but it's
> not necessarily violence.
> Need time to be "alone" on occasion.
> That this kind of stuff is not an important part of my thinking.
> Passion for other things in life beside family or personal issues.
> Your thoughts and ideas have relevance.
> Take our actions at face value; don't always think there's more to it.
> Outwardly we act one way, inwardly we can act/feel differently.
> Our moods, both up and down.
> Our need to be in control.
> Candor of a good relationship is often compromised by the need to
> be "politically correct."
> That male values and goals are similar but they need not be discussed
> so much, nor articulated so clearly.
> Our belief that in regard to nurturing and caregiving, there may be a
> time to begin to let go in order to let the individual develop and
> learn independence and self-reliance, and women might place that
> time later in the child's development.

These men offer boys a validation of boys' strengths as individuals, for example, personal autonomy. They also validate boys' "physicality," their need for "alone time" and "space," and their having less need to "talk" about these things ("This kind of stuff is not an important part of my thinking.") While there is an echo of the boys' "Please see my heart" ("Outwardly we act one way, inwardly differently"), much of that frank expression of the men's yearning for connection is more submerged and denied ("Take our actions at face value; don't always think there's more to it.") To validate the relational qualities of boys in their schools, the men teachers would need to be validated for the presence and expression of their own relational yearnings, by men and women both.

These women and men teachers are part of what we call "the hidden curriculum of gender," operating strongly but more or less invisibly in the classrooms of these boys and girls, reflecting invisibilities in the "normal" culture.

The "Hidden Curriculum" of Gender

Schools have a hidden curriculum of gender (an "invisible" curriculum, like our "invisibilities of gender" in the dialogues).[2] Gender differences and their impact on relationships between boys and girls operate in powerful ways in the classroom and outside but are rarely, if ever, explicitly addressed. Schools and classrooms can be seen as a network of relationships, where connections and disconnections shape students' personal and academic growth. Many of these connects and disconnects are impacted by gender—and by other significant factors such as race, ethnicity, class, and sexual preference.

Schools reflect the broader cultural challenges to the full relational development of each gender. Over and over we see the collision of the two pathways of development. Many schools place primary value on individual achievement, objectivity, and outspokenness, while not explicitly rewarding achievement *with* others or participating in a community where everyone feels included and respected. This is what Goleman[3] has called "emotional intelligence," which we might include in the concept of "relational intelligence." While elementary schools may evaluate students for "working well with others" and "helping others work," these characteristics are rarely rewarded explicitly in middle school and beyond. "Classroom participation" may be graded in terms of how frequently a child raises his or her hand, but this may not reward those students—often girls—who participate more quietly, in more subtle ways, in building the classroom group culture. The qualities of connection and disconnection in the classroom, often shaped by gender relations, have everything to do with how individuals participate, learn, and grow.

The Connected Classroom: Using the Connection Model to Create a New Vision of Coeducation

Most schools have not envisioned a true coeducation, where differences between boys and girls could add—that is, lead to healthy, mutually empowering connections. Rather, boys and girls participate in what might be called a "separate but unequal" educational system. Schools "shortchange girls"—denying, among other things, their relational ways of working and learning, especially in science and math; they also "shortchange boys" by rewarding boys' more individualistic path of development and ways of learning and de-emphasizing boys' more relational qualities.

Schools are making important efforts toward gender equity in education but generally not very much toward gender mutuality. That is, while they try to treat boys and girls equally and provide equal opportunity, they make fewer efforts to see if the differences between boys and girls in schools, acknowledged and brought into dialogue, could *add,* so that school could be a place where boys and girls can grow and learn *from* and *with* each other.

Helping boys and girls and teachers to "shift to the 'we'" in the classroom and outside could be helpful in creating a mutual, truly "co"-education in each class, and even in a whole school system. We have begun to work on this process in middle school classes and—taking the advice of the seventh- and fourth-graders—with elementary school classes. The steps toward connection are much like those suggested for men and women in couples, applied to the classroom:

Building classroom "we" awareness.

Building classroom "boy" and "girl" (gender) awareness.

Learning to talk "connect" and "disconnect" in the classroom (moving through disconnection to connection).

Nourishing and empowering the classroom "we."

Using these steps in middle school, we are developing a curriculum on relationship and gender, where the students and the teacher are developing a shared concept and application of the "classroom we." We are particularly indebted to Nancy Beardall and Carol Phillips for their collaboration. In building classroom "we" awareness, for example, students might create a class map or quilt or imaginary band to build an image and sense of the "we." Teachers might create with students a basic contract of individual responsibilities, empowering the class to decide or to advise on rewards and penalties. In one group, a different student was designated to observe the overall process of the group and to recognize students who contributed and participated constructively during that class meeting.

When this framework has been developed, for example, rather than a teacher asking the girls "Why don't you girls raise your hands?" the teacher might say, "I'm noticing that some girls are not raising their hands. How can 'we' understand and work with this?" The issues of participation in class, sports, grading, discipline, and so on—all can be reframed in terms of the class "we," along with building an awareness of the effect of gender on that "we."

In one kindergarten class, we suggested that each boy and girl play or work for twenty minutes a day with another child, randomly selected, to move them out of their habitual relationships. Each, then, would talk to the whole class about: How did they decide what to play? Who compromised and why? What did they learn from playing with the other person? Could they create a new game or activity that came out of both of their interests and skills? It is important to look at the process of working together so as not to simply replicate typical gender patterns of interaction. For example, one cross-gender pair of kindergartners were challenged to find a way to deal with the girl's greater ease with compromising. For older children, this exercise could be done in working together academically, for instance on a science project.

One of the most striking facts of elementary education is that most of the teachers are women. Recently a woman teacher said that she had been having trouble working with the boys in the class. The principal, a man, said, "Maybe we need to get a man in here, to get the boys under control and show them how to act." Even though the teacher felt she was skilled at the process of relationship with her students and in helping students to grow in relationship, she acceded to this. "Boys will be boys," she thought, "boys need men." The result was that rather than valuing and strengthening the relational skills of boys, their more traditional roles, focus on the individual, power hierarchies, and their reluctance to engage with girls and women were not challenged.

The potential for change is tremendous if we can validate and empower women teachers to use their relational skills in their classrooms to encourage the boys—as well as the girls—to put connection first and to hold the connection through disconnection and impasses. If we could validate boys' yearning for connection throughout these "years of missed chances," we might, by continuing to explore relationship *between* boys and girls, transform them into "the years of good connections," and help them arrive at adolescence without the genders being so mysterious to each other.

Much pain and suffering might be avoided; the school culture, and then the larger culture, might begin to move toward a more connection-centered enterprise rather than a self/other one. Validating women elementary school teachers in strengthening the teacher–boy relationship has great potential, as does validating mothers in the mother–son relationship.

Using the language of "connect" and "disconnect" is another step to take in the classroom. Seventh-graders absorb these ideas easily. Using these terms can shift the dialogue greatly. Again, they can learn the idea, and experience the movement from a disconnect to a better connect. Children are receptive to the idea that it's not just what you do, it's what you do *next* that really matters—how you grow and learn in connection, through understanding one's impact on others. Childhood is one long process of trying, retrying, retrying.

Finally, there are many ways in the classroom—and in the school system—to nourish and empower the "classroom we" and the "school we" through purpose statements and value statements and by creating projects and socially responsible activities together. As we have worked in more depth in schools, we've taken to heart what high school students have said, that we have to work with all three groups: students, teachers, and parents. In our lectures and dialogues with parents, women outnumber men by at least four to one. Especially in elementary classrooms the women teachers predominate. High school boys in dialogue have asked us "Where are the men in the school who are willing to talk with us about these issues as men who can model different kinds of authority? Are there any men like this?" Such men need to get involved.

It is necessary not only for students to use the resource of same-gender experience and cross-gender experience but for teachers as well. If each elementary school class had two teachers, a man and woman, the students in that class could learn about their relationship to the same-gender adult and also see a healthy cross-gender relationship at work, with each person respecting the other and supporting the other's growth through working on differences. The students could learn about real male–female relationships, in ways other than how advertising, movies, and popular music portray them. In several schools we've seen that one gender or the other is considered dominant. One private high school, which originally was a boys' school and now is coed, said that "there is definitely a male headwind. The boys own the hallways." In the reverse situation, much more rare, a girls' school now admitting boys, "the dominant voice here is feminist."

It has become clear to us that if we cannot create a truly mutual, coeducational environment, single-gender schools may be a good alternative.

But if we can coeducate, much as we've seen the shift toward mutuality in couples, "The sky's the limit!" It would be a bold creation of the twenty-first century, especially as our culture becomes more diverse, to find ways to use differences of all kinds to create mutual connections in our schools.

The Connected Corporation: Using the Connection Model to Create a New Vision of Business

The Connection Model can be applied to any setting where differences may not be well acknowledged or worked with. Corporations are a good example. For the past several years we have worked in a small corporation, a partnership of men and women who were quite diverse in terms of nationality, culture, class, and ethnicity. It has been remarkable to find how much the same model, and the same strategies, are of use in the business world. Businesspeople often say that the most crucial element in their success is "good relationships." If differences in the business arena can be brought into dialogue, they can add. If the people of a company learn to "hold the we through a disconnection," it can lead to a better connection, both within the company and in the company's relation to clients. At first we took it on faith that if the connections were right, profit and growth would follow. Now we have data that suggests this to be true. Much has been written in the business literature on the value of "team building." We believe the Connection Model has much to offer in such an enterprise. The Connected Corporation would be one that builds a corporate "we" awareness, a corporate "man" and "woman" and other group awareness, one that learns to talk corporate "connect" and "disconnect" and that nourishes and empowers the corporate "we." Nowhere is it clearer how a system of mutual relationship could challenge more traditional hierarchical, power-over systems to move toward mutual, shared-power systems. To create mutuality in power-over systems is one of the great challenges of our age.

Mothers and Sons, Fathers and Daughters

This book is about using differences to create connections. We have focused on differences of gender, but "the shift to the 'we'" might well happen in dialogue around any difference, such as race, ethnicity, sexual preference, class, and so on, where issues of power can be included in the dialogue.

Much work needs to be done in same-gender dialogue—mother–daughter and father–son. Much attention has been paid to this in the culture. We ourselves do not attempt a dialogue around gender without taking this first step of getting the men (or boys) together and the women (or girls) together to work on issues in same-gender relationships. Only then, after affirming shared experience, can the two genders work creatively together. This is a necessary step. However, this step is not sufficient. We feel strongly that great power for change can come from cross-gender dialogue between mother and son, father and daughter.

The mother–son relationship has the possibility of helping the son and mother hold the idea of ongoing good connection, which will keep alive the son's deep yearning for growth in connection and affirm that boys can grow to a fuller potential in healthy connection than in isolation.[4] The mother's belief in this needs validation and support, for in the past mothers have been pathologized and vilified for "holding on to sons." Affirming the value of that yearning and growth in connection has great power. If boys are free to express these parts of themselves, connection may start to be validated in schools, the workplace, government, and so on, as a way of being and working together.

The father–daughter relationship has the possibility of helping the daughter and father hold the idea of ongoing good connection, which will allow the daughter's true and authentic "voice" to be heard loud and clear as she negotiates the culture that often seeks to silence it. Through this process, a father's yearning for growth in connection may also be validated. One father described his enormous growth in appreciating and respecting his daughter's relational strengths through their talk during weekly ten-mile runs together. Because fathers are members of the dominant group in terms of economic and social power, there is the possibility of men's using their political clout—in schools and governments—to change things for the better. If daughters are having trouble in schools, fathers can get involved. When fathers get involved, institutions may listen better.

Mothers and fathers together. The most important "we" to a child is the one right before his or her eyes: married or not. The way that sons and daughters learn about relationship is not only by relationship to each parent but by seeing the relationship between parents, and between parents and other adults. Our strategies to find ways to move to mutual, to shift to "we," to use gender, personal, and cultural difference to grow through and toward connection, will be useful in building mutuality in families. We all have to walk the walk.

.   .   .

If we are to live "human-sized lives"[5] rather than as mythic "heroes," if we are to be of the Earth rather than on separate planets, these suggestions may turn out to be urgent imperatives for the twenty-first century. Globally, we are increasingly connected; economically, politically, and through cyberspace. We are more and more connected as we grow in awareness of the ecological crises we have created and must solve together. Our ability to begin to live and work in mutual relation, as part of the we, may be the crucial factor in the survival of our own and other species and our Earth as we know it.

We have high and grand hopes for the future of this work as part of a whole body of work contributing to changing the paradigm from self/other to we, from part to whole, and from sickness to wellness.[6] By helping people make good connections, we have seen bitterness and anger transformed to compassion, shame to curiosity, guilt to the essential healing of shared sorrow, and hatred to love. We have seen people rooted in self come to the edge and realize that to continue in that disconnection is death and destruction and the spread of suffering down through generations. We have seen self-centeredness melt, expand, embrace the "we," and start to move in relation and heal.

Once we begin to see not only the "things" in the world but the "connections" in the world—from defining and locating atoms by their relationship to each other to seeing the rain forest as the lungs of our planet; once we start to see not only the people, the men and boys and women and girls, but the relationships between them; once we start to shift our seeing from separate "I's" and "you's" to "we's," our whole world changes and we can never go back. We can forget knowledge—computers may be taking over that function of our brain—but we can never forget what we come to truly see and understand. Growth in connection transforms, unforgettably.

Now, on our journey as six-year-old cross-cultural parents of a daughter born in China, we too are holding a faith in mutuality, holding our connection to our daughter's culture of origin and to a shared purpose with her unknown birth parents. There is much, every day, within us and in the world that threatens and challenges our holding our connections.

We as a couple are sustained by all the couples we have listened to. When we get into fights and disconnections—and we do—we hear their voices, see their faces, see our daughter's concerned face watching us, and we do our best to shift to the "we," understand that each of us as a man and as a woman are still struggling to see clearly ourselves, each other, and our We. We then try to move from blame to shared responsibility, try to use the words "connection" and "disconnection." It is often hard to do in a difficult or exhausted moment. But we struggle to hold the "we" through the disconnection, to trust the process, no matter what.

And that is the hope for the future, the challenge, and the gift: to walk through the pain and sorrow together, "we" seeing, and being, and moving together. To come back from the fork in the path that we could not help but take as young boys and girls, to recover from the inevitable disconnections, the shifts away from "we," and by holding the "we" through all the tragic and violent disconnects create a new and enlarged mutual connection to hold for the next generation.

Notes and References

Introduction

1. J. Jordan, "The Meaning of Mutuality," in J. Jordan, A. G. Kaplan, J. B. Miller, I. P. Stiver, and J. Surrey, *Women's Growth in Connection: Writings from the Stone Center* (New York: Guilford, 1991), p. 89.

2. J. Jordan, A. G. Kaplan, J. B. Miller, I. P. Stiver, and J. Surrey, *Women's Growth in Connection: Writings from the Stone Center* (New York: Guilford, 1991). See also J. Jordan, ed., *Women's Growth in Diversity: More Writings from the Stone Center* (New York: Guilford, 1997); J. Miller and I. Stiver, *The Healing Connection: How Women Form Relationships in Therapy and in Life* (Boston: Beacon Press, 1997); *Work in Progress,* Stone Center Working Paper Series (Wellesley, MA: Stone Center, Wellesley College).

3. C. Gilligan, *In a Different Voice* (Cambridge, MA: Harvard University Press, 1982). See also C. Gilligan, A. G. Rogers, and D. Tolman, eds., *Women, Girls, and Psychotherapy: Reframing Resistance* (New York: Haworth Press, 1991).

4. S. Bergman, "Men's Psychological Development: A Relational Perspective," *Work in Progress,* Stone Center Working Paper Series no. 48 (1991). See also T. Real, *I Don't Want to Talk About It* (New York: Scribner, 1997); K. Weingarten, *The Mother's Voice: Strengthening Intimacy in Families,* 2d ed. (New York: Guilford, 1997); O. Silverstein, *The Courage to Raise Good Men* (New York: Viking, 1994).

5. R. Bly, *Iron John* (Reading, MA: Addison-Wesley, 1990).

6. S. Keen, *Fire in the Belly* (New York: Bantam, 1991).

7. E. Fein and S. Schneider, *The Rules* (New York: Warner, 1996).

8. D. Tannen, *You Just Don't Understand* (New York: Morrow, 1990).

9. J. Gray, *Men Are from Mars, Women Are from Venus* (New York: HarperCollins, 1992).

10. J. Herman, *Trauma and Recovery* (New York: Basic Books, 1992).

11. R. Eisler, *The Chalice and the Blade* (New York: HarperCollins, 1987).

12. J. Kabat-Zinn and M. Kabat-Zinn, *Everyday Blessings: The Inner Voice of Mindful Parenting* (New York: Hyperion, 1997). See also D. S. Hopson and D. P. Hopson, *Friends, Lovers, and Soulmates: A Guide to Better Relationships Between Black Men and Women* (New York: Simon and Schuster, 1994); G. Hendricks and K. Hendricks, *Conscious Loving: The Journey to Co-commitment* (New York: Bantam, 1990); H. Hendrix, *Getting the Love You Want* (New York: Henry Holt, 1988); J. Welwood, *Journey of the Heart: Intimate Relationships and the Path of Love* (New York: HarperCollins, 1990); T. Moore, *The Care of the Soul* (New York: HarperCollins, 1992).

13. D. Stern, *The Interpersonal World of the Infant* (New York: Basic Books, 1985).

14. L. Evers, ed., *Between Sacred Mountains: Navajo Stories and Lessons from the Land* (Tuscon and London: Sun Tracks and the University of Arizona Press, 1982).

1. Differences Between Men and Women

1. Judith Jordan has written of this concept in a number of working papers in *Work in Progress*, Stone Center Working Paper Series (Wellesley, MA: Stone Center, Wellesley College): see, e.g., "Relational Development: Therapeutic Implications of Empathy and Shame," no. 39 (1989); "Courage in Connection," no. 45 (1991); "Relational Resilience," no. 57 (1992).

2. Ada Maria Isasi-Diaz, of the Mudflower Collective, *God's Fierce Whimsy* (New York: Pilgrim Press, 1985), p. 128.

2. How We Got Here

1. B. Thorne, *Gender Play* (New Jersey: Rutgers University Press, 1993).

2. D. Stern, *The Interpersonal World of the Infant* (New York: Basic Books, 1985).

3. The Connection (or Relational) Model has been developed at the Stone Center, Wellesley College. The *Work in Progress* publications may be ordered by contacting the Wellesley Centers for Women Publications Office at (617) 283–2510. We are following the definitions of J. Miller and I. Stiver, *The Healing Connection: How Women Form Relationships in*

Therapy and in Life (Boston: Beacon Press, 1997). *Connection* connotes an interaction between two or more people that is mutually empathic and empowering; a *disconnection* is an encounter that works against mutual empathy and mutual empowerment. A relationship exists over time and inevitably is characterized by connections and disconnections.

4. J. Miller, *Toward a New Psychology of Women* (Boston: Beacon Press, 1976).

5. J. Jordan, A. G. Kaplan, J. B. Miller, I. P. Stiver, and J. Surrey, *Women's Growth in Connection: Writings from the Stone Center* (New York: Guilford, 1991).

6. J. Jordan, "The Meaning of Mutuality," in Jordan et al., *Women's Growth in Connection.*

7. Miller and Stiver, *Healing Connection,* p. 17.

8. J. Surrey, "What Do You Mean by Mutuality in Therapy?" in J. Miller, J. Jordan, A. Kaplan, I. Stiver, and J. Surrey, "Some Misconceptions and Reconceptions of a Relational Approach," *Work in Progress,* Stone Center Working Paper Series no. 49 (Wellesley, MA: Stone Center, Wellesley College, 1991), p. 10.

9. Jordan, "The Meaning of Mutuality," p. 89.

10. C. Heyward, *Touching Our Strength: The Erotic as Power and the Love of God* (New York: Harper and Row, 1989), p. 191.

11. S. Bergman and J. Surrey, "The Woman–Man Relationship: Impasses and Possibilities," *Work in Progress,* Stone Center Working Paper Series no. 55 (1992). See also S. Bergman and J. Surrey, "Couples Therapy: A Relational Approach," *Work in Progress,* no. 66 (1994); J. Surrey, "Self-in-Relation: A Theory of Women's Development," *Work in Progress,* no. 13 (1985). For a detailed description of men's psychological development, see S. Bergman, "Men's Psychological Development: A Relational Perspective," *Work in Progress,* no. 48 (1991); and for women's psychological development, see Surrey, "Self-in-Relation," and J. Miller, "The Development of Women's Sense of Self," *Work in Progress,* no. 12 (1981).

12. J. Miller, "What Do We Mean by Relationships?" *Work in Progress,* no. 22 (1986).

13. Miller and Stiver, *Healing Connection.* See also J. Jordan, "A Relational Perspective for Understanding Women's Development," in J. Jordan, ed., *Women's Growth in Diversity: More Writings from the Stone Center* (New York: Guilford, 1997).

14. Ibid. See also J. Jordan, "Relational Awareness," *Work in Progress,* no. 76 (1994).

15. Bergman, "Men's Psychological Development." See also Surrey, "Self-in-Relation."

16. Bergman, "Men's Psychological Development."

17. Ibid.

18. C. Gilligan, *In a Different Voice* (Cambridge, MA: Harvard University Press, 1982). See also R. Levant and W. Pollack, eds., *A New Psychology of Men* (New York: Basic Books, 1995); T. Real, *I Don't Want to Talk About It* (New York: Scribner, 1997); T. Kupers, *Revisioning Men's Lives* (New York: Guilford, 1993).
19. Bergman, "Men's Psychological Development."
20. O. Silverstein, *The Courage to Raise Good Men* (New York: Viking, 1994).
21. Ibid. See also P. Caplan, *Don't Blame Mother: Mending the Mother–Daughter Relationship* (New York: Harper and Row, 1989); K. Weingarten, *The Mother's Voice: Strengthening Intimacy in Families,* 2d ed. (New York: Guilford, 1997).
22. C. Dooley and N. Fidele, "Uncharted Waters: The Mother–Son Relationship," paper presented at the Stone Center, Wellesley, MA, April 1998.
23. Jean Baker Miller, personal communication with authors.
24. S. Osherson, *Finding Our Fathers* (New York: Fawcett, 1987).
25. D. Tannen, *You Just Don't Understand* (New York: Morrow, 1990).
26. J. Miller, "Connections, Disconnections, and Violations," *Work in Progress*, no. 33 (1988).
27. J. Jordan, "Relational Development: Therapeutic Implications of Empathy and Shame," *Work in Progress*, no. 39 (1989).
28. Gilligan, *In a Different Voice.* See also M. Pipher, *Reviving Ophelia: Saving the Selves of Adolescent Girls* (New York: Putnam, 1994); C. Steiner-Adair, "When the Body Speaks: Girls, Eating Disorders, and Psychotherapy," in C. Gilligan, A. G. Rogers, and D. Tolman, eds., *Women, Girls, and Psychotherapy: Reframing Resistance* (New York: Haworth Press, 1991).
29. Jordan, "The Meaning of Mutuality."
30. Surrey, "Self-in-Regulation."
31. Gilligan, *In a Different Voice.*
32. AAUW Education Foundation, *How Schools Shortchange Girls* (New York: Marlowe, 1992).

3. Women's Yearning Meets Men's Dread

1. S. Bergman and J. Surrey, "The Woman–Man Relationship: Impasses and Possibilities," *Work in Progress*, Stone Center Working Paper Series no. 55 (Wellesley, MA: Stone Center, Wellesley College, 1992). See also J. Miller and I. Stiver, *The Healing Connection: How Women Form Relationships in Therapy and in Life* (Boston: Beacon Press, 1997); I. Stiver, "A Relational Approach to Therapeutic Impasses," *Work in Progress*, Stone Center Working Paper Series no. 58 (1992).
2. J. Miller, "Connections, Disconnections, and Violations," *Work in Progress*, Stone Center Working Paper Series no. 33 (1988).

3. J. Jordan, "The Meaning of Mutuality," in J. Jordan, A. G. Kaplan, J. B. Miller, I. P. Stiver, and J. Surrey, *Women's Growth in Connection: Writings from the Stone Center* (New York: Guilford, 1991).

4. S. Bergman, "Men's Psychological Development: A Relational Perspective," *Work in Progress,* Stone Center Working Paper Series no. 48 (1991).

5. J. Jordan, "Courage in Connection," *Work in Progress,* Stone Center Working Paper Series no. 45 (1991). See also J. Miller and J. Surrey, "Revisioning Women's Anger: The Personal and the Global," *Work in Progress,* Stone Center Working Paper Series no. 43 (1990).

6. D. Tannen, *You Just Don't Understand* (New York: Morrow, 1990).

7. Ibid.

8. Z. Luria, presentation at the Dedication Conference, Stone Center, Wellesley College, MA, 1981.

9. P. Caplan, *They Say You're Crazy: How the World's Most Powerful Psychiatrists Decide Who's Normal* (Reading, MA: Addison-Wesley, 1995).

10. D. Tannen, *The Argument Culture* (New York: Random House, 1998).

11. *Alcoholics Anonymous,* 3d ed. (New York: AA World Services, 1976).

12. J. Herman, *Trauma and Recovery* (New York: Basic Books, 1992).

13. J. Katz, "How Does Feminism Help Men?" lecture presented at the Wellesley Center for Women, Wellesley, MA, 1997.

4. Getting to "We"

1. S. Bergman and J. Surrey, "Couples Therapy: A Relational Approach," *Work in Progress,* Stone Center Working Paper Series no. 66 (Wellesley, MA: Stone Center, Wellesley College, 1994). See also J. Jordan, "Relational Resilience," *Work in Progress,* Stone Center Working Paper Series no. 57 (1992); J. Surrey, "Relationship and Empowerment," *Work in Progress,* Stone Center Working Paper Series no. 30 (1987); J. Miller, "Connections, Disconnections, and Violations," *Work in Progress,* Stone Center Working Paper Series no. 33 (1988).

2. J. Jordan, "Relational Awareness: Transforming Disconnections," *Work in Progress,* Stone Center Working Paper Series no. 76 (1994).

3. J. Jordan, "Courage in Connection," *Work in Progress,* Stone Center Working Paper Series no. 45 (1991). See also J. Miller, *Toward a New Psychology of Women* (Boston: Beacon Press, 1976); J. Miller, "The Construction of Anger in Women and Men," *Work in Progress,* Stone Center Working Paper Series no. 4 (1982).

4. J. Jordan, "The Meaning of Mutuality," *Work in Progress,* Stone Center Working Paper Series no. 23 (1985). See also J. Surrey, "Self-in-Relation: A Theory of Women's Development," *Work in Progress,* Stone Center Working Paper Series no. 13 (1985); J. Miller and I. Stiver, *The Healing Connection:*

How Women Form Relationships in Therapy and in Life (Boston: Beacon Press, 1997).

5. I. Stiver and J. Miller, "From Depression to Sadness in Women's Psychotherapy," *Work in Progress*, Stone Center Working Paper Series no. 36 (1988).

6. I. Stiver, "The Meaning of Dependency in Female–Male Relationships," *Work in Progress*, Stone Center Working Paper Series no. 7 (1983).

7. D. S. Hopson and D. P. Hopson, *Friends, Lovers, and Soulmates: A Guide to Better Relationships Between Black Men and Women* (New York: Simon and Schuster, 1994).

5. How Couples Grow

1. J. Miller and J. Surrey, "Revisioning Women's Anger: The Personal and the Global," *Work in Progress*, Stone Center Working Paper Series no. 43 (Wellesley, MA: Stone Center, Wellesley College, 1990). See also J. Jordan, "Courage in Connection," *Work in Progress*, Stone Center Working Paper Series no. 45 (1991).

2. Merle Bombadieri, personal communication with the authors.

3. J. Borysenko, *Minding the Body, Mending the Mind* (Reading, MA: Addison-Wesley, 1987). See also B. Siegal, *Love, Medicine, and Miracles* (New York: HarperCollins, 1995); H. Benson, *The Relaxation Response* (New York: Bantam, 1975); D. Ornish, *Love and Survival* (New York: HarperCollins, 1998); J. Kabat-Zinn, *Wherever You Go, There You Are* (New York: Hyperion, 1996).

4. D. S. Hopson and D. P. Hopson, *Friends, Lovers, and Soulmates: A Guide to Better Relationships Between Black Men and Women* (New York: Simon and Schuster, 1994).

5. C. Heyward, *Touching Our Strength: The Erotic as Power and the Love of God* (New York: Harper and Row, 1989).

6. J. Kabat-Zinn and M. Kabat-Zinn, *Everyday Blessings: The Inner Voice of Mindful Parenting* (New York: Hyperion, 1997).

7. N. Morton, *The Journey Is Home* (New York: Pilgrim, 1982).

7. Boys and Girls Together

1. B. Thorne, *Gender Play* (New Jersey: Rutgers University Press, 1993).

2. AAUW Education Foundation. AAUW Education Foundation, *How Schools Shortchange Girls* (New York: Marlowe, 1992).

3. D. Goleman, *Emotional Intelligence* (New York: Bantam 1995).

4. O. Silverstein, *The Courage to Raise Good Men* (New York: Viking, 1994). See also C. Dooley and N. Fidele, "Uncharted Waters: The

Mother–Son Relationship," paper presented at the Stone Center, Wellesley, MA, April 1998.

5. Mary Watkins, personal communication with the authors.

6. J. Macy, *Despair and Personal Power in the Nuclear Age* (Philadelphia: New Society, 1983). See also C. Heyward, *Touching Our Strength: The Erotic as Power and the Love of God* (New York: Harper and Row, 1989); V. Thakar, *The Eloquence of Living* (San Rafael, CA: New World Library, 1989).